Wiltshire Record Society

(formerly the Records Branch of the Wiltshire
Archaeological and Natural History Society)

VOLUME 73

Sketch of the monument to two children of Thomas Crockford in Fisherton Delamere church, pasted into the first Stockton parish register. It was made in 1826 by R.F. St Barbe, rector of Stockton (see p. xxxviii).

THE PARISH REGISTERS
OF THOMAS CROCKFORD
1561–1633

edited by

JOHN CHANDLER

from translations by

CHRISTOPHER NEWBURY
and
STEVEN HOBBS

CHIPPENHAM

2020

Published on behalf of the Wiltshire Record Society,
c/o Wiltshire and Swindon History Centre,
Cocklebury Road, Chippenham SN15 3QN

www.wiltshirerecordsociety.org.uk

by The Hobnob Press,
8 Lock Warehouse, Severn Road,
Gloucester GL1 2GA

www.hobnobpress.co.uk

Typeset by John Chandler

CONTENTS

ABBREVIATIONS

CCEd	Clergy of the Church of England Database (online)
HMC	Historic Manuscripts Commission
ODNB	*Oxford Dictionary of National Biography* (online)
TNA	The Natonal Archives, Kew
VCH	*Victoria County History*
WSA	Wiltshire & Swindon Archives

PREFACE

The three parish registers which Thomas Crockford (1580-1634) began and continued until shortly before his death, covering Fisherton Delamere (where he was vicar from 1613) and its neighbours on either side, Wylye and Stockton, have long interested historians and topographers.[1] Sir Richard Colt Hoare in 1824 described the Stockton register as 'the most curious one which has yet fallen under our observation' and quoted from three entries (**1135, 1160, 1202**).[2] An anonymous author published a description and extracts from the Stockton register in 1832.[3] In 1913 a transcript (but not translation) of the Wylye register made by two local antiquaries was published by the rector.[4] R.B. Pugh, when writing the history of Fisherton for the Victoria County History in 1963, described Crockford as 'a happy instance of a reading clergyman,' and that 'he kept the registers in florid Latin and noted in them many personal details about his parishioners'.[5] Martin Ingram made extensive use of the Wylye register in his study of evidence from church courts relating to the parish, published in 1990.[6] The Wiltshire Family History Society, as part of a countywide programme, has published basic genealogical information derived from these registers.

In 1992 Christopher Newbury translated the first Stockton register

---

1 They are now in the Wiltshire & Swindon Archives maintained at Wiltshire & Swindon History Centre, Chippenham, as folllows: Fisherton Delamere (WSA 522/1); Stockton (WSA 203/1); Wylye (WSA 521/2).

2 Hoare, Sir R.C., *Modern Wiltshire*, vol. 1, pt. 2 (Heytesbury Hundred, 1824), 248; curiously he described the Fisherton register as containing nothing of particular interest, apart from a single entry (**572**).

3 *British Magazine*, vol. 2, 351-5. The author may have been Roger St Barbe, rector of Stockton, who wrote notes about Crockford and drew the monument to his children at around this time (see Frontispiece to this volume).

4 G.R. Hadow (ed.), *The Registers of the Parish of Wylye . . . from transcripts made by T.H. Baker and J.J. Hammond* (1913). Baker and Hammond had already published their transcripts of five entries relating to Thomas Bower and his family (**1391, 1769, 1820, 1836, 1839**) in *Somerset & Dorset Notes & Queries*, vol. 12 (1911), 220-2.

5 *VCH Wilts*. vol. VIII (1965), 45.

6 M. Ingram, *Church Courts, Sex and Marriage in England, 1570-1640* (1990).

from its beginning by Crockford in 1589 to its final entries in 1712. His translation was not published, but he donated a typescript copy to the Wiltshire Record Office (now Wiltshire & Swindon History Centre), and this has been, and remains, available to researchers. He subsequently agreed to the society's suggestion that he prepare translations of the Crockford material in the Fisherton and Wylye registers for publication as a volume in this series, subject to the constraints imposed on him by a busy public life. Because of the other demands on his time it was agreed in 2018 that he would complete his translation of the Wylye register, while the society's former general editor, Steven Hobbs, assisted by Penelope Rundle, would prepare a translation of the Fisherton register. My role would be to edit the volume for publication and to see it into print.

Thus there has been a division of labour, and this is reflected in the wording of the title page. The hard graft of translating difficult Latin texts, without which this volume would not have been possible, has fallen to Mr Newbury and Mr Hobbs; but they cannot be held responsible for the shortcomings of the translations published here, which are the result of my attempts to impose consistency on the material and to present it in the manner to be expected of a modern edition of records of this period and this nature. Apart from checking the translation of every entry against the original registers and adding some pre-1600 material that we had previously planned to exclude, I have numbered and annotated the entries, and prepared the introduction and the indexes. For the errors, mistranslations and omissions that remain I am solely to blame.

It is my pleasant duty to acknowledge on the society's behalf, first and foremost the work of Mr Newbury, Mr Hobbs and Miss Rundle, but also the help and co-operation of the staff of the Wiltshire & Swindon History Centre, where the registers are deposited. In addition I should like to thank Claire Skinner, the society's general editor, and her fellow committee members and officers, for their support.

Members will notice some small changes to the physical format of this volume, compared with its predecessors in the series. In common with other similar bodies, the society has had to cope with rising costs over the last few years, and these changes are designed to reduce printing costs. It should be added that the original registers have all been filmed and are available to view online on the Ancestry website.

John Chandler

INTRODUCTION

THE SETTING

The texts translated in this edition describe, sometimes in intimate detail, the lives and deaths of the inhabitants of five neighbouring villages in a south Wiltshire valley between about 1560 and 1630, recorded by one who, at least in the later decades, would have known every family. These five communities all lived close to the River Wylye, which rises beyond Warminster to the north-west and flows to Wilton in the south-east, where its waters join and are lost in the River Nadder. Living halfway between these two towns, the villagers looked to them both, but also to places along the Dorset border to the south-west – Shaftesbury, Mere and Gillingham – and northwards across Salisbury Plain, to Westbury and Edington (see map, p. xxviii).

Three of the five villages – Stockton, Bapton and Wylye – stood south of the river (see map, p. xxix). For Stockton, the river was its boundary, and the parish did not extend beyond it. Bapton was not a parish in its own right, although it may have been larger than Fisherton (Fisherton Delamere, to give its name in full), which was its counterpart north of the river, and in whose parish it lay. Fisherton's parish, therefore, straddled the river, as did that of Wylye, whose counterpart and dependent on the north was Deptford. So, five villages in three parishes. Occasionally, at times of flood or the destruction of a bridge, parishioners could not reach their own church across the river, so that Bapton people resorted to Wylye, and Deptford people to Fisherton. In other ways, too, through family, farming and business interests, these communities were bound together, far more so than with their neighbours upstream (Sherrington and the Codfords), and downstream (the Langfords).

In a pattern repeated along many chalkland valleys, not only in Wiltshire, each settlement possessed a strip of territory, seen on the map as an irregular rectangle, which was defined by boundaries of venerable antiquity and which have remained unaltered, in many places, into the 21st century.[1] The lands of Fisherton and its neighbours extended southwards

---

1   This and the following paragraphs are derived principally from parish histories in *VCH Wilts*, vol. VIII, 34-46 (Fisherton); vol. XI, 212-23 (Stockton); vol. XV, 295-305 (Wylye).

as far as the watershed with the next valley system, marked by a wandering prehistoric earthwork; to the north their limit was an ancient routeway leading across Salisbury Plain.

This regularity reflected, and was influenced by, that of the valley itself. Rich, flat meadows of alluvial soil flank the river, with bands of gravel deposits beyond forming slightly higher ground at the foot of the valley slopes. The terrain then rises in a typical chalkland landscape of gentle hillsides and steeper dry coombes to rolling downland north and south, capped on the southern hilltop by thin flinty soil. The land most suitable for cultivating crops lay on the lower hillsides, enriched by nutrients filtered down from the poorer soils beyond, and here each community had its great open arable fields. On the higher ground above the fields was rough grazing pasture for sheep, and where the flint outcropped along the southern edge woodland flourished. The sheep flocks provided not only wool, meat and milk, but were folded on the fields to manure the soil and improve the yields of wheat and barley. This sheep-and-corn husbandry predominated across south Wiltshire for many centuries until the Victorian period.

Along the gravel terraces, elevated a little above the river in spate, stood the settlements and ran the lanes connecting them. Deptford and the western part of Stockton were ranged along their lanes, and Bapton and Fisherton lined streets parallel to them. Wylye's plan was more complex and perhaps evolved from two settlements, east and west, which joined in a minor grid of streets. Stockton too had a second settlement, a knot of buildings around its church, which stands east of the main centre. And in the registers Bapton was often distinguished between the main village, Bapton street, and a satellite, Bapton by the leap-gate or field-gate, which we may assume was the hamlet later called Little Bapton. The territories of Wylye and Stockton were roughly twice as wide as their neighbours, and both maintained two sets of open fields, east and west, perhaps reflecting their dual origins.

A static and timeless rural landscape, superficially, but changes and innovations were taking place. By 1600 the two principal owners of Stockton were families of clothiers, and thereafter a disproportionate number of parishioners described themselves as weavers or tailors. Around the same time a new manor house was built on part of Stockton common marsh, and the meadowland around it was inclosed. The principal landholding in Bapton changed hands twice, in 1625 and 1627. Wylye's demesne farm was divided up into eight separate holdings c.1626, and a row of eight small farmhouses was built to replace the old farmstead. A

Stockton man was employed by the landowner to construct floated water meadows (among the earliest in Wiltshire) at Wylye in 1632 in order to improve the grass crop, and may have done the same at Stockton.

In 1621 the Fisherton tithingmen presented that in their parish they had no recusants, no absentees from church, no inns or alehouses nor drunken persons, no unlawful weights or measures, no neglect of hues and cries, no roads out of repair, no wandering rogues or idle persons, and no inmates of whom they desire reformation, 'thancks be to Almighty God theirefore'.[1] This may be taken at face value or, as seems more likely, as an attempt to dissuade authority from meddling in parochial affairs. Next door in Wylye the church court records reveal that the arrival of the puritan John Lee as rector in 1619 (**1846**) caused widespread resentment and dissension.[2] Crockford's registers say nothing directly about this or any other matter of social cohesion or conflict, but they provide the backcloth to everything that was going on, and all that may be discovered from other sources of the period.

THOMAS CROCKFORD

Crockford, familiar to anyone concerned with the Anglican church, is a surname derived from a place, probably Crockford (Bridge) near Addlestone, in Chertsey (Surrey). Richard de Crocford is recorded in Surrey in 1214,[3] but in the early modern period the surname was most prevalent in north Hampshire and Berkshire, with an outlying cluster in Somerset. John Crockford (1824/5–1865), who first published his *Clerical Directory* in 1858, haled from Somerset,[4] and no connection has been found with Thomas, the compiler of the registers edited in this volume.

Much of what we know about Thomas Crockford he tells us himself in the 'bare bones' of an autobiography written when he was in his thirties, and included in the Fisherton register (**680**).[5] His father Richard (*c.*1533–1602) was a husbandman or small farmer living in Wargrave (Berks.) between Reading and Henley, who married his mother, Elizabeth Nash

1 HMC, *Report on MSS in Various Collections*, pt. 1, (vol. 55, 1901), 93, cited by Pugh in *VCH Wilts*, vol. VIII, 36.

2 M. Ingram, *Church Courts, Sex and Marriage in England, 1570-1640* (1990), 120-3.

3 P. Hanks *et al* (eds.), *Oxford Dict. of Family Names in Britain and Ireland* (2016), 475, 482. Croxford, also found in the same area, appears to be a variant form of the same name.

4 *ODNB*.

5 Details not otherwise referenced in this section are from entry **680**.

(1547–*c*.1595) in her home parish of Basildon, in the Thames valley, a few miles upstream beyond Reading.[1] Richard had come from Rotherfield Peppard, a nearby village in Oxfordshire, where his father William, also a husbandman, had died in 1573, leaving most of his possessions to Richard's brother.[2]

Thomas Crockford was born at Wargrave in October 1580 and attended a school conducted in the quire of St Mary's parish church by Thomas Baker, the curate from the nearby village of Ruscombe.[3] When Mary Crockford, his mother, died, Thomas took up a position in 1595, presumably as children's tutor, in the service of the local squire, John Mochett (d. 1605), moving with the household not far away to Crowsley in Shiplake (Oxon.) when Mochett purchased the manor in the same year.[4] From Shiplake, after two years, Thomas went up, as Mochett's protégé, to Magdalen College, Oxford, where he remained under the tutelage of Isaac Pocock, a fellow some ten years his senior. Both men left Oxford in 1602, Pocock for ordination and a clerical career as vicar of a parish in rural Sussex;[5] Crockford, following his father's death in August, to take up the post of schoolmaster at Stockton before the end of the year.[6]

No other Stockton schoolmaster occurs in the registers here edited, before or after Crockford, but the post carried an ample salary, and the boys' school may have been the initiative of the parish's erudite rector, John Terrie, with whom he lodged for the first five or six years, thus until *c*.1608. Terrie, whom Crockford held in very high regard, took an interest in education, and left a bequest in his will as an encouragement to the parish clerk to give the youth and children of the parish religious instruction in church between Sunday morning and evening prayer.[7]

Alongside his duties teaching school, Crockford was ordained deacon at the end of 1604 and priest in 1605.[8] He began to serve, perhaps

1   details from indexes accessed via Find my Past.
2   Oxon. Wills Index, 185.199, accessed via Find my Past. By 1613 Crockford had promoted his late father to the staus of yeoman (**811**).
3   Baker graduated BA from Magdalen Hall, Oxford in 1586, and left Ruscombe in 1596 or 1597 to become vicar of Dorney near Eton (Bucks.) until 1614 or later (CCEd).
4   *VCH Oxon*, vol. XX, forthcoming.
5   Foster, *Alumni Oxon*.; CCEd.
6   He subscribed to the 39 articles as a schoolmaster on 2 Dec. 1602: WSA D5/9/1.
7   TNA, PROB 11/146/163.
8   WSA D1/2/19.

unofficially, as curate in nearby parishes, including Codford, Wylye and Great Wishford (**680**). A wedding in 1606 may have been responsible for opening a new horizon in his life. The steward at the rectory where he was living married the daughter of a clothier from Mere, Thomas Alford (**801**, cf. **1208**). Grace Alford, the bride, was one of ten or more sisters (**814**), and a little over six years later it was the youngest, Joan, who became Crockford's wife, in January 1613 (**811**). They were married for 21 years, and she outlived him.

A tenth daughter brought perhaps little in way of a dowry, and initially the couple relied on the local Stockton gentry, the Toppes and Potticaries, to augment Thomas's teaching stipend. His break came with the not unanticipated death,[1] in November 1613, of the vicar of Fisherton Delamere, Joel Doughty, and Crockford's presentation to the living by the patron, the marquis of Winchester (**679, 680**). His teaching role continued until 1616, but thereafter he settled into his life as vicar of Fisherton, assistant (*coadjutor*) to his clergy neighbours on either side, in Wylye and Stockton, family man, small farmer, and chronicler of everyone's affairs.

Thomas and Joan Crockford produced seven children in all between 1618 and 1632, five daughters and two sons. The first son, in 1622, was stillborn, and the difficult birth left Joan in grave danger (**721**); the third daughter, in 1624, died in infancy while farmed out to a wet nurse (**331, 730**). Both were buried in the children's section of Fisherton graveyard, and the Crockfords erected a touching memorial to them with Latin epitaph, which was mounted on the outside wall of the chancel until moved inside the church in 1902, where it remains.[2] The other five children, age 15 down to 2 years old, and their mother, outlived Thomas, who died in April 1634. He withdrew from parish duties in Wylye in 1629,[3] and from Stockton in 1631. His last entries in the Fisherton register were made in April 1633 (**386, 387**), by which time his handwriting had been deteriorating for several years. He made his will in September 1633, 'beinge reasonable well of bodye & of indifferent good memorie', just short of his fifty-third birthday, and died seven months later.

From his will and probate inventory (see *Appendix*) details of the Crockfords' domestic life emerge. Fisherton vicarage house was relatively

1 Doughty had made his will nearly three years earlier, in January 1611: WSA P2/8Reg/195.

2 See note to **721**, p. xxxviii, and frontispiece to this volume.

3 This must have caused a problem, as the rector obtained a dispensation for absence around the same time, and for a while there was no curate in place to serve the parish (**360**).

modest, just a kitchen, hall and buttery with three chambers above, but it was also the centre of a working small farm. Its barn contained wheat, barley, malt and hay, and wheat and oats were growing in the field. He also ran a flock of fifty sheep, along with four pigs and three head of cattle. Noteworthy was Crockford's library, totalling 338 books,[1] and his possession of a musket with its accoutrements, and a sword.

Also recorded in Crockford's will is a leasehold house in Warminster, and it is likely that his widow and young family moved there after his demise. Their eldest daughter, Mary, was buried in Warminster in 1640, a little before her 22nd birthday, and her youngest sister, Elizabeth, was married there in 1655. The surviving son, John Crockford, may be identified with one of that name living in Salisbury in 1653 when he married in Marlborough.[2] Nothing more has been discovered of Crockford's widow, Joan.

CROCKFORD'S REGISTERS

The requirement to maintain a register of marriages, christenings and burials conducted in each parish was made by Thomas Cromwell in his mandate of 1538.[3] Responsibility lay with the parish clergy, who were to enter details of the parties to these events in a book each Sunday in the presence of a churchwarden, and the book was to be kept securely in a locked coffer or chest. In the febrile atmosphere of the 1540s and 1550s many parishes may have been disinclined to keep such a record, fearing that it would be used to impose a tax; even when kept, parish registers, bound or on loose paper sheets, were easily mislaid or destroyed through the negligence of transient clergy. In only six Wiltshire parishes have original registers, commencing in 1538, survived.

The major reason for the loss of early registers was a new set of requirements imposed by a constitution of Canterbury approved in 1598. It ordered parishes to purchase books of parchment into which the earlier registers were to be copied, from 1538 where they existed, but especially from the beginning of Elizabeth's reign, 1558. Henceforth entries were to be made each Sunday, by the minister or parish clerk, in the presence of

1   John Terrie, Crockford's long-term neighbour and friend, and a distinguished theologian, bequeathed his books to a son (TNA, PROB 11/146/163), but it is possible that some of his library was acquired subsequently by, or had been given before Terrie's death, to Crockford.
2   Parish registers, via Ancestry.
3   See W.E. Tate, *The Parish Chest* (1969 edn.), 43-6; S. Hobbs (ed.) *Gleanings from Wiltshire Parish Registers* (Wilts Record Soc. vol. 63, 2010), ix-x.

both churchwardens, who were to sign each page, and the entries were to be read out in church. A copy was to be sent each year to the diocesan authorities, the so-called bishop's transcripts, at Easter – amended in 1603 to within a month of Lady Day, 25 March.

In Wiltshire, as elsewhere, the surviving records of many if not most of the marriages, baptisms and burials which occurred before 1598 are transcripts copied into parish registers begun as a result of this Canterbury constitution order. In a few registers (including those for Broad Chalke, Highworth, Idmiston and Warminster) this process was begun promptly and is stated explicitly.[1] In some other places it was undertaken several years later, as at Wilcot (1605), Bishop's Cannings (1607), West Harnham (1608), Froxfield (1609) and Inglesham (1614).[2] At Patney the copy was not made until 1636, and then only because the old register, from 1592, was found in the parson's garden.[3]

The 1598 instruction to make copies of earlier parish registers undoubtedly gives the context for Crockford's work. When he arrived in Stockton as schoolmaster in 1602 the rector, John Terrie, had been keeping the registers scrupulously since his institution to the living in May 1589 but, apparently, had inherited none from his predecessor. It must have been Terrie who before 1613 set Crockford to work on copying the Stockton registers, because when he began he described himself as schoolmaster, not as vicar of Fisherton.[4] He would not have been the first in Wiltshire to have been given such a task: in 1598 Jerard Prior, schoolmaster of Melksham, copied the registers there from 1568,[5] and at Stanton St Bernard, when an old torn register was found in the vicarage house which few could make sense of, 'a young scholar scribbled it forth' from 1568 to 1604.[6] In fact the handwriting of Crockford's Stockton register gives the impression of a fair copy until about 1608 or 1609, after which variations in pen, ink and spacing suggest that thenceforth he was recording events as they occurred. This he continued to do for the rest of Terrie's incumbency and for a few years after his death in 1625, until giving up in February 1631.

His institution as vicar of Fisherton in November 1613 gave Crockford responsibility for another set of parish registers which, he tells

1   Hobbs, *op. cit.*, 29, 125, 131, 247.
2   *ibid.*, 272, 18, 265, 110, 132.
3   *ibid.*, 183.
4   p. 87 below.
5   Hobbs, *op. cit.*, 163-4.
6   *ibid.*, 217.

us in the preamble to his transcript, were incomplete and inaccurate.[1] They did, however, extend back a further generation beyond those of Stockton and Wylye, to the 1560s. He cannot have worked on them before he became vicar, as is clear from this preamble, and internal evidence suggests that he did not begin his copy (or at least, that he did not 'catch up' with contemporary events) until some years later. In the long autobiography that he included in the burial register at the point where he succeeded the previous vicar (**680**) he tells us that he continued as schoolmaster at Stockton for nearly 14 years, having begun there late in 1602. This would bring him to 1616, the earliest date that he could have written the entry (which relates of course to 1613). And when he recorded the burials for 1616 he must still have been copying from earlier records, as one was incomplete (**691**), although he knew that full details had been included in the bishop's transcript sent to Salisbury. As with Stockton, the regularity and spacing of the handwriting suggest that Crockford was copying up to a certain point – in Fisherton the change comes around 1618 – after which entries were added as they happened. A marked deterioration sets in around the end of 1631, so that during 1632 and 1633 it appears that he was struggling to write. The last entry included in this edition of the Fisherton burial register, and the only one he did not compose himself, was written in April 1634, and records his own death (**760**).

During 1618 Crockford took on the role of assistant (*coadjutor*) to his neighbour, Thomas Bower, rector of Wylye (**1840**). Bower died in February 1619, three months after his wife (**1839, 1836**), so it is likely that the burden of parish affairs during that year, including the keeping of the registers, fell on Crockford, and this task he continued to perform under the incumbency of Bower's successor, John Lee, until 1629. He found that the existing registers, which began in 1581, the year before Bower arrived in Wylye, were imperfect and inaccurate;[2] he would hardly have written these criticisms at the head of his transcript while Bower was still alive. It is obvious that some of the imperfections were of recent origin – relatively few events were recorded in Crockford's transcripts between 1611 and 1617. He left a space for burials in 1615, 1616 and part of 1617, presumably in the (unrealised) hope that a page missing from Bower's register would be found. But from 1618, when Crockford took charge of registration, the entries are full and of similar character to those in his Fisherton and Stockton registers. How soon after Bower's death he began transcribing records into the new register is unclear. Only after 1625 or 1626 does the

1   p. 1 below.
2   p. 147 below.

orderly transcription hand become varied and haphazard, suggesting that entries were thereafter added when they happened.

This analysis has suggested that Crockford began the Stockton register before about 1608, the Fisherton register before about 1618, and the Wylye register before about 1625. Having transcribed all the earlier entries he could find he then continued each of them by adding events as they were celebrated, until 1629 (Wylye), 1631 (Stockton) and 1633 (Fisherton).

There are hints about Crockford's methodology and scope – if not his purpose – in the preambles to the three registers, and sprinkled elsewhere among the entries. Embarking on the Wylye transcripts he explained that he would call on the memory of trustworthy men still alive, and there is a specific example of this where he corrected the baptismal date of a Potticarie son on information from the boy's nurse (**1398**). Very often he would add 'as it was asserted' or a similar phrase to qualify a statement. When elderly Ambrose Cockerell died in 1610 at Stockton he tried to find out about the family's origins, as they were commemorated in the church, but the older people could remember nothing (**1160**). Frequently in his Wylye registers, but occasionally also in Fisherton, he left spaces when important details, usually of forenames or places, were lacking in his source, hoping no doubt to discover them from family or neighbours. Many such spaces remain, but in at least four instances it is clear that he was able to add information later, since the pen or ink are different,[1] and there are other places where he corrected a name or added an entry. He left gaps for whole years, and sometimes a run of years, for which he had discovered no events.

The Wylye registers, especially for the years before 1618, when Crockford became more closely involved in running the parish, have a somewhat scrappy appearance, suggesting that discovering reliable information had proved irksome. The task in Stockton must have been much easier, as John Terrie, the orginator of the old register which he was transcribing, was still alive and could be consulted. The Fisherton registers that he inherited and copied seem to have been well kept, if restricted to basic details, although a few early years were absent. Crockford, after a short time as their vicar, would have known intimately all the families whose older members and ancestors were chronicled. He would have had little trouble checking, correcting and augmenting the entries as he copied them into his new register.

None of the old registers from which he compiled the three books

---

1 Elizabeth in **1524**, second in **1625**, 10 in **1810**, Robert in **1890**.

edited here have survived, so it is impossible to know to what extent he copied them and how much additional information he supplied from other sources. There are three extant bishop's transcripts, however, for Fisherton covering 1605 and 1608 in Latin, and for Wylye covering 1611–12 in English, which should be exact copies of the relevant portions of the superseded registers. Of nineteen Fisherton entries recorded in the bishop's transcripts all the dates correspond with Crockford's register, but he corrected one surname (from Hoskins to Rebeck: **223**) and added a missing surname (**224**); in every case he supplied additional details, such as occupations, mother's names, parentage and age, which are not recorded in the bishop's transcripts. As an example, the bishop's transcript records that on 1 April 1605 Henry Eyles alias Hix of Bapton was buried; Crockford (**655**) adds the information that he was a husbandman, head of a household, almost in his seventies, who made a will on 15 March 1604 and died on Easter Sunday, 31 March. All these details had been gleaned about a man whose death took place more than eight years before Crockford became vicar. The bishop's transcript for Wylye probably reflects the inadequacy of Thomas Bower's recording. Of the four baptismal entries Crockford corrected the forenames of two, from Jane to John (**1526**), and from John to James (**1528**), and the date of a third, from 29 to 19 April (**1529**). And he enhanced the five burial entries, as he had for Fisherton, so that to the bald 'John Selwood was buried 25 August 1611', he added (**1805**) that the deceased was a little boy, second son of John Selwood of Deptford, tailor and husbandman at the same time, and of Jane his wife – and all of this information he rendered into Latin.

Many parish registers of Crockford's era were written in Latin, and this would have posed little difficulty for parish clerks and churchwardens, as the knowledge needed of Latin vocabulary to make a satisfactory basic register entry was extremely limited. Crockford's Latin, that of a schoolmaster and scholar, was far more extensive, and has been described as 'florid'.[1] But his carefully composed exercises of 'florid' Latin prose were usually restricted to laudatory passages accompanying the burials of the gentry, clergy and other parish notables. In particular, the registers include four extended encomia, three to his fellow clergy Joel Doughty in 1613 (**679**), Thomas Bower in 1619 (**1839**), and John Terrie in 1625 (**1239**); and one to Mary Toppe, wife of the Stockton squire (**1202**). Crockford tells us that he himself gave the address at Bower's funeral (**1839**) and it may be, therefore, that the tribute to Bower included in the register was in effect the essence (or even a *verbatim* transcript) of that address, whether

1 R.B. Pugh, in *VCH Wilts*, vol. VIII, 45.

delivered in Latin or English. The same may be true of the other encomia and of some of the shorter tributes. It should be noted that Crockford never used his Latin to cloak derogatory remarks about the upper echelons of local society – who might be able to read Latin (and may indeed have learnt it from him). But this medium of Latin empowered him to make more candid verdicts on some of the lower orders without fear of reprisals.

Although it is possible to draw tentative conclusions as to when and how Crockford achieved his registers edited here, there is little to suggest what might have been his motive for undertaking such a task. But we can perhaps gauge how his ideas had developed by comparing the three preambles. The earliest, for Stockton (before 1608, we suggest), describes the work he was embarking on as merely a faithful copy of John Terrie's original register.[1] When he began work on Fisherton (before 1618?) he was aiming to include also the most noteworthy parochial matters, secular as well as ecclesiastical.[2] By the time he took on Wylye (before 1625?) his grandiose project was to produce a book chronological, topological and tropological of parochial affairs, chiefly ecclesiastical.[3] What he meant by the Latin words *topologicus* and *tropologicus*, is not entirely clear, and he may even have invented the former. The latter had a specialist meaning of a figurative interpretation of the moral meaning of scripture, but Crockford presumably intended by this euphonius pairing to indicate more generally that he was concerned with places, and with their inhabitants' morals or way of life.[4]

If that was his intention, ill health or the disordered state of the Wylye records may have cut short his enthusiasm, since he hardly ever referred to secular matters as such, nor to customs, popular beliefs or social concerns. Everything we learn from him about his three parishes is through the prism of the individuals' lives whom he buried, married or baptised.[5]

---

1 below, p. 87.

2 below, p. 1.

3 below, p. 147.

4 If this was the case, he prefigured Richard Gough, whose *Human Nature Displayed in the History of Myddle* (1834) is regarded as a classic social history of a Shropshire village: see David Hey, *An English Rural Community: Myddle under the Tudors and Stuarts* (1974). Gough was born less than a year after Crockford died, and wrote his account of every family in his parish in 1700.

5 Two exceptions were perhaps his comment on a plague which afflicted Wylye in 1603 (**1786**), and fires at Stockton in 1609 and 1610 (**1167**), but these both involved loss of life and so related to events in the registers.

THE PARISHIONERS

Crockford's descriptions of his parishioners to a large extent reflected their status in local society.[1] Heading the elite were those in control of the manors, whether as resident lords, or as 'farmers', who leased the demesnes. At Stockton the Toppe family had owned the principal manor since 1585, and they also leased Fisherton manor (from the marquesses of Winchester) from 1574. The Potticaries acquired a significant estate in Stockton in 1592, which they regarded as a second manor, and by 1626 were also leaseholders in Wylye (**1638**, etc) from its owner, the earl of Pembroke. Bapton manor was leased by the Hoskins family until 1627, when John Davies of North Wraxall acquired it, having married Joan Hoskins the year before (**357, 486**). Deptford belonged to a prominent county family, the Mompessons, but they did not reside, and several lessees are mentioned in the registers (**360, 757, 1435, 1525**). To these gentry or freeborn families he was respectful and, in the case of the Toppes and Potticaries sometimes effusive in praising their virtues.[2] When Mary Toppe, chatelaine of Stockton, died in 1617 Crockford wrote her obituary as if she warranted beatification (**1202**).

It was through the influence of the Toppes and Potticaries that Crockford believed he owed his preferment to Fisherton vicarage, and he and his fellow clergy – all resident at this period – stood next in the local hierarchy as men of influence. The most eminent was John Terrie (d. 1625), rector of Stockton, who proclaimed his Calvinist and anti-Catholic doctrine in a substantial work, *The Triall of Truth*, published in three volumes (1600, 1602, 1625).[3] Thomas Bower, rector of Wylye until his death in 1619, also had a distinguished career, having served as domestic chaplain in the court of Elizabeth (**1839**). Crockford had less to say about his own predecessor at Fisherton, Joel Doughty (d. 1613), a man of humbler attainments, whose impact on the local community lay more in the number of his progeny who remained living and working there.

Most male inhabitants of the three parishes, as in rural Wiltshire generally, made their living by agriculture, and in the registers they were divided into three categories, yeomen, husbandmen and labourers. The distinction between the yeoman class of leaseholders and larger farmers,

---

1 This paragraph relies on *VCH Wilts*, vol. VIII, 34-46 (Fisherton); vol. XI, 212-23 (Stockton); vol. XV, 295-305 (Wylye).

2 They were, of course, along with the local clergy, the most likely to be able to read Latin.

3 *Oxford DNB*.

and the husbandmen – the copyholders and small farmers – seems not to have been clear-cut, and individuals moved from one category to the other. When Crockford married in 1612 he described his late father Richard as a yeoman (**811**), although the following year, when he became vicar, he called him a husbandman (**680**), which is how Richard described himself in his will. The term husbandman (*agricola*) occurs many more times in the registers than yeoman (443 instances compared with 173), and more than labourer (*operarius*, 314 instances). Many labourers were resident, employed on the farms, and sometimes described as servants of yeomen (e.g. **443, 478, 705, 1883**) or of husbandmen (**824, 1841**); others were seasonal workers, 'incomers', who came to help with the harvest (**691, 726**, etc) or to work on the demesne (**287, 291**, etc).

The largest group of 'specialist' farmworkers were shepherds, although there were probably only one or two for the flocks of each village. Some were part-time, described also as husbandman (**297, 1559**) or labourer (**687**), and one employed an assistant (**688**). There were families of shepherds, notably the Rockesborroughs and the Skydmores. The Knight family of Stockton were ploughwrights, and John Sutton, a ploughwright from Shrewton, settled in Wylye in 1623 (**1330, 1627**, etc). Richard Wayle was a sieve-maker in Wylye (**1547**, etc), and William Style, also of Wylye, a carter or carrier (**1467**, etc). Stockton once had a common oxherd, who died at a great age in 1623 (**1233**).

There were mills at Fisherton and Wylye, and the millers were significant men who served as churchwardens. Christopher Smyth and his son, described as yeomen, were proprietors of the manorial mill at Fisherton, which they held by a specified legal agreement (**371, 716, 731**, etc); Wylye mill was used for fulling as well as corn, and its 'master', Joel Girdler, was described as a clothier (**1331, 1546**, etc). Crockford's parishes lay between and away from Wiltshire's two main clothmaking centres, around Salisbury in the south and the Westbury and Trowbridge area in the west, but several fulling mills existed on the River Wylye, from Bishopstrow down to Wilton. The Potticaries, settled in Stockton and Wylye, and described many times in the registers as gentlemen clothiers, owned a fulling mill nearby at Boyton, and were linked by marriage to the Whitakers, a leading family of clothiers from Bratton and Edington, near Westbury (**812, 1022**). The Toppes also owed their wealth to cloth, as London merchants, although Crockford never alluded to this. Two fullers were recorded at Wylye (**1318, 1671**), but these were far outnumbered by weavers and tailors. No fewer than 30 tailors were listed, principally in Wylye, although living in Stockton, Bapton and Deptford also, and from nearby parishes; 21 weavers were recorded too, half living in Stockton, but others in Wylye and Fisherton. These numbers seem far in excess of local needs and so may be connected with the Potticaries' business.[1]

Other trades and crafts appear in the registers far less frequently. Each village had its blacksmith, and in Bapton and Stockton there were two. Four butchers were named, but only one or possibly two shoemakers. There were brewers in Deptford and Wylye, where there was an inn. A few other tradesmen worked in construction, as carpenters, builders, tilers and woodworkers. Servants apart, few women's occupations are noted.

Not everyone recorded in the registers was living in the three parishes. Besides the marriage partners who came from elsewhere, strangers occasionally died or gave birth while passing through. In 1625 a soldier from Frome fell ill while returning home and died at Fisherton (**733**), while at Stockton in 1621 occurred the death of the newborn daughter of a couple returning from Somerset to Romsey (**1224**). Two Wylye burials are of unusual interest. In 1622 a Somerset man in his nineties died at the inn on his way home after giving evidence in a lawsuit in London (**1871**). Three years later an unnamed cap-maker from London, who was suffering from the plague, died on the road and (at his request) was rapidly buried in a field on the outskirts of the village (**1889**).

LIFE AND DEATH

Aside from their relationships to each other and their occupations, Crockford at his most expansive in the 1620s, and sometimes earlier, recorded other information about his flock – their age, cause of death, personal circumstances and religious beliefs.

The frequent deaths of neonatal and young infants, especially if they were twins, and in at least six instances of their mothers also as a result of childbirth, was a distressing but inevitable fact of 17th-century life. In such circumstances it was sometimes necessary to arrange an impromptu private baptism (**306, 327**, etc). The Crockfords themselves experienced two such bereavements, and Joan's life was in danger after a stillbirth (**721, 730**). The misfortunes endured by the Vargeis (*alias* Pierson) family may be traced through the index and make pitiful reading. Crockford once referred to the contemporary belief in a nine-year cycle through life, the climacteric (**1872**), which envisaged a critical decline around the age of 63, but in truth many of his parishioners died much younger. Despite this there were notable survivors, and he recorded thirteen instances of

---

1   Three 'woolworkers' were described as servants employed by Christopher Potticarie (**829, 834, 1218**).

elderly inhabitants claiming to be in their nineties or thereabouts, or even older. Marriages were often contracted between younger men and older women, and *vice versa*, and there are three instances (**493, 828, 837**) where an elderly man took a young bride, probably to secure her 'free bench' widow's tenure of a copyhold when he died.[1]

Illegitimacy was comparatively rare – only sixteen women were identified as bearing bastards – including Amy Potticarie (**1648**), whose predicament must have embarrassed her high-status family – and only two produced more than one; both were described as prostitutes (**1069, 1664**). Crockford occasionally recorded with disapproval pre-nuptial pregnancy (**290, 325, 492, 1664**), although detailed comparison of baptism and marriage entries would probably show that, here as elsewhere, it was a common, if not a normal occurrence. Within marriage it was not unusual for a wife to bear six or more children – Mary Potticarie of Stockton and Eleanor Potticarie of Wylye each had ten (**1053, 1872**). We have noted that Joan Crockford was one of at least ten sisters. Four instances of children born posthumously were recorded (**351, 884, 973, 1512**).

At the time of parishioners' burials Crockford, particularly during the 1620s, usually attempted to sum up their lives in terms of their fortune or misfortune, and aspects of their character. Unless they were of yeoman class or above his assessment was generally brief and frank, sympathetic to their plight (e.g. **707, 1838**) and complimentary or censorious regarding their morals. Concerning the higher echelons he was more circumspect, presumably because they might understand his Latin, so that he praised their public-spiritedness, their piety and their good nature, often in extravagant terms, and it is hard to determine his genuine feelings. Some, including Mary Toppe (**1202**) and John Terrie (**1239**), he clearly regarded with affection and respect, but what should we make of his enigmatic verdict on John Potticarie (**1872**), who 'suffered the varying fickleness of the world, and the frightening blows of the Devil himself'?

Crockford was rarely specific as to the precise cause of death, although he cited a wasting disease eight times and a fever five. Plague was held responsible (retrospectively) for a spate of deaths in Wylye in 1603 (**1786**), and also killed a stranger (**1889**), as we have noted. Dropsy, epilepsy, jaundice, paralysis, dysentery and quinsy were also diagnosed (once each), and perhaps dementia (**744**).[2] Elizabeth Skydmore, a poor

---

1 Explained by J.H. Bettey, 'Marriages of convenience by copyholders in Dorset during the 17th century', *Proc. Dorset NHAS*, vol. 98 (1976), 1–5.

2 *fera senio*: 'wildness in old age. For references to the other conditions see the general index.

shepherd's wife, starved to death in 1619 (**1216**). Misadventure was a relatively uncommon cause of death: a child was scalded (**1255**), a young carpenter succumbed to a blow on the head (**1220**), and two fatal accidents occurred to parishioners visiting local towns (**752, 1888**). Crockford noted a strange coincidence, when Sarah Smyth, the Fisherton miller's wife, died in 1624 at almost the same hour on the same day as her sister at Hale, near Fordingbridge (**731**). The sad end of Richard Taylour of Wylye in 1626 was also worth recording: He was suddenly snatched by death, and he died unseen in his bed at night in a storm (**1898**).

EDITORIAL NOTE

This text is presented as a translation of Crockford's Latin into modern English, including everything that he wrote apart from some phrases of common form. Except where cramped, his writing is usually clear and consistent, in a bold secretary hand with italic influences, although occasionally abbreviations and suspensions cannot be expanded with confidence. As commonly at this period, initial capitals were sprinkled arbitrarily, and they have been ignored. Where information was not to hand, he was in the habit of leaving spaces, and these have been indicated either in the footnotes (for Wylye, where they are numerous), and /or as a dash in the text. In his later years he included details of the clergy and churchwardens who, as required by the 1598 instruction, had authenticated the registers, even when there were no entries, and these are included.

Crockford's Latin is generally unambiguous, although his registers present certain difficulties for the translator. Occasionally the writing itself has become illegible through damage – rubbing and fading – but only on one page of the Wylye baptismal register (containing entries **1411-23**) has significant information been lost. In his set-piece encomia to deceased clergy and gentry, and his autobiographical summary (**679, 680, 1202, 1239, 1839**), as well as in many of his shorter tributes, he relished his grandiloquence, piling on synonyms and convoluted sentences. They make for imposing Latin, but are less easily rendered faithfully in impressive English, so that sometimes, although the general meaning is clear, the syntax is confusing.

The interpretation of two expressions calls for specific comment. Crockford frequently uses *oriund'* to denote a place or family origin. When describing a place this has been translated by 'raised in' or a similar phrase, and when linked to a family by 'descended from'. But in the latter case *oriund'* often does not have overtones of a long pedigree – he is merely telling us the maiden name or parentage of a married woman. Another favourite word is *aerumnosus*, which has the root meaning 'burdened' and is regarded by all authorities as denoting 'wretched' or 'troubled'. But Crockford almost invariably uses the word to describe a mother or father, apparently as a compliment, and so it seems likely that he is translating back into Latin the English word 'careful', which in his time could mean 'full of care', but also 'taking care', as is the modern idiom. Although 'careful' invariably fits the context in the registers, this translation retains 'troubled' or a synonym, because of the lack of any corroborative evidence from elsewhere to the contrary.

Apart from 'yeoman', for which Crockford had no Latin equivalent and thus expresses in English, occupations are nearly always given in Latin. The most common are *operarius*, translated as 'labourer', and *agricola*, translated as 'husbandman'. The Latin *firmarius*, translated as 'farmer', does not carry the modern meaning, but should be understood as a leaseholder (usually of a manor). Other crafts and trades have been rendered consistently, and the Latin equivalent of each is given in the general index.

Common forenames have been rendered from Latin into their usual modern equivalent, and their spelling standardised (e.g. Anne, Anthony, Catherine, Cecily, Eleanor, Jeffery, Matthew, Susan). Some less familiar names have also been spelled consistently, including Amy (for *Amica*), Avice (*Avisia*), Dionise (not Denise, for *Dionisia*), Ellis (*Elizeus*), Frances (*Francisca*) Honor (*Honoria*), Julian (always feminine: *Juliana*) and Tamsin (*Thomasina*). *Matilda*, although occasionally found at this period as an English name, has been rendered as Maud, and *Christiana* as Christian (always feminine), since both occur in these forms attached to the same individuals later in the Fisherton register when it was written in English. The relatively few uncommon forenames have been left in the spellings found in the registers, even when two entries, spelled differently, appear to relate to the same individual. One name, Vargeis (and variants), is of interest because it was used frequently as an *alias* surname for the family also known as Pierson. It seems to have originated as the Celtic forename Fergus (**45, 564**), modified by west-county dialect, and Latinised by Crockford as *Vargesius*; the Fisherton individual to whom it belonged left a will in which he was named Fergus Parsons (see **564n**). The delightfully named Crescens Moonday (**1504**) is not a Latin translation; the forename derives from the New Testament!

Surnames have been retained in the spellings found in the register (even when different spellings occur in the same entry), although variants of the same name have been grouped together in the index, with the alternative spellings noted in parenthesis and cross-referenced where necessary. Occasionally, but inconsistently, Crockford hyphenated surnames, but this practice has not been retained, except where it clearly denoted two separate names.

Dates, which Crockford generally wrote out in full, have been converted to modern usage, as 15 May, etc, but days of the week and feast days have been retained if included in the registers. Mistakes and impossible dates have been noted in the footnotes. Crockford insisted that the year began at the feast of the Incarnation, 25 March, and his reckoning of years in the registers consistently run from that date until the following 24 March (as was customary at this period). His arrangement has been followed, but the headings have been restyled in the form 1604/5 etc. as an aid and caution to the reader.

Baptisms and burials are usually stated simply, as *baptizatus(a) fuit* and *sepultus(a) fuit*, but for the marriage ceremony Crockford fairly consistently (though sometimes in heavily abbreviated form) used three different constructions for the three parishes, as follows: *solemni matrimonio consummaverunt* (Fisherton); *solemni matrimonio coniuncti sunt* (Stockton); *matrimonio ritu solemni celebraverunt* (Wylye). In this translation all have been rendered simply as 'married' or 'were married'.

As a general rule any unusual or problematic Latin word or passage has been transcribed in a footnote, with a comment where appropriate. The notes have also been used to describe and explain other textual anomalies and difficulties.

MAPS AND ILLUSTRATIONS

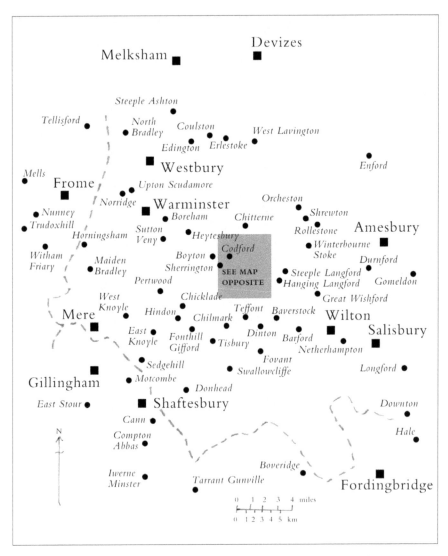

Map of south Wiltshire and adjoining counties, showing places mentioned in the text

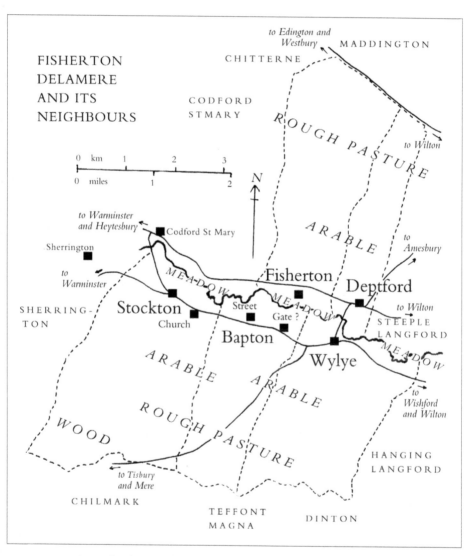

Map of Fisherton Delamere and its neighbours, Stockton and Wylye

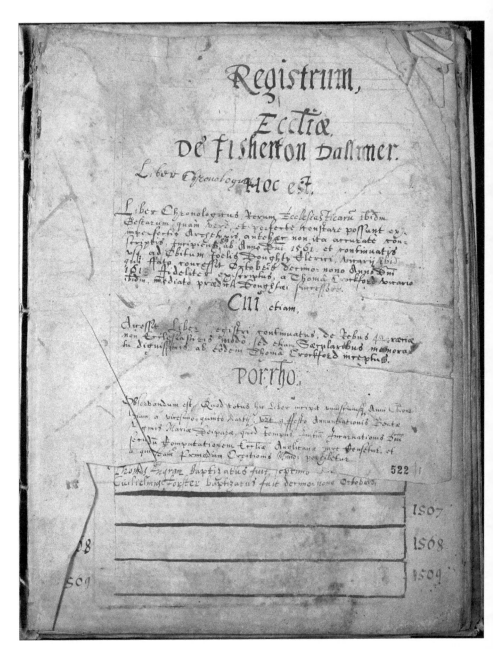

*The preamble to Crockford's Fisherton Delamere register, setting out his intention. He has ruled out the years, but has found no baptismal entries for 1567-9. On the next page he has copied entries for 1561, 1565 and 1566: see **1-16**.*

Part of a page of marriage entries from the Wylye register. Note that in 1606 Crockford has left a space after Elizabeth, in the hope of discovering the bride's surname. He found no record of marriages for several years, and so left spaces (see entries 1296–1309).

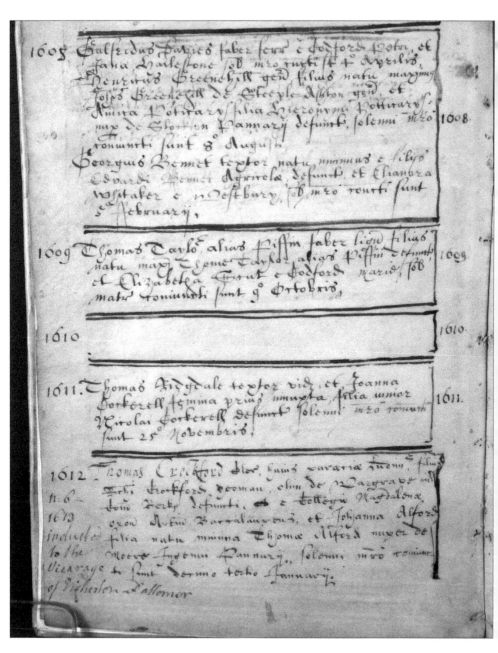

*Part of a page of the Stockton marriage register. The last entry on the page records the marriage of Thomas Crockford to Joan Alford of Mere, and has a marginal annotation by a later hand (see entries **806–11**).*

*Part of a page of the Stockton burial register devoted to Crockford's encomium of Mary Toppe, wife of John Toppe, the lord of Stockton manor, who died in 1617 (see entry **1202**). Her effigy, alongside her husband and six children (all named on this page), is in Stockton parish church (see p. xxxvii below).*

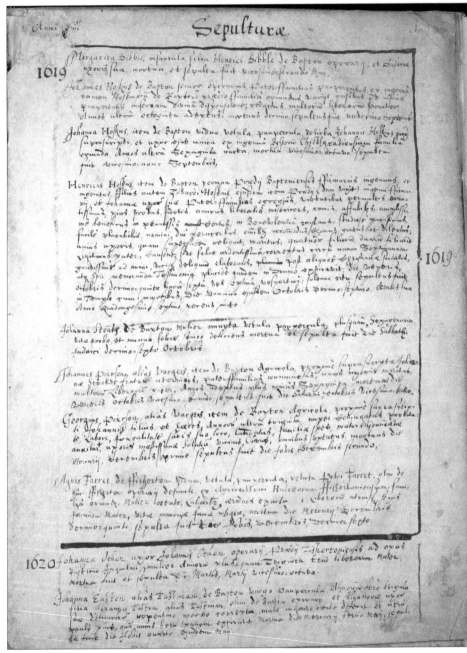

*A typical page illustrating Crockford's brief biographies accompanying records of burials in the Fisherton Delamere register. His obituary of Henry Hoskins, an important landholder in Bapton, is particularly well crafted and informative (see entries **706–15**).*

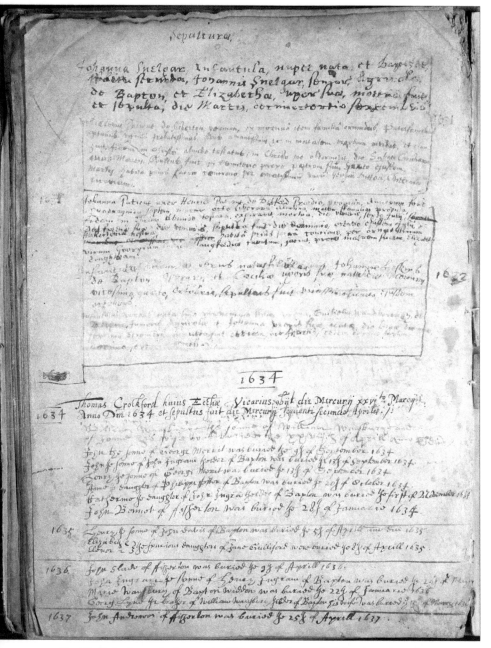

Crockford's final contributions to the Fisherton Delamere burial register show the deterioration in his handwriting as he approached his death, which is recorded as the first entry under 1634 (see entries **755–60**). *Thereafter the register was kept in English.*

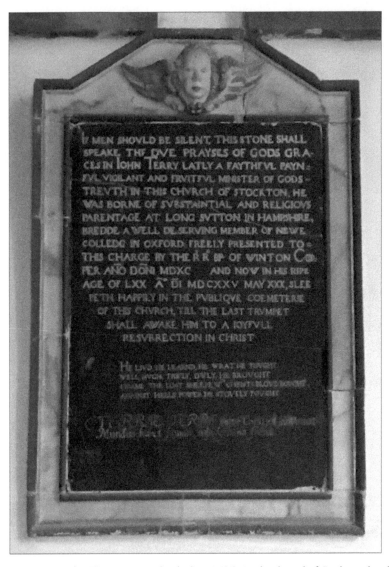

*Monument to John Terrie, rector, who died in 1625, in the chancel of Stockton church. Crockford had lodged with him and held him in high regard (see entry **1239**).*

The monument to John and Mary Toppe in Stockton church depicts their six children, boys John the elder, John the younger, and Edward, and girls Anne, Mary and Elizabeth. All are recorded in Crockford's register.

*Monument in Fisherton Delamere church to Alice Crockford and her unnamed stillborn brother (see entries **721**, **730**, and frontispiece to this volume). The inscription consists of a six-line elegy, consisting of three elegiac couplets, carefully constructed in Latin metre (alternate hexameters and pentameters), followed by five lines in Latin prose. A literal translation, which unfortunately loses the elegance of the Latin, is as follows:*

No name was attached to you, son, and you,
Daughter, are written Alice in the records;
But in the book of life you both as equals have a name,
Which God recognises is sufficient for you.
You, boy, have seen no light, and you, girl, only a small amount
On earth, but the light of heaven is extended to you both.

Infant boy and infant girl, first son and third daughter of Thomas Crockford, vicar, and of Joan his wife. The stillborn boy was buried on Sunday 1 September 1622; the girl, two months old, was buried on Wednesday 26 May 1624.

FISHERTON DELAMERE

This is the Register of the Church of Fisherton Delamere[1]

A book in chronological order of church matters which can be truly and completely established to have taken place there, derived from the incomplete originals of his predecessors, which were not so accurately written. It begins in the year 1561 and continues up to the death of Joel Doughty, clerk, vicar there, who met his end[2] on 19 October in the year of our Lord 1613. It has been faithfully copied out[3] by Thomas Crockford, the forementioned Doughty's immediate successor as vicar there.

To which has been added a continuation[4] to the register book, about the most noteworthy parochial matters that are not only ecclesiastical but also secular, begun by the same Thomas Crockford.

Furthermore, it should be observed that this book begins the chronology of each year from 25 March, the feast of the Annunciation of the Blessed Virgin Mary, Mother of God,[5] which date is rightly considered by the reckoning of the Anglican church to be the beginning of our Lord's incarnation, from which the first ordering of the world's creation took place.[6]

Baptisms

or a chronological catalogue of the infants in the church of Fisherton Delamere through the sacrament of baptism, in a register listing Christian people from the year of the Incarnation of our Lord Christ 1561.

1561

1   Cecily Ingram, baptised 13 July.

2   Judith Forster, baptised 19 August.

1   *Dallimer*
2   *qui fato concessit*
3   *exscriptus*
4   *continuatus*
5   *Deiparae*
6   *a quibusdam primordium creationis mundi perhibetur*

3   John Hodder, baptised 5 September.

4   John Robinson, baptised 16 November.

1562–4 [no entries][1]

1565

5   Richard Farret, baptised 9 April.

6   Christopher Pinfold, baptised 10 April.

7   Alice Eyles, baptised 10 May.

8   Elizabeth Colman, baptised 1 August.

9   William Passion, baptised 1 October.

10   Thomas Hicks, *alias* Eyles, baptised 13 October.

1566[2]

11   Eleanor Andrewes, baptised 15 February.

12   John Nightinghall, baptised 16 February.

13   Agnes Snelgar, baptised 19 February.

14   Margery Wandsborrough, baptised 4 September.

15   Thomas Ingram, baptised 7 October.

16   William Forster, baptised 19 October.

1567–9 [no entries]

---

1   *Tecilia Ingram bap* has been written against 1562, presumably repeating in error the entry from 1561

2   This appears to relate to the year beginning 1 January

1570

17   Mary Hicks, *alias* Eyles, baptised 9 July.

18   William Pinfold, baptised 6 September.

19   Amy Farret, baptised 1 October.

20   John Wansborrough, baptised 6 November.

1571

21   Stephen Mabill, baptised 8 October.

22   Margaret Andrewes, baptised 26 November.

1572

23   John Snelgar, son of Henry Snelgar, baptised 1 October.

1573

24   Amy, daughter of Mark Eyles, baptised 15 August.

25   Henry Hoskins, son of Edwards Hoskins of Bapton, yeoman, baptised 26 August.

26   Alice Hewlet, daughter of Stephen Hewlett, baptised 23 September.

1574

27   Jane Pinfold, daughter of Thomas Pinfold, baptised 1 February, which should be reckoned 1573.[1]

28   Philip Foster, son of Thomas Foster, baptised 1 June 1574.[2]

29   William Wandsborrough, son of John Wansborrough, baptised 23 July.

1   i.e. it should have been entered before the 1574 heading
2   the year added to avoid confusion with previous misplaced entry

30   Joan Spring, daughter of Henry Spring, baptised 19 August.

31   Philip Andrewes, son of William Andrewes, baptised 4 September.

32   John Dibble, son of John Dibble, baptised 2 November.

33   Thomas Eyles, son of Mark Eyles, baptised 23 December.

34   Susan Druse, daughter of Thomas Druse, baptised 28 December.

1575

35   Alice Passion, daughter of William Passion, baptised 10 April.

36   Thomas Hoskins, son of Edward Hoskins, yeoman, baptised 20 July.

37   Margery Hewlett, daughter of Stephen Hewlet, baptised 7 November.

38   Thomas Farret, son of Peter Farret, baptised 9 November.

1576

39   Agnes Everley, daughter of John Everley, baptised 19 September.

40   Helena or Eleanor Wansborrorough,[1] daughter of John Wansborrough, baptised 9 October.

41   Henry Rebeck, son of Thomas Rebeck, baptised 2 November.

42   Philip Spring, son of Henry Spring, baptised 3 November.

1577

43   Margery Andrewes, daughter of John Andrewes, baptised 3 May.

44   Elizabeth Eyles, daughter of Henry Eyles, baptised 28 May.

1   *sic*

1578/9

45 Fergus[1] and Mark, sons of William Passion, baptised 2 June.

46 Thomas Hoskins, son of John Hoskins, baptised 3 August.

47 John Hewlet, son of Stephen Hewlet, baptised 3 October.

48 Richard Rawlins, son of Brian Rawlins, baptised 7 October.

49 Agnes Passion, daughter of Robert Passion, baptised 23 September.

50 Honor Farret, daughter of Peter Farret, baptised 2 November.

51 Margaret Bennet, daughter of John Bennet, baptised 9 November.

52 Amy Eyles, daughter of Mark Eyles, baptised 23 January.

53 Joan Andrewes, daughter of John Andrewes, baptised 3 February.

1579/80

54 John Wallice, son of John Wallice, baptised 30 August.

55 Elizabeth Forster, daughter of Thomas Forster, baptised 30 October.

56 John Everley, son of John Everley, baptised 28 December.

57 Amy Eyles, daughter of Henry Eyles, baptised 9 January.

1580/1

58 John Frie, son of Thomas Frie, baptised 13 July.

59 Elizabeth Foster, daughter of William Foster, baptised 30 July.

60 James Rebeck, son of Thomas Rebeck, baptised 16 September.

1 *Vergasius*: see **564**. Vargeis was used as an *alias* surname by members of this family, and is presumably derived from the forename Latinised here.

61   Robert Kerby, son of Richard Kerby, baptised 12 January.

62   Margaret Farret, daughter of Peter Farret, baptised 23 March.

1581/2

63   Thomas Edmunds, son of William Edmunds, baptised 26 March.

64   Amy Wheeler, daughter of Thomas Wheeler, *alias* Young, also baptised 26 March.

65   Joan Rawlins, daughter of Brian Rawlins, baptised 16 May.

66   John Andrewes, son of John Andrewes, baptised 22 May.

67   Henry Wallice, son of John Wallice, baptised 8 October.

68   Guy Everley, son of John Everley, also baptised 8 October.

1582/3

69   Joan Bennet, daughter of John Bennet, baptised 22 May.

70   Henry Passion, son of William Passion, baptised 1 July.

71   Mary Hoskins, daughter of John Hoskins, baptised 8 August.

72   Philip Hewlet, son of Stephen Hewlet, baptised 31 January.

73   Alice Forster, daughter of Thomas Forster, baptised 21 February.

1583/4

74   Margaret Andrewes, daughter of John Andrewes, baptised 13 June.

75   Amy Rawlins, daughter of Brian Rawlins, baptised 16 June.

76   William Kerby, son of Richard Kerby, baptised 3 August.

77   Elizabeth Farret, daughter of Peter Farret, baptised 23 August.

78   Katharine Williams, daughter of Philip Williams, clerk, vicar of this church, 5 September.

79   John Frie, son of Thomas Frie, baptised 6 October.

80   Thomas Bennet, son of John Bennet, baptised 12 October.

81   Edward Hoskins, son of John Hoskins, baptised 20 November.

82   John Bengman, son of John Bengman, baptised 24 March.

1584/5

83   Mary River, daughter of William River, baptised 3 July.

84   Joan Forster, daughter of William Forster, baptised 6 July.

85   John Dourneford, son of James Dourneford, baptised 3 September.

86   Margaret Williams, daughter of Philip Williams, clerk, vicar of this church, 10 September.

87   Dorothy Bennet, daughter of John Bennet, baptised 9 October.

88   Joan Everley, daughter of John Everley, baptised 13 December.

89   Philip Mungy, son of Thomas Mungy, baptised 16 January.

90   Joan Hill, daughter of Richard Hill, baptised 23 January.

1585/6

91   Nicholas Passion, son of William Passion, baptised 1 August.

92   Jane Hewlet, daughter of Stephen Hewlet, baptised 6 August.

93   George Mathew, son of William Mathew, baptised 22 August.

94   Helena or Eleanor Hoskins, daughter of John Hoskins, baptised 3 September.

95   John Waddle, son of John Waddle, baptised 6 September.

96   Richard Kerby, son of Richard Kerby, baptised 7 September.

97   Agnes Williams, daughter of Philip Williams, clerk, vicar of this church, baptised 29 September.

98   Reginald Eyles, son of William Eyles, baptised 23 January.

99   Alexander Maurice, son of John Maurice, baptised 13 February.

1586/7

100   Philip Andrewes, son of John Andrewes, baptised 5 April.

101   Elizabeth Pierson, *alias* Vargis, daughter of John Pierson etc, baptised 10 April.

102   Christopher Bennet, son of John Bennet, baptised 2 September.

103   Henry Fry, son of Thomas Fry, baptised 12 November.

104   Philip Passion, son of William Passion, baptised 2 December.

105   Michael Bengman, son of John Bengman, baptised 19 December.

106   Eleanor Hoskins, daughter of John Hoskins, baptised 8 January.

1587/8

107   Philip Otherich, son of Richard Otherich, baptised 30 March.

108   Eleanor Bennet, daughter of John Bennet, baptised 20 September.

109   John Hoskins, son of John Hoskins, baptised 21 October.

110   William Farret, son of Peter Farret, baptised 15 October.

111 Agnes Hoskins, daughter of Edward Hoskins, baptised 5 November.

112 Thomas Whattle, son of John Whattle, also baptised 5 November.

113 Richard Soppe, son of John Soppe, baptised 1 January.

114 John Pierson, *alias* Vargis, son of John Pierson, etc, baptised 9 February.

115 Catherine Hill, daughter of Richard Hill, baptised 25 February.

1588/9

116 John Williams, son of Philip Williams, clerk, baptised 25 March.

117 Mark Hulet, son of Stephen Hulet, baptised 22 August.

118 Agnes Bennet, daughter of John Bennet, baptised 25 September.

119 Thomas Wallis, son of John Wallis, baptised 3 October.

120 Edmund Ingram, son of John Ingram, baptised 4 November.

1589/90

121 Edward Hoskins, son of John Hoskins, baptised 13 April.

122 William Maurice, son of John Maurice, baptised 25 September.

123 Agnes Blackman, daughter of Christopher Blackman, baptised 29 September.

124 Agnes Wandsborrough, daughter of William Wandsborrough, baptised 28 October.

125 William Abbat, son of William Abbat, baptised 31 November.[1]

126 Mark Brether, son of John Brether, baptised 10 December.

1 *sic*

127   Elizabeth Hulet, daughter of Stephen Hulet, baptised 21 February.

1590/1

128   Philip Williams, son of Philip Williams, clerk, baptised 2 July.

129   John Merriot, son of John Merriot, baptised 15 July.

130   John Bennet, son of John Bennet, baptised 3 September.

131   William Soppe, son of John Soppe, baptised 17 November.

132   Elizabeth Ingram, daughter of John Ingram, baptised 28 November.

133   Eleanor Rawlins, daughter of Brian Rawlins, baptised 28 December.

134   Joan Estman, daughter of John Estman, baptised 25 January.

1591/2

135   Susan Wandsborrough, daughter of William Wandsborrough, baptised 25 September.

136   Agnes Mascoll, daughter of George Mascoll, baptised 29 September.

137   Henry Meriot, son of John Merriot, baptised 10 January.

1592/3

138   Richard Holoway, son of William Holoway, baptised 20 August.

139   Joan Brether, daughter of John Brether, baptised 22 September.

140   Agnes Pierson, *alias* Vargeis, daughter of John Pierson erc, baptised 25 December.

141   William Clerk, son of John Clerke, baptised 6 January.

142   Agnes Ingram, daughter of John Ingram, baptised 20 January.

143   Alice Williams, daughter of Philip Williams, clerk, baptised 25 February.

1593/4

144   Eleanor Eyles, daughter of Henry Eyles of Bapton, yeoman, baptised 17 July.

145   Philip Mascoll, son of George Mascoll, baptised 11 August.

146   Philip Bennet, son of John Bennet, baptised 29 October.

147   Elizabeth Soppe, daughter of John Soppe, baptised 10 January.

148   Agnes Ingram, daughter of John Ingram, baptised 2 March.

149   Elizabeth Wansborrough, daughter of William Wandsborrough, baptised 15 March.

1594/5

150   George Merriot, son of John Merriot, baptised 5 April.

151   John Pierson, *alias* Vargeis, son of John Pierson, etc, baptised 7 April.

152   Henry Peareman. son of Richard Peareman, baptised 6 August.

153   Elizabeth Jacob, daughter of James Jacob,[1] baptised 10 November.

154   Elizabeth Maurice, daughter of John Maurice, baptised 12 November.

155   Edward Bennet, son of John Bennet, baptised 16 February.

1595/6

156   Susan Davies, daughter of William Davies, baptised 21 March.

1   *Jacobi Jacob,* implying that the surname was Jacob, not James

1596/7

157   Henry James, son of Edward James of Bapton, blacksmith, baptised 15 May.

158   Elizabeth Pierson, *alias* Vargeis, daughter of John Pierson, etc, baptised 4 June.

159   John Doughtie, son of Joel Doughtie, clerk, vicar of this church, born 24 June, baptised 29 June.

160   Ralph Bennet, son of John Bennet of Fisherton, husbandman, baptised 30 July.

1597/8

161   Alice Ingram, daughter of John Ingram the elder, of Bapton street, husbandman, baptised 20 May.

162   Joan Slade, daughter of John Slade of Fisherton, husbandman, baptised 22 May.

163   Mary Wandsborrough, daughter of William Wandsborrough the elder, of Bapton, husbandman, baptised 9 August.

1598/9

164   Joan Hoskins, daughter of John Hoskins the elder, of Bapton, craftsman,[1] baptised 30 March.

165   John Pembridge, son of John Pembridge, baptised 5 April.

166   Susan Lambert, daughter of John Lambert, *alias* Eustace, miller, baptised 14 September.

167   John Morely, son of Edward Morely, baptised 13 December.

168   George James, *alias* Mason, son of Edward James, etc, blacksmith,

1   *opificis*

baptised 13 January.

169   Roger Smyth, son of Christopher Smyth, baptised 31 January.

170   Joan Pierson, *alias* Vargeis, daughter of John Pierson, etc, baptised 18 March.

1599/1600

171   Christopher Passion, illegitimate son of Alice Passion and (so she says) Thomas Gulliford of Deptford, baptised 26 September.

172   Margaret Kent, daughter of Thomas Kent of Deptford in the parish of Wylye, yeoman, baptised in this church 1 December.

173   John Ingram, son of John Ingram the elder of Bapton street, husbandman, baptised 28[1] February.

174   Edward, illegitimate son of Henry Eyles of Bapton, yeoman, and acknowledged by him[2] (as it appears) (I do not find the name of the woman), baptised 3 March.

1600/1

175   William Wandsborrough, son of William Wandsborrough of Bapton, the elder, husbandman, baptised 22 April.

176   Henry Hoskins, firstborn son of Henry Hoskins, yeoman, the farmer of Bapton, baptised 22 May.

177   Elizabeth Slade, daughter of John Slade of Fisherton, husbandman and head of a household, baptised 23 May.

178   William Imber, son of Edward Imber of Deptford, parish of Wylye, husbandman, baptised in this church 29 May.

179   Sarah Toppe, daughter of Alexander Toppe, gentleman, descended from the gentry family of Topps of Stockton, the farmer of Fisherton

1   *ultimo*
2   *ab eodem agnitus*

manor by free right for life, baptised 20 July.

180   Mary James *alias* Mason, daughter of Edward James *alias* Mason, blacksmith of Bapton near the Lipp-yate, baptised 10 October.

181   Elizabeth Beachin, daughter of William Beachin, carpenter and master builder,[1] who was raised in Kent, but working on a dwelling-house in Bapton,[2] baptised 7 December.

182   Eleanor Pierson *alias* Vargeis, daughter of John Pierson *alias* Vargeis of Bapton, husbandman, baptised 6 March.

1601/2

183   James Rebeck, son of Henry Rebeck of Bapton, husbandman, baptised 25 October.

184   William Hoskins, son of John Hoskins the elder of Bapton, baptised 13 December.

185   Melior Slade, daughter of John Slade of Fisherton, husbandman, baptised 24 January.

186   William Court, son of Thomas Court of Fisherton, labourer, baptised 27 January.

187   Henry Ingram, son of John Ingram of Bapton at the Lippyat, husbandman, baptised 31 January.

1602/3

188   Elizabeth Beachin, daughter of William Beachin, carpenter of Bapton, baptised 2 May.

189   Eleanor Rockesborrough, daughter of John Rockesborrough, shepherd, baptised 2 May.

190   Robert Head, son of Richard Head, appointed the farmer of the

1   *fabri-lignarii et architecti*
2   *Baptoniae conducentis habitaculum*

Rectory,[1] baptised 1 August.

191 Thomas Baker *alias* Chate, son of Robert Baker *alias* Chate, baptised 8 August.

192 Stephen Hoskins, second son of Henry Hoskins, yeoman, etc, baptised 29 January.

193 Margaret Foster, daughter of Philip Forster of Bapton, husbandman, baptised 30 January.

194 Margaret Imber, daughter of Edward Imber, husbandman, baptised 6 February.

1603/4

195 Alexander James, son of Edward James *alias* Mason of Bapton, blacksmith, baptised 8 April.

196 Thomas Ingram, son of John Ingram the elder of Bapton street, husbandman, baptised 10 April.

197 William Andrewes, son of John Andrewes of Fisherton, husbandman, baptised 24 August.

198 Magdelena Pierson *alias* Vargeis, daughter of John Pierson, etc, baptised 12 October.

199 Henry Rebeck, son of Henry Rebeck of Bapton, husbandman, baptised 16 October.

200 George Slade, son of John Slade of Fisherton, baptised 20 November.

201 Elizabeth Smyth, daughter of Christopher Smyth of Deptford within Wylye, baptised 15 January.

1604/5

202 Roger Potticarie, son of John Poticarie, gentleman and clothier,

1 *Rectoriae ffirmar' deput'*

who is descended from the freeholding Potticaries of Wilton through his father, and the gentry family of the Topps of Stockton through his mother; by right the lessee[1] of the farm of Fisherton manor for a term of years, baptised 25 March.

203 Agnes Ingram, daughter of John Ingram of Bapton at the Lippe-yate, the younger, husbandman, baptised 15 November.

204 John Harding son of James Harding of Fisherton mill, baptised 29 January.

205 Eleanor Andrewes, daughter of John Andrewes, husbandman, baptised 1 March.

1605/6

206 Anne or Agnes Forster, daughter of Philip Forster of Bapton, husbandman baptised 9 May.

207 Amy Potticarie, daughter of John Potticarie, gentleman, etc, baptised 16 June.

208 Joan Hoskins, first daughter of Henry Hoskins of Bapton, yeoman, baptised 10 August.

209 Martha James, daughter of Edward James *alias* Mason of Bapton, blacksmith, baptised 1 December.

210 Eleanor Wandsborrough, daughter of William Wandsborrough of Bapton the elder, husbandman, baptised 15 January.

211 Margaret Rebeck, daughter of Henry Rebeck of Bapton, husbandman, baptised 21 February.

212 Anne Slade, daughter of John Slade of Fisherton, husbandman, baptised 26 February.

213 Henry son of Anne Court, a poor widow, baptised 19 March.

1   *jure conductorio*

1606/7

214 Dorothy and Cecily, twin daughters of a certain Clement Isaake,[1] baptised 30 May.

215 Alice Forster, daughter of Philip Forster of Bapton, husbandman, baptised 7 June.

216 John Borrough, son of John Borrough, labourer, baptised 20 October.

217 Henry Pierson, son of John Pierson *alias* Vargeis of Bapton, husbandman, baptised 24 December.

218 Susan Potticarie, daughter of John Potticarie, gentleman, etc, baptised 1 February.

1607/8

219 John Rockesborrough, son of John Rockesborrough, shepherd, baptised 11 April.

220 Christopher Slade, son of John Slade of Fisherton, husbandman, baptised 9 August.

221 Elizabeth Hoskins, daughter of William Hoskins of Bapton, weaver, one of the sons of Edward Hoskins yeoman, formerly, while he lived, the farmer of Bapton manor, baptised 1 November.

222 Catherine Ingram, daughter of John Ingram of Bapton at Lippyate, the younger, baptised 29 November.

223 Anne Rebeck, daughter of Henry Rebeck of Bapton, husbandman, baptised 12 March.

1608/9

224 Anne James, daughter of Edward James *alias* Mason of Bapton, blacksmith, baptised 18 September.

1 the spelling of the name is uncertain

225   Josiah Doughtie, son of Joel Doughtie, labourer, the son of Joel Doughtie, clerk etc, baptised 25 September.

226   John Hulet, son of Philip Hulet, shepherd, of Bapton, baptised 30 October.

227   Thomas Rockesborrough, son of John Rockesborrough, shepherd, of Fisherton, who was in truth the son of Thomas Rockborrough of Stockton, an old man, also a shepherd, baptised 18 February.

1609/10

228   Anne Forster, daughter of Philip Forster of Bapton, husbandman, baptised 25 June.

229   James Borrough, son of John Borrough, labourer, baptised 7 September.

230   Mary Passion, daughter of Henry Passion of Fisherton, husbandman, baptised 21 September.

231   William Eyles, son of Robert Eyles *alias* Hickes of Fisherton, husbandman, baptised 15 October.

232   Thomas Rebeck, son of James Rebeck of Bapton, husbandman, baptised 4 March.

1610/11

233   Elizabeth Doughtie, daughter of Joel Doughtie, labourer, who is actually[1] the son of Joel Doughtie, clerk, vicar of this church, baptised 17 February.

1611/12

234   Joan Flemming, daughter of Nicholas Flemming of Fisherton, labourer, baptised 27 March.

---

1   *nempe*

235   Thomas Ingram, son of John Ingram the elder of Bapton at Lippe-
yate, husbandman, baptised 14 April.

236   Joan James, daughter of Edward James *alias* Mason of Bapton,
blacksmith, baptised 15 April.

237   Joan Ingram, daughter of John Ingram the younger of Bapton at
Lyppeyate, husbandman, baptised 29 May.

238   Mary Hoskins, daughter of John Hoskins the younger of Fisherton,
labourer, baptised 30 May.

239   Judith Heliar, daughter of Thomas Heliar of Fisherton, labourer,
baptised 14 June.

240   Philip Hulett, son of Philip Hulett, shepherd, of Bapton, baptised 8
September.

241   John Peniecote, son of Henry Peniecote of Fisherton, labourer,
baptised 18 September.

242   Henry Eyles, son of Robert Eyles *alias* Hicks of Fisherton,
husbandman, baptised 19 January.

243   Richard Forster, son of Philip Forster of Bapton, husbandman,
baptised 2 February.

1612/13

244   Roger Rebeck, son of James Rebecke of Bapton, husbandman,
baptised 25 March.

245   William Passion, son of Henry Passion of Fisherton, husbandman,
baptised 24 May.

246   Robert Hayter, only son of Thomas Hayter, yeoman, who was
raised in Great Wishford; by his wife Eleanor, daughter of Henry Eyles,
formerly of Bapton, yeoman, baptised 11 October.

247   Nicholas Flemming, son of Nicholas Flemming of Fisherton, labourer, baptised 21 October.

248   Henry Dibble, son of Henry Dibble of Bapton, labourer, baptised 28 October.

1613/14

249   Joan Steevens, daughter of Josiah Steevens of Fisherton, weaver, baptised 12 September.

250   John Wandsborrough, son of William Wandsborrough, husbandman, who is the son of John Wandsborrough, formerly of Bapton, butcher, born 12 and baptised 17 October.

251   Jane Doughtie, daughter of Joel Doughtie of Fisherton, labourer, born 9 and baptised 12 December.

252   Another Henry Dibble, son of Henry Dibble of Bapton, husbandman, born and baptised 24 December.

253   John Hoskins, son of John Hoskins of Bapton, labourer, who is the son also of John Hoskins the elder of Bapton, baptised 31 December.

254   Anne Rebeck, daughter of James Rebeck of Bapton, husbandman, born 8 and baptised 13 March.

255   [register signed by] Joel Doughtie, vicar, Thomas Crockford, vicar. William Wandsborrough, John Andrewes, churchwardens.

1614/15

256   Christopher Hoskins, son of Henry Hoskins of Bapton, yeoman etc, born 25 and baptised 27 March.

257   Eleanor James, daughter of Edward James *alias* Mason of Bapton, blacksmith, born 20 and baptised 21 May.

258   Henry Forster, son of Philip Forster of Bapton, husbandman, born and baptised 2 November.

259 Sarah Eyles, daughter of Robert Eyles *alias* Hickes of Fisherton, husbandman, born 28 December and baptised 1 January.

260 Philip Cheverill, son of Edward Cheverill of Bapton, from Tisbury, tailor, born 18 and baptised 19 March.

261 Edmund Dibble, son of Henry Dibble of Bapton, labourer, born 18 and baptised 22 March.

262 John Ingram, son of John Ingram the younger of Bapton at Lippeyate, husbandman, born 21 and baptised 22 March.

263 [register signed by] Thomas Crockford, vicar.
Josiah Steevens for Mary Wandsborrow and Richard Coombs for Elizabeth Doughtie widow, churchwardens.

1615/16

264 Agnes Steevens, daughter of Josiah Steevens of Fisherton, weaver, born 31 May and baptised 4 June.

265 Joan Hoskins, daughter of John Hoskins the younger of Bapton, labourer, born 29 June, which is the feast of Peter, and baptised 2 July.

266 Judith Thomson, daughter of John Thomson of Fisherton, but from Teffont, husbandman, born 6 and baptised 10 September.

267 John Passion, firstborn son of John, the son of William Passion, husbandman of Fisherton, born 1 and baptised 4 October.

268 Joan Rebeck, daughter of James Rebeck of Bapton, husbandman, born 2 and baptised 4 January.

269 Philip and Bridget Hevell, son and daughter of Francis Hevell, shepherd, whose mother died from the exertion of giving birth to twins,[1] were born and baptised 20 of the previous[2] August.

270 [register signed by] Thomas Crockford, vicar

1 *mater moribunda gemino enixa est partu*
2 *e pred'*, to indicate that the entry is misplaced

Henry Hoskins of Bapton, yeoman and William Passion of Fisherton husbandman, churchwardens.

1616/17

271 Richard Flemming, son of Nicholas Flemming labourer of Fisherton, born 26 and baptised 31 May.

272 Grace Doughtie, daughter of Joel Doughtie of Fisherton, labourer, born 7 and baptised 9 February.

273 Elizabeth Bush, daughter of Philip Bush of Deptford within the parish of Wylye, labourer, born likewise in Deptford 17 February, and baptised in our church here at Fisherton 23 February (because the way to Wylye was blocked off by flood water).[1]

274 [register signed by] Thomas Crockford, vicar.
Nicholas Flemming for John Toppe, esquire, and Henry Ingram of Bapton, churchwardens.

1617/18

275 Edward Hoskins, fourth son of Henry Hoskins of Bapton, yeoman, born 1 and baptised 4 May.

276 William Wandsborrough, second son of William Wandsborrough of Bapton, husbandman, and of Jane his wife, born 14 and baptised 17 August.

277 Philip Forster, son of Philip Forster, husbandman, and of Anne his wife, born 22 September shortly before morning,[2] and baptised 28 September.

278 William Passion, second son of John Passion of Fisherton, labourer, and of Elizabeth his wife, born on the same day, 22 September, shortly before night,[3] and baptised at the same baptismal service[4] on 28 September.

---

1   *aquaru' enim irruptio iter ad Wiliam intercluserat*
2   *sub mane*
3   *sub noctem*
4   *baptisterio*

279 John Soppe, son of Richard Sopp of Fisherton, shepherd, and of Grace his wife, born 24 and baptised 26 November.

280 Alice Rebek, daughter of James Rebeck of Bapton, husbandman etc, and of Alice his wife, born 4 and baptised 7 December.

281 George Vargeis, illegitimate son of Elizabeth Vargeis, the younger daughter of John Vargeis *alias* Pierson of Bapton, husbandman, born 17 and baptised 19 December.

282 [register signed by] Thomas Crockford, vicar.
John Snelgar the elder, for Joan Snelgar, widow, his stepmother of Bapton, and John Tomsin, husbandman, for the tenement of Nicholas Steevens of Fisherton, churchwardens.

1618/19

283 Note that Christopher Maurice, first son of Alexander Maurice of this Fisherton, weaver, and of Anne his wife, was born at Edington 24 March 1617, and baptised there 27 March 1618.[1]

284 Bridget Hoskins, daughter of John Hoskins, now of Fisherton, labourer, but the son of John Hoskins the elder of Bapton, from the freeholding Bapton family of Hoskins; and of Margaret his wife, born 7 and baptised 11 April.

285 Mary Crockford, firstborn daughter of Thomas Crockford, clerk and vicar of this church, and of Joan his wife, born Monday 8 June around the second hour after midnight, and baptised Wednesday 24 June, the feast of St John the Baptist.

286 Margaret Dibble, daughter of Henry Dibble of Bapton, labourer, and of Susan his wife, born 25 and baptised 27 June.

287 Nicholas Rodeford, son of John Rodeford, labourer, an incomer working as a farm servant[2] on Fisherton manor, born 24 February and baptised 7 March.

1   i.e. three days later, 24 and 27 March 1617/18
2   *ad opus agriculturae famuli inquilini*

288 [register signed by] Thomas Crockford, vicar.
John Hevell of Fisherton, husbandman and shepherd, and Henry Dibble of Bapton, labourer,[1] for the tenement of widow Everley, churchwardens.

1619/20

289 Richard Maskoll, son of Philip Maskoll of Fisherton, weaver, and of Emma his wife, born 30 April, baptised 1 May.

290 Henry Goodinough, son of Thomas Goodinough of Sherrington, labourer, and of Eleanor, who was formerly his mistress but now is his wife. She is actually the daughter of John Hoskins the elder of Bapton, labourer, and the child was conceived[2] in Sherrington, as is reported, before marriage, but born after marriage in Bapton 22 May and baptised 23 May at Fisherton.

291 John Othen, son of John Othen, labourer, an incomer employed as a farm worker[3] on Fisherton manor, who is descended from the Othens, once a freeholding family[4] from Salisbury in Wiltshire; and of Joan his wife, born 23 and baptised 27 June.

292 Edward Aford, illegitimate son of Mary Aford, the daughter of a certain Roger Aford of Motcombe, Dorset, and (as she strongly claimed) of Edward Hoskins, tailor, the son of John Hoskins of Bapton the elder, labourer, born and baptised 30 July.

293 Robert Wandsborrough, third son of William Wandsborrough of Bapton, husbandman, and of Jane his wife, born Thursday 14 and baptised Sunday 17 October.

294 Jane Patient, first daughter of John Patient *alias* Passion of Fisherton, husbandman, and of Elizabeth his wife, born Sunday 19 December, and baptised the following Sunday, 26 December, the feast of St Stephen the first martyr.

---

1 laborer (in English)
2 *genitus*
3 *ad opus rusticum inquilini*
4 *quondam ingenuis*

295 Edmund Ingram, third son of John Ingram of Bapton at the field gate,[1] commonly called Lyppe-yate, husbandman, born Saturday 11 and baptised Sunday 12 March.

296 [register signed by] Thomas Crockford, vicar.
William Eyles of Fisherton, husbandman, and Philip Foster of Bapton for Joan Ingram, widow, churchwardens.

1620/1

297 Melior Soppe, second daughter of Richard Soppe of Fisherton, sometimes a husbandman, sometimes a shepherd,[2] and of Grace his wife, born Friday 7 and baptised Sunday 9 April.

298 William Cock, firstborn son of William Cocke the younger of Bapton, labourer, nephew of William Cocke the elder of Fisherton, labourer, originally from Devonshire; and of Elizabeth his wife, born Wednesday 19 and baptised Saturday 22 April.

299 John Rebeck, third son of James Rebeck of Bapton, husbandman, and of Alice his wife, born Saturday 22 and baptised Sunday 23 April.

300 John Doughty, second son of Joel Doughty, now of Fisherton, labourer, and of Jane his wife. He was the nephew of Joel Doughty, deceased, who while he lived was clerk and vicar of this church. John was born Friday 28 and baptised Sunday 30 April.

301 Another Margaret Dibble, second daughter of Henry Dibble of Bapton, labourer, and of Susan his wife, born Thursday 5 and baptised Friday 6 October.

302 Anne Crockford, second daughter of Thomas Crockford, clerk, vicar of this church, and of Joan his wife, born Monday 26 February, a little before midday, and baptised Tuesday 6 March.

303 [register signed by] Thomas Crockford, vicar.
William Patient of Fisherton and Philip Foster of Bapton, husbandman, churchwardens.

1   *apud porta' agrariam*
2   *modo agricolae modo pastoris oviu'*

1621/2

304   Thomas Wandsborrough, fourth son of William Wandsborrough of Bapton, husbandman, and of Jane his wife, born the first Sunday of Advent, 2 December, baptised Wednesday 5 December.

305   [register signed by] Thomas Crockford, vicar.
John Hulett of Fisherton and James Rebecke of Bapton, husbandmen, churchwardens.

1622/3

306   William Wandsborrough, the smaller of male twins,[1] second son of William Wandsborrough of Bapton the younger, husbandman, and of Joan, his wife. The birth was premature and his brother was stillborn, but he emerged alive and unharmed.[2] He received, by the grace of God, the sacrament of baptism at the hands of the vicar at a private ceremony in great haste,[3] around the hour of eight in the evening on Friday 26 April.

307   Elizabeth Maurice, firstborn daughter of Alexander Maurice of Fisherton, weaver, and of Anne his wife, born Thursday 9 and baptised Sunday 12 May.

308   Eizabeth Farret, firstborn daughter of William Farret of Fisherton, labourer, and of Mary his wife, born Tuesday 11 and baptised Thursday 13 June.

309   Susan Meriot, firstborn daughter of George Meriot of Bapton, labourer, and of Catherine his wife, born Thursday 4 and baptised Sunday 7 July.

310   Thomas, firstborn son of Thomas Battin, labourer, an incomer employed as a farm worker[4] on Fisherton manor, and of Edith his wife, born Saturday 13 and baptised Sunday 14 July.

1   *e duobus masculis gemellis, natu minor*
2   *partu praematuro (post fratrem exanimem) in lucem prodiit vivus idem at salvus.* The last two words are indistinct and uncertain
3   *sum'a cum festinatione privato ritu*
4   *ad opus rusticum inquilini*

311 Emma Mascall, first live-born daughter of Philip Mascall of Fisherton, weaver, and of Emma his wife, born Tuesday 30 and baptised Wednesday 31 July.

312 James Hoskins, firstborn son of Edward Hoskins of Bapton, tailor, and of Elizabeth his wife, born Monday 4 and baptised Sunday 10 November.

313 Edward, the second illegitimate son of Eleanor Goodynough of Bapton, a poor woman. Whether she is a wife or widow is uncertain, but what is certain is that she was married to a scoundrel who deserted her a long time ago,[1] Thomas Goodynough, formerly of Sherrington, labourer. When the mother was examined in the usual way[2] about her bastard son she named Henry James *alias* Mason of Bapton, blacksmith, to be the father. It appears that the boy was born prematurely[3] on Monday 13 January and baptised publicly in the church font on Tuesday 14 January.

314 Alice Patient, second daughter of John Patient of Fisherton, husbandman, and of Elizabeth his wife, born Monday 17 February and baptised on Sunday, the Sunday of Lent,[4] 23 February.

315 [register signed by] Thomas Crockford, vicar.
John Bennett of Fisherton, yeoman, and James Rebecke of Bapton, husbandman, chuchwardens.

1623/4

316 John Cocke, second son of William Cocke, labourer, an incomer employed as a farm worker[5] on Fisherton manor, and of Elizabeth his wife, born Monday 21 and baptised Wednesday 23 April.

317 Joel Doughtie, firstborn son of John Doughtie of Fisherton, yeoman, and of Joan his wife, born Monday 19 May, baptised Thursday, the feast of the Lord's Ascension, 22 May. He was given his name in grateful and

1 *uxor' an viduae incertu' est, certu' est relictae mariti sui nebulonis diu abhinc fugitivi*
2 *de more*
3 *immaturus*
4 *in carniprivio*
5 *ad opus rusticu' inquilini*

reverential memory of his paternal grandfather Joel Doughtie, the former vicar of this church.

318 James Wandsborrough, third son of William Wandsborrough of Bapton the younger, husbandman, and of Joan his wife, born Saturday 9 and baptised Sunday 10 August.

319 Joan Hoskins, firstborn daughter of Edward Hoskins of Bapton, tailor, and of Elizabeth his wife, born Thursday 6 and baptised Sunday 9 November.

320 Christian Rebecke, fourth daughter of James Rebecke of Bapton, husbandman, and of Alice his wife, born Monday 22 December, and baptised Wednesday, the eve of the Lord's Nativity, 24 December.

321 [register signed by] Thomas Crockford, vicar.
John Ingram of Bapton at the Lipe-yate, and John Slade the younger of Fisherton, husbandmen, churchwardens.

1624/5

322 Alice Crockford, third daughter of Thomas Crockford, clerk, vicar of this church, and of Joan his wife, born on Monday in Easter week, 29 March, between the first and second hours of the afternoon, and baptised Friday in the same week, 2 April.

323 Thomas Dibble, fourth son of Henry Dibble of Bapton, labourer, and of Susan his wife, born Friday 28 May, baptised Saturday 29 May.

324 John Snelgar, firstborn son of John Snelgar of Bapton, the elder, husbandman, and of Elizabeth his wife, born Friday 27 August, baptised Sunday the 14th after Trinity, 29 August.

325 Agnes Hoskins, firstborn illegitimate[1] daughter of William Hoskins of Bapton, tailor, and of Elizabeth his wife, born Tuesday, the feast of Saint Mathew, 21 September, baptised Friday 24 September.   .

---

1   *illegitima*, written instead of *notha*, the usual word for an illegitimate child: William and Elizabeth had married on 2 August, some seven weeks before the birth (**482**).

326   Edith Guilbert, firstborn daughter of John Guilbert of Fisherton, husbandman, and of Eleanor his wife, born Friday 1 October, baptised Sunday, the 20th after Trinity, 10 October.

327   Thomas Meriot, a small, sick and very delicate child, the second son of George Meriot of Bapton, labourer and of Catherine his wife, born before he was expected.[1] He arrived on Saturday evening, and was baptised semi-privately,[2] the best which could be done, with all due haste,[3] at the hands of the vicar of this church on the same day, Saturday 30 October.

328   John Doughtie, second son of John Doughtie of Fisherton, yeoman, one of the churchwardens this year, and of Joan his wife, born Monday, the feast of St John the Evangelist, 27 December, and baptised Thursday 30 December.

329   Joan Maurice, second daughter of Alexander Maurice of Fisherton, weaver, and of Anne his wife, born and baptised Sunday, the second after Epiphany, 16 January.

330   [register signed by] Thomas Crockford, vicar.
Thomas Moore of Bapton and John Doughtie of Fisherton, yeomen, churchwardens.

1625/6

331   Joan Crockford, the fifth child and fourth daughter of Thomas Crockford, clerk, vicar of this church, and of Joan his wife, born on Sunday 8 May between the hours of nine and ten before noon, and baptised Saturday 14 May.

332   Nicholas Steevens, firstborn son of Nicholas Steevens of Fisherton, husbandman, and of Joan his wife, born Thursday 14 July, baptised Sunday 17 July.

333   Anne Merriot, second daughter of George Merriot of Bapton, labourer, and of Catherine his wife, born Wednesday 14 December, baptised Thursday 15 December.

1   *natus partu nondum expectato*
2   *demi privato baptisterio*
3   *sum'a qua fieri potuit, matura festinatione*

334   Christopher Hinwood, second son of Hugh Hinwood of Deptford, blacksmith, and of Maud his wife, born at Deptford Tuesday 13 December, and baptised at our Fisherton (as the way to Wylye was impassable because a bridge had collapsed),[1] on Sunday 18 December.

335   Robert Wandsborrough, fourth son of William Wandsborrough of Bapton the younger, husbandman, and of Joan his wife, born Saturday 18 February, baptised Sunday 19 February, the Sunday before Lent.[2]

336   [register signed by] Thomas Crockford, vicar.
Anthony Balard of Bapton and Nicholas Steevens of Fisherton, yeomen, churchwardens.

1626/7

337   Joan and Elizabeth Doughtie, twin young infants born prematurely (as it is alleged), the first and second daughters of John Doughtie of Fisherton, yeoman, and of Joan his wife, On the day of their birth and as quickly as possible,[3] they were legitimately baptised in a private baptismal service at the hands of the vicar on Palm Sunday, 2 April.

338   Roger Patient, third son of John Patient of Fisherton, husbandman, and of Elizabeth his wife, born Monday 3 April, and because the mother was in grievous danger[4] baptised on Tuesday 4 April.

339   Sarah Guilbert, second daughter of John Guilbert of Fisherton, husbandman, and of Eleanor his wife, born Wednesday 3 May, baptised Friday 5 May.

340   Bridget Farret, second daughter of William Farret of Fisherton, labourer, and of Mary his wife, born Thursday, the feast of the Ascension of the Lord, and baptised on the following Sunday 21 May.

341   Elizabeth Bennett, firstborn daughter of Ralph Bennett of Bapton, but from Fisherton, husbandman, and of Alice his wife, born Friday 23

1   *quippe pontu' disjectio iter ad Wiliam impedierat*
2   *d'nico in carnisprivio*: it was the Sunday followed by Ash Wednesday and the start of Lent.
3   *die nata fuerunt, et quam expedite fieri potuit*
4   *lugubri matris periculo*

June, baptised Sunday 25 June.

342 George Merriot, third son of George Merriot of Bapton, labourer, and of Catherine his wife, born on Sunday the eve of Christ's nativity, and baptised on Monday the feast of the nativity, 25 December.

343 Bridget Mascall, third daughter of Philip Mascall of Fisherton, weaver, and of Emma his wife, born Thursday 11 January, baptised Friday 12 January.

344 John Crockford, sixth child and second son of Thomas Crockford, clerk, vicar of this church, and of Joan his wife, born Monday 31 January, a little after the hour of seven in the morning, and baptised on the following Sunday, 4 February, the Sunday before Lent.

345 Henry Doughtie, third son of John Doughtie of Fisherton, yeoman, and of Joan his wife, born Monday 12 March, baptised on Palm Sunday 18 March.

346 [register signed by] Thomas Crockford, vicar.
Christopher Smyth of Fisherton[1] the elder, and Henry Rebecke of Bapton, yeomen, churchwardens.

1627/8

347 Mary Cocke, first daughter of William Cocke now of Vennhampton, Devon,[2] husbandman, and of Elizabeth his wife, born at Bapton Saturday 21 July, baptised in the public baptismal service of our church of Fisherton on Sunday 22 July.

348 Mary Snelgar, firstborn daughter of John Snelgar the elder of Bapton, husbandman, and of Elizabeth his wife, born Wednesday 5 September, baptised Sunday 9 September.

349 Edward Hoskins, first son of Edward Hoskins of Bapton, tailor, and of Elizabeth his wife, born Thursday 11 October, baptised Sunday 14 October.

1 Fisherton mill in bishop's transcript
2 *Fenne-hampton*: presumably Vennhampton, a settlement in Norton Fitzwarren, Somerset, is intended.

350   Susan Steevens, second daughter of Nicholas Steevens of Fisherton, husbandman, and of Joan his wife, born Friday 26 October, baptised Saturday 27 October.

351   Ralph Bennet, second child, but first and only posthumous son of Ralph Bennet, formerly of Bapton, husbandman, deceased, and of Alice his former wife, now widow, was born and baptised Sunday, the third after the feast of Epiphany of the Lord, 27 January.

352   Alice Hoskins, second legitimate daughter of William Hoskins of Bapton, tailor, and of Elizabeth his wife, born Monday 18 February, baptised Friday 22 February.

353   Elizabeth Patient, third daughter of John Patient of Fisherton, husbandman, and of Elizabeth his wife was born and baptised on the first Sunday in Lent,[1] 2 March.

354   John Guilbert, firstborn son of John Guilbert of Fisherton, husbandman, and of Eleanor his wife, born Monday 3 March, baptised Friday 7 March.

355   [register signed by] Thomas Crockford, vicar.
William Patient of Fisherton, and William Wandsborough the elder of Bapton, yeomen, churchwardens.

1628/9

356   Dorothy Doughtie, third daughter of John Doughtie of Fisherton, yeoman, and of Joan his wife, born Saturday 9 August, baptised on the ninth Sunday after Trinity, 10 August.

357   John Davies, firstborn son of John Davies of North Wraxall, free tenant of the manor of Bapton by right of co-emption,[2] born in the same manor on Wednesday 15 October, baptised in a public baptismal service at Fisherton on the following Wednesday, 22 October.

---

1   *Quadragesima*
2   *iure coemptitio*. The root meaning of *coemptio* appears to relate to acquiring property through marriage. Davies purchased the manor soon after he married Joan Hoskins, daughter of the previous leaseholder (see **486**).

358   Anne Dibble, third[1] daughter of Henry Dibble of Bapton, labourer, and of Susan his wife, born Friday 23 January, baptised Saturday 24 January.

359   [register signed by] Thomas Crockford, vicar.
Robert Eyles *alias* Hicks of Fisherton, and William Wandsborrough the younger of Bapton husbandmen, churchwardens.

1629/30

360   Richard Tillie firstborn Son of Richard Tillie now of Deptford manor, but from Erlestoke,[2] tailor, and of Mary his wife, born at Deptford on Saturday 21 March 1628, baptised at our Fisherton (partly through the lack of a curate at Wylye, but also because of a flood between Deptford and Wylye),[3] on Thursday 26 March 1629.[4]

361   Charles Merriot, fourth son of George Merriot of Fisherton, labourer, and of Catherine his wife, born Wednesday 1 April, baptised Saturday, the eve of Easter, 4 April.

362   Thomas Doughtie, third son of Joel Doughtie of Fisherton, labourer, parish clerk of this church, was born and baptised on Tuesday in Pentecost week, 26 May.

363   John Wandsborrough, fifth son of William Wandsborrough the younger of Bapton, husbandman, and of Joan his wife, born Monday 27 July, baptised Saturday 1 August.

364   Sarah Smith, firstborn daughter of Christopher Smyth the younger of Fisherton mill, yeoman, and of Phoebe his wife, born on Thursday 27 August, baptised on Sunday 31 August.[5]

---

1   a space is left in the register, but third is given in the bishop's transcript
2   *Stoake Comitis*
3   *tam p'pter defectum curati apud Wiley, quam p'pter illuvie aquae inter Detford et Wiley*
4   The years are given because of the start of the year on 25 March by the Julian calendar; baptism took place five days after birth.
5   *recte* 30 August.

365   William Doughtie, fourth son of John Doughtie of Fisherton, yeoman, and of Joan his wife, was born and baptised on Monday, the feast of the Innocents, 28 December.

366   John Ingram, firstborn son of John Ingram of Bapton street, yeoman, and of Anne his wife, born on Thursday 7 January, baptised Sunday 10 January.

367   Thomas Guilbert, second son of Nicholas Guilbert of Fisherton, husbandman, and of Eleanor his wife, born Tuesday 9 February during Lent,[1] baptised Thursday 11 January.

368   John Steevens, second son of Nicholas Steevens of Fisherton, husbandman, and of Joan his wife, born the fourth Sunday in Lent, 7 March, baptised Wednesday 10 March.

369   [register signed by] Thomas Crockford, vicar.
Stephen Hoskins of the manor of Bapton, yeoman, and John Andrews of Fisherton, husbandman, churchwardens.

1630/1

370   Nicholas Hoskins, first son of William Hoskins of Bapton, tailor, and of Elizabeth his wife, born Friday 6 August, baptised Sunday 8 August.

371   Christopher Smyth, first son of Christopher Smyth of Fisherton mill, the younger, yeoman (and nephew of Christopher Smyth the elder, also of the mill, yeoman), and of Phoebe his wife, born Thursday the feast of Saint Mathias the Apostle,[2] baptised the first Sunday in Lent, 27 February.

372   [register signed by] Thomas Crockford, vicar.
Henry Dibble for Mary Ingram of Bapton, yeoman, and [illegible] for Frances [?Hev]ell of Fisherton, husbandman, churchwardens.

1631/2

373   Elizabeth Guilbert, third daughter of John Guilbert of Fisherton,

1   day and date missing from register, supplied from bishop's transcript.
2   24 February

husbandman, and of Eleanor his wife, born Wednesday 11 May, baptised, by urgent necessity at home in a private baptism in place of a public one by the ministry of the vicar on Friday 13 May.

374 John Farret, first son of William Farret of Fisherton, labourer, and of Mary his wife, born Sunday 7 August, baptised Saturday 13 August.

375 Joan Snelgar, second daughter of John Snelgar the elder of Bapton, husbandman, and of Elizabeth his wife, born Thursday 8 September, baptised Sunday 11 September.

376 Elizabeth Doughtie, fourth daughter of John Doughtie of Fisherton, yeoman, and Joan his wife, born Wednesday 26 October, baptised Sunday 30 October.

377 Edward James, firstborn son of Henry James *alias* Mason of Fisherton, blacksmith, and of Mary, who is now his wife, born Saturday 5 November, baptised Sunday 6 November.

378 Anne Foster, firstborn daughter of Thomas Foster of Fisherton, but from Bapton, husbandman, and of Agnes, who is now his wife, born Friday 18 November, baptised Saturday 19 November.

379 Elizabeth Crockford, fifth daughter, but in fact the seventh child of Thomas Crockford, vicar of this church, and of Joan his wife, born Thursday 26 January within the hours of one and twelve[1] in the afternoon, and baptised Monday following, 30 January.

380 Elizabeth Ingram, first daughter of John Ingram of Bapton, husbandman, and of Anne his wife, born Thursday 23 February, baptised on St Mathias' day, 25 February.

381 [register signed by] Thomas Crockford, vicar.
William Patient of Bapton, husbandman and John Snelgar the elder of Fisherton, yeoman, churchwardens.

1632/3

382 Eleanor Rocksborrough, first daughter of John Rocksborrough of

1   *sic: intra horas primam et duodecimam pomeridianos*

Fisherton manor, shepherd, and of Eleanor his wife, born Saturday 16 June, baptised Sunday 17 June.

383   Francis Guilbert, third son of John Guilbert of Fisherton, husbandman, and of Eleanor his wife, born and baptised on Wednesday 27 June.

384   William Hoskins, third son of Edward Hoskins of Bapton, tailor, and of Elizabeth his wife, born Thursday 20 September, baptised Friday the feast of St Matthew, 21 September.

385   Eleanor Steevens, third daughter of Nicholas Steevens of Fisherton, yeoman and Joan his wife, born Wednesday, before daylight, and baptised at afternoon prayers[1] on Sunday 30 September.

1633/4

386   John Hoskins, second son of William Hoskins of Bapton, tailor, and of Elizabeth his wife, born Wednesday 3 April, baptised Friday 5 April.

387   Thomas Ingram, first son of Thomas Ingram of Fisherton, but from Bapton, husbandman, and of Dorothy his wife, born Sunday 7 April, baptised the following Friday 12 April.

388   [register signed by] Thomas Crockford, vicar.
Robert Green and John Hullet, yeomen, churchwardens.

There follow seven 1633 baptisms in English written in the same hand as that which recorded Crockford's burial, presumably added after his death. The record of baptisms in this register continues in English until 1693.

1   *praecibus pomeridianis*

Marriages

or, a chronological catalogue of the men and women who have completed[1] their marriage contract by a religious service in the church of Fisherton Delamere, from the year of our Lord's incarnation 1566.

1566

389 Thomas Eve and Agnes Merriot, married 9 January.

390 Henry Callaway and Helena Light, married 25 January.

1567

391 John Randoll and Joan Forster, married 4 November.

1568

392 Thomas Druse and Mary Hoskins, married 6 July.

393 Edward Hoskins and Mary Andrewes, married 16 November.

394 John Batt and Elizabeth Parker, married 24 November.

1569

395 Henry Eyles and Helena or Eleanor Hoskins, married 13 September.

396 William Andrewes and Joan Mascoll, married 13 November.

397 Thomas Mascoll and Eleanor Knee, married 5 November.

398 Edward Hoskins and Joan Eyles, married 20 November.

399 John Hoskins and Joan Ingram, married 25 November.

---

1   *consummaverunt*, completed, not consummated in the modern sense

1570-2 [no entries]

1573

400   Stephen Hulet and Margery Hevell, married 27 September.

1574

401   Thomas Stoning and Agnes Comeles, married 25 April.

402   Henry Spring and Agnes Hoskins, married 3 May.

403   John Merriot and Elizabeth Abbat, married 7 June.

404   Thomas Dibble and Elizabeth Hoskins, married 13 November.

405   John Bowles and Alice Ingram, 20[1] November.

1575-6 [no entries]

1577/8

406   Thomas Forster and Joan Wandsborrough, married 10 August.

407   Thomas Frie and Agnes Humphrey, married 25 August.

408   William Hevell and Elizabeth Hulett, married 10 November.

409   John Wallice and Elizabeth Fish, married 30 January.

410   William Passion and Margaret Eyles, married 23 February.

1578/9 [no entries]

1579/80

411   Robert Howell and Elizabeth Forster, married 25 January.

412   John Hoskins the elder and Christian West, married 2 February.

1   a space is left after *vicesimo*

1580-1 [no entries]

1582/3

413 Philip Williams, clerk, vicar of this church, and Margaret Eyles, *alias* Hicks, married 30 June.

1583/4

414 John Bengman and Florence Mathew, married 2 October.

415 Robert Lock and Joan Horder, *alias* Taylor, married 28 January.

1584/5

416 William Cooke and Elizabeth Payne, married 5 October.

417 Richard Hill and Alice Eyles, married 13 November.

1585/6

418 William Mathew and Margaret Rogers, married 11 May.

419 John Pierson, *alias* Vargeis, and Catherine Humphreys, married 1 July.

420 John Estman and Eleanor Stokes, married 21 November.

1586-7 [no entries]

1588/9

421 Henry Gantlet and Radican[1] Frowd, married 27 May.

422 Nicholas Sturgis and Agnes Pembright, married 6 September.

423 William Lake and Bridget Sandis, married 27 September.

1 *Radicana*

424 John Brether and Eleanor Gaynons or Genings, married 18 November.

1589/90

425 Anthony Eyles and Susan Wandsborrough, married 9 April.

426 John Merriot and Agnes Humphreyes, married 2 October.

427 John Ford and Elizabeth Eylis, married 22 October.

428 Michael Fricker and Agnes Ingram, married 3 November.

1590/1 [no entries]

1591/2

429 William Holoway and Agnes Pettie, married 25 October.

430 John Minety and Agnes Wandsborrough, married 29 November.

431 George Smyth and Joan Andrewes, married 24 February.

1592/3 [no entries]

1593/4

432 Richard Steevens and Margaret Andrewes, married 11 June.

433 William Steving[1] and Margaret Andrewes, married 23 September.

434 John Cross and Joan Petty, married 12 February.

1594/5

435 Henry Snelgar and Joan Takle, widow, married 27 May.

1595/6 [no entries]

---

1   the name is unclear

1596/7

436   Richard Gibbons and Catherine Clement, both of this parish, married 31 October.

1597/8

437   John Wandsborough the younger, son of John Wandsborough of Bapton, butcher, and Julian Aylewood of Cloford,[1] Somerset, married 30 May.

438   Stephen Hibard of Barford, yeoman, and Joan Hoskins, widow, relict of Edward Hoskins, formerly of Bapton, married 4 September.

439   William Wickham of Boreham in the parish of Warminster, and Elizabeth Imber of this parish, married 24 October.

1598/9 [no entries]

1599/1600

440   Henry Hoskins, yeoman, the farmer of Bapton, son of Edward, and Joan Gerish, widow, relict of John Gerish formerly of Melksham,[2] yeoman, deceased, married 2 July.

441   John Dew of Wylye, husbandman, and Elizabeth Hoskins, daughter of the foresaid Edward and sister of the foresaid Henry, married 22 October.

442   John Tanner of Tellisford,[3] Somerset, and Agnes Snelgar of Bapton, married 1 December.

1600/1

443   Edward Imber, labourer, servant of Henry Barnes of Deptford in the parish of Wylye, yeoman, and Melior Mathew, daughter of John Mathew, also of Deptford, married in our church of Fisherton Delamere 7 April.

1   *Clowford*
2   *Milsham*
3   *Telsford*

444   George Hodder of Bapton, husbandman and tailor, and Agnes Rebeck, widow, relict of Thomas Rebeck of Bapton, husbandman, married 30[1] June.

445   Edward Barter of Deptford in the parish of Wylye and Joan Edridge of this Fisherton parish, married 23 February.

1601/2

446   Thomas Court, labourer, and Alice Smyth, both of this parish, married 18 May.

447   William Norman of Mells, Somerset, dyer, and Elizabeth Forster, daughter of Thomas Forster of Bapton, husbandman, married 9 June.

1602/3

448   Henry Rebeck, husbandman, and Elizabeth Norton, both of Bapton, married 10 August.

1603/4

449   Thomas Eyles and Joan Foyle, both of this parish, married 11 September.

450   John Hulett of Fisherton, husbandman, and Margaret, illegitimate daughter of Henry Eyles *alias* Hicks of Bapton, husbandman,[2] married 18 December.

451   John Soppe of Fisherton, shepherd, son of John Soppe of Fisherton, shepherd, and Alice Passion, daughter of William Passion the elder, and sister of William Passion the younger of Fisherton, husbandman, married 20 February.

1604/5

452   Edward Chevers or Cheverill of Tisbury, tailor, and Joan Forster,

1   *ultimo*
2   husbandman written in English

daughter of Thomas Forster of Bapton, husbandman, by his second wife, that is to say Joan, Wandsborow's daughter, married 11 November.

1605/6

453 Robert Skydmore of Stockton, shepherd, and Elizabeth Forster of Bapton married 24 June.

454 John Andrewes of Maiden Bradley, husbandman, and Eleanor Wandsborrough, daughter of John Wandsborrough of Bapton, butcher, married 1 July.

1606–7 [no entries]

1608/9

455 Joel Doughtie the younger, labourer, son of Joel Doughtie the elder, clerk, vicar of this church, and Jane Hulet, daughter of Stephen Hulet of Fisherton, husbandman, deceased, married 29 June.

456 Henry Passion, husbandman, son of William Passion the elder of Fisherton, husbandman, and Joan Doughtie, daughter of Joel Doughtie, clerk, vicar of this church, married 25 December, that is to say on the feast of the birth of the Lord Christ.

1609/10

457 Thomas Heyter, son of Robert Heyter of Great Wishford, yeoman, and Eleanor Eyles *alias* Hicks, legitimate daughter of Henry Eyles *alias* Hicks, of Bapton, yeoman, married 8 January.

458 John Hoskins the younger, labourer, son of John Hoskins the elder, of Bapton, labourer, and Margaret Farret, daughter of Peter Farett of Fisherton, labourer, deceased, married 29 January.

1610/11

459 John Hooper of Stockton, husbandman, son also[1] of John Hooper, formerly of the same Stockton, husbandman; and Alice Forster, daughter

1   *itidem*, an allusion presumably to them sharing the same name

of Thomas Forster, formerly of Bapton, husbandman, by his wife Joan, Wandsborrow's daughter, married 18 June.

460   John Ingram of Bapton at the Lippeyate, the elder, husbandman, and Amy Farret, daughter of Peter Farret of Fisherton, labourer, deceased, married 4 February.

1611/12

461   William Coales of Witham Friary,[1] Somerset, shepherd, and Agnes Mascoll, daughter of George Mascoll of Fisherton, deceased, married 25 November.

462   Thomas Hoskins of Hanging Langford[2] within the parish of Steeple Langford, tailor, one of the sons of Edward Hoskins, formerly the farmer[3] of Bapton, deceased, and Catherine Doughtie, one of the daughter of Joel Doughtie, clerk, vicar of this church, married 27 January.

1612/13

463   John Rowden of Hanging Langford within the parish of Steeple Langford, yeoman, and Elizabeth Doughtie, daughter of Joel Doughtie, clerk, vicar of this church, married 31[4] May.

464   William Knight the elder, of Stockton, ploughwright, and Tamsin Heywood, a woman not previously married, maidservant of Henry Hoskins, the farmer of Bapton, married 26 October.

1613/14

465   John Bennet of Fisherton yeoman, twice widowed, and Elizabeth Smithfield, daughter of Thomas Smythfield, of Heytesbury, yeoman, married 26 April.

466   Thomas Cooke of Steeple Langford, tailor[5] and Elizabeth Wickham

1   *Charter-house Witham*
2   *Langford pendent*
3   *Fermarii*
4   *ultimo*
5   *vestar'*

of Fisherton, widow, married 23 June.

467 John Passion, only son of William Passion of Fisherton, husbandman, and Elizabeth Haylock, daughter of Robert Haylock of Tisbury, husbandman, married 26 October.

1614/15 [no entries]

1615/16

468 William Knight of Fisherton, the younger, ploughwright, son of William Knight likewise of Fisherton, the elder, ploughwright, and Elizabeth Hulet, daughter of Stephen Hulet, formerly of Fisherton, husbandman, deceased, married 31 July.

469 Walter Greene of Compton,[1] Dorset, labourer, and Anne Furnell *alias* Rogers, daughter of Richard Furnell *alias* Rogers of Chilmark, labourer, actually a maidservant of John Bennet of Fisherton, yeoman, married 17 November.

1616/17

470 Anthony Ballard of Stockton, husbandman, descended from the Ballards of Steeple Ashton, and Margaret Eyles *alias* Hicks, widow, relict of Henry Eyles *alias* Hicks, formerly of Bapton, husbandman, deceased, married 28 October.

1617/18

471 Richard Passion of Sherrington, husbandman, widower, and Elizabeth Ingram, firstborn[2] maiden daughter of John Ingram, formerly of Bapton, husbandman, deceased, married 28 April.

472 Nicholas Flemming of Fisherton, a labourer from Stockton, and Margaret Scammell from Wylye, married 26 October.

---

1 probably Compton Abbas near Shaftesbury
2 *natu maxima*

1618/19

473 Richard Grumbold, a young labourer, and Judith Doughty, youngest daughter of Joel Doughty, clerk, deceased, sometime vicar of this church, and of Elizabeth his wife, married 13 July.

1619/20 [no entries]

1620/1

474 Henry Hoskins, a young bachelor and freeholder, more than 20 years old, firstborn son of Henry Hoskins, yeoman, deceased, formerly the farmer of Bapton, and of Joan his wife; and Frances Blacker, a maiden in the flower of her youth,[1] that is to say only just 17 years old or very little more,[2] the only daughter of Edmund Blacker of the hamlet of Pierston[3] in Gillingham parish, Dorset, yeoman, and of Jane his wife, married in Gillingham church on Monday 9 October.

475 George Merriot, a young unmarried labourer, almost 26 years old, born and spent almost his whole life in Bapton;[4] and Catherine Benham, a young girl almost 20 years old, daughter of William Benham of Steeple Langford, shepherd, married on Monday 22 January.

1621/2

476 William Farret of Fisherton, an unmarried labourer, more than 33 years old, born in Fisherton, and spent almost his whole life there; and Mary Aford, a girl of almost thirty, daughter of Robert Aford of Motcombe, Dorset, married on Monday 9 April.

477 William Wandsborrough of Bapton, a young unmarried husbandman, almost 22 years old, son and heir of William Wandsborrough, formerly of Bapton, husbandman, deceased, and of Mary his wife, now his widow and still living; and Joan Hooper of Stockton, a girl 30 years old, one of the daughters of John Hooper, formerly of Stockton, husbandman,

1   *in tenore aetatis flora virgo*
2   *inutpote annorum fere septemdecem [. . .] exiguo supra.* The word obscured by an ink-blot may be *vel.*
3   *de Peereston viculo;* Pierston Farm stands west of Milton on Stour.
4   *fere perpetuo educatus*

and of Elizabeth his wife, both deceased. It is reported that they were married in the peculiar[1] parish church of Ansty, on Monday in Lent, 4 March.

1622/3

478 Robert Philippes, a young unmarried labourer, almost 26 years old more or less, the living-in servant of John Bennet of Fisherton, yeoman, employed in farm work,[2] descended from a labouring family in Shrewton; and Elizabeth Farret, a woman not previously married, 40 years old more or less, descended from a labouring family here in Fisherton, married on Thursday, the feast of St James, 25 July.

479 John Doughtie of Fisherton, a bachelor and freeholder, a little over 26 years old, youngest son of Joel Doughtie, clerk, former vicar of this church, deceased, and of Elizabeth his wife, who has also died; and Joan Goddard of Upton Lovell, a girl 30 years old more or less, descended from a working family there, married by licence on Monday 12 August.

480 Edward Hoskins of Bapton, an unmarried tailor a little more than 33 years old, one of the sons of John Hoskins the elder, formerly of Bapton, deceased, who was descended from a freeholding family there, and of Joan his wife who has also died; and Elizabeth Weekman, a woman more or less 36 years old, descended from a family of carpenters[3] from Clatford near Andover (as is reported), were married (after the banns had been legally published in advance) on Monday 23 September.

1623/4

481 John Guilbert of Fisherton, an unmarried husbandman, almost 30 years old, descended from a farming family of Maiden Bradley; and Eleanor Andrewes, a girl almost 19 years old, the only daughter of John Andrewes of this Fisherton, husbandman, and of Eleanor his wife, were married (after the banns had been legally published in advance) on Monday 10 November.

1   *exempta.* The Knights Hospitallers had peculiar jurisdiction over Ansty church, which passed in 1546 to the manorial lords and was retained until the 19th century (*VCH Wilts*, xiii, 98).

2   *ad opus rustic' famulus domesticus*

3   *lignaria*

1624/5

482   William Hoskins, an unmarried tailor, almost 23 years old, the youngest born son of John Hoskins the elder, formerly of Bapton, labourer, deceased, and of Joan his wife; and Elizabeth Bridmore, a woman more or less 26 years old, one of the daughters of Peter Bridmore, now of Winterbourne Stoke, shepherd, and of Alice his wife. She was in the domestic service[1] of Anthony Ballard of Bapton, husbandman, and Margaret his wife, and they were married (after the banns had been legally published in advance) on Monday 2 August.

483   Henry Baker of Sherfield [English], Hampshire,[2] yeoman, once widowed, more or less 50 years old; and Joan Ingram, only daughter of Henry Ingram of our Bapton, yeoman, and of Mary his wife, a maid almost 30 years old, married (after the banns had been legally published in advance) on Monday 15 November.

484   Luke Snowe of Tisbury, a husbandman once widowed, almost 60 years old; and Honor Deere, descended from a farming family of Dinton, domestic servant of widow Joan Hoskins of Bapton manor, a woman not previously married, almost 40 years old, married (after the banns had been legally published in advance) on Monday 22 November.

1625/6

485   Ralph Bennet of Fisherton, unmarried husbandman, almost 30 years old, the last born son of John Bennet also of Fisherton, yeoman, and of Agnes, who was formerly his wife; and Alice Ingram, a woman not previously married, the last born daughter of John Ingram of Bapton street, yeoman, deceased, and of Joan his wife. They were married (after the banns had been legally published in advance) on Monday 21 November.

1626/7

486   John Davies of North Wraxall in north Wiltshire, unmarried yeoman, a little more or less than 30 years old; and Joan Hoskins, a maiden

1   *e domestico autem famulitio*
2   *Shirefield in com' Australis Hantoniae*

nearly 21 years old, the firstborn daughter of Henry Hoskins formerly of Bapton, yeoman, deceased, and of Joan his wife now his widow. They were married (after the banns had been legally published in advance) on Monday 12 June.

487 John Hunt alias Church-howse of Horningsham, a once widowed husbandman, conjectured to be over 30 years old; and Rose Barber, a maidservant[1] almost 40 years old (so it is affirmed), from the house of Philip Hulet of Bapton, shepherd, and commonly believed[2] to be descended from a Hindon family. They were married (after the banns had been legally published in advance) on Monday 18 October.

1627/8 [no entries]

1628/9

488 John Ingram of Bapton street, an unmarried young yeoman, almost 29 years old, son and successor of John Ingram, formerly of Bapton street, yeoman, and of Joan his wife; and Anne Rebecke, second daughter of Henry Rebecke of Bapton, yeoman, and of Elizabeth his wife, a girl 21 years old, married (after the banns had been legally published in advance) on Monday 28 July.

489 Christopher Smyth the younger of this Fisherton mill, bachelor, almost 28 years old, the third son of Christopher Smyth of the same place, yeoman, and of Sara formerly his wife, now deceased; and Phoebe Stoakes, a 24-year-old woman not previously married, who was descended from a freeholding family of Erlestoke,[3] married (after the banns had been legally published in advance) on Monday 10 November.

1629/30 [no entries]

1630/1

490 Edward Ingram of Bapton street, a young unmarried yeoman, more than 30 years old, first son of Henry Ingram also of Bapton, yeoman, and

---

1   *ancilla*
2   *plebieia vero*
3   *Stoake Com's*

of Mary his wife; and [—][1] Candie, more than 20 years old, one of the daughters of Richard Candie of Swallowcliffe, yeoman, and of W— his wife. They were married on Thursday (as it is reported) 17 June in the church of the foresaid Swallowcliffe.

491   Stephen Hoskins of Bapton manor, a young unmarried yeoman, the second son of Henry Hoskins who was formerly (while he lived) farmer of the same manor, and of Joan his then wife, but now his widow; and Jane Flower daughter[2] of William Flower of Melksham yeoman and — his wife.[3] They were married by licence, as it is reported, in the — church[4] of Salisbury on Monday 21 June.

492   John Hoskins of Bapton street, labourer, once widowed, slightly more or less than 47 years old; and Cecily Izaake, who was previously his mistress[5] and, as it turned out, pregnant,[6] a woman slightly more or less than 24 years old in the domestic service of John Hulet of Fisherton, husbandman. They were married (after the banns had been legally published in advance) in our Fisherton church on Thursday 21 October.

1631/2

493   Thomas Mountague of Baverstock,[7] widowed husbandman, over 60 years old; and Elizabeth Cockerill, a maiden almost 25 years old, daughter of Ambrose Cockerill, formerly of Stockton, husbandman, deceased, and of Elizabeth who was then his wife, but is now the wife of Robert Greene of Bapton, husbandman. They were married by licence in our Church on the Monday of Easter week, 11 April.

494   Thomas Hascall from the household[8] of Nicholas Steevens of our Fisherton, yeoman, descended from a farming family of Cann next to Shaftesbury,[9] who is himself an unmarried husbandman more than 30

---

1   a space has been left for the unknown forename
2   a space has been left after *filia*
3   a space has been left for the wife's forename
4   a space has been left after *ecclesia*
5   *amasia*
6   *et ut eventus praebuit pregnans*
7   *Baberstoke*
8   *famulitio*
9   *Cam, iuxta Shaston*

years old; and Dorothy Izaak, a woman about 25 years old, previously unmarried, in the domestic service[1] of John Hulet, husbandman, also of Fisherton. They were married (after the banns had been legally published in advance) on Monday 13 June.

1632/3

495   Stephen Francisce[2] of Maddington, woodworker,[3] almost 20-year-old son of Thomas Francisce also of Maddington, carpenter; and Eleanor Wandsborrough, youngest born daughter of Mary Wandsborrough of our Bapton, almost 27 years old. They were married (after the banns had been published in advance) on Saturday 4 November.

There are no entries in 1633. Marriage entries continue in English in this register from 1634 until 1707.

---

1   *familia*
2   *Francisco* in bishop's transcript
3   *faber lignaeus*

Burials

This is a chronological catalogue of the Christian people who died in this parish of Fisherton Delamere and who had their place of burial in the church or graveyard of this same parish with due funeral rites, from the year of our Lord Christ's Incarnation 1569.

1569

496 Edmund Ingram, buried 25 March.

497 Isabel Andrewes, buried 28 March.

498 Agnes Pierson, buried 2 April.

499 Margery Hoskins, buried 8 June.

500 Agnes Hodder, also buried 8 June.

501 — Wandsborrough,[1] buried 20 June.

1570 [no entries]

1571/2

502 Alice Forster, buried 10 March.

1572/3

503 Thomas White, buried 15 November.

504 John Eyles, buried 15 February.

1573/4

505 John Everley, buried 25 March.

1   a space is left for the forename

506 Joan Hoskins, buried 29 September.

1574/5

507 John Robinson, buried 30 October.

508 Agnes Eyles, buried 19 December.

509 Richard Passion, 4 February.

1575/6

510 John Fisher, buried 16 April.

511 John Dibble, buried 20 April.

512 Joan Forster, buried 9 July.

513 William Forster, buried 20 July.

514 Richard Bennet, buried 23 September.

515 Christian Everley, buried 7 October.

516 John Dibble, buried 26 November.

517 Margery Pinfold, buried 1 December.

518 James Pinfold, buried 8 December.

519 Margery Scarlet, buried 20 December.

520 Elizabeth Snelgar, buried 11 January.

521 John Apersey, buried 5 February.

522 Joan Rebeck, buried 22 March.

1576/7

523   Eleanor Dibble, buried 26 April.

524   Margaret Forster, buried 13 May.

525   Catherine Sheepheard, buried 23 May.

526   Alice Mable, buried 20 July.

527   William Bayley, buried 23 July.

528   Agnes Tockstaffe, buried 28 December.

529   Eada, or Edith, Farret, buried 13 January.

1577/8

530   Cecily Passion, buried 2 June.

531   Mark Passion, buried 30 June.

532   Joan Forster, buried 9 July.

533   Mark Passion, buried 19 September.

534   Thomas Hoskins, buried 5 December.

535   Margaret Bennett, buried 19 January.

1578/9

536   Margery Andrewes, buried 9 June.

537   John Forster, buried 10 August.

538   William, or Williams (it is uncertain),[1] buried 7 December.

1   *Guilielmus, sive Guilielmiades, incert' est, Anglice (Williams),* presumably Crockford was uncertain whether the English name he found in the register was William as a forename, or Williams as a surname.

539 John Everley, buried 29 December.

1579/80

540 William Meryweather, buried 15 June.

541 John Tockstaffe, or Doyctafe, buried 28 July.

542 Jerome Rawlins, buried 5 August.

543 Elizabeth Eyles, buried 5 August.

544 Frideswide[1] Eyles, buried 23 November.

545 Robert Kerby, buried 20 February.

1580-1 [no entries]

1582/3

546 Alice Eyles, buried 26 March.

547 German[2] Andrewes, buried 1 April.

548 Juliana Bennet, buried 27 May.

549 Thomas Forster, buried 8 July.

550 Christian Hoskins, buried 12 August.

551 Mary Hoskins, buried 15 August.

552 Agnes Eyles, buried 16 November.

1583/4

553 Maud Brayne, or rather (as I think)[3] Bryan, buried 2 April.

1   *Fridiswida*
2   *Germanus*
3   *(ut opinor)*

554   Catherine Williams, buried 8 September.

555   John Fry, buried 6 October.

1584/5

556   John Snelgar, buried 18 September.

557   Margaret Williams, buried 3 October.

558   William Kerby, buried[1] 18 October.

559   John Durford, buried 25 October.

560   Dorothy Bennet, buried 29 October.

561   John Everley, buried 13 December.

562   Philip Mountjoy, commonly Mundy, buried 14 January.

563   Joan Hill, buried 4 March.

1585/6

564   Fergus[2] Pierson, buried 15 April.

565   Elizabeth Cornelius, buried 6 March, but uncertain whether this year or next.

1586/7

566   John Hopes, or (as I conjecture) Hobbs, buried 23 April.

567   Agnes Robyson, buried 19 May.

568   William Andrewes, buried 7 June.

---

1   *sepultus fuit* is repeated
2   *Vargeisius*: that this is an attempt to render the forename Fergus is confirmed by his will. where he is called Fergus Parsons (WSA, P2/7Reg/19B). See also **45**.

569 Edward Hoskins of Bapton, yeoman, buried 21 September.

570 Christopher Bennet, buried 13 October.

571 Philip Passion, buried 17 February.

572 Thomas Toppe, yeoman, descended from the Stockton gentry family of the Toppes, but the freehold farmer of Fisherton manor under the lord marquis,[1] buried 18 February.

1587/8

573 Eleanor Bennet, buried 10 November.

574 John Williams, buried 20 December.

575 John Eastman, buried 10 January.

576 Thomas Hulet, buried 21 January.

577 James Robyson, buried 30 January.

578 John Brethers, buried 5 February.

1588/9

579 Margaret Passion, buried 3 June.

580 Elizabeth Fish, buried 14 June.

581 Robert Pierson, buried 27 July.

582 Mark Hulet, buried 16 September.

583 A certain Agnes —,[2] a poor little woman, buried 21 November.

1589/90

1 *Fishertoniensis praedii liber sub d'no marchione furmarius*
2 a space is left for the surname

584   Agnes Bennet, buried 2 October.

585   Mark Brethers, buried 16 December.

1590/1

586   William Hevell, buried 18 May.

587   Philip Williams, buried 23 July.

588   Agnes Blackman, *alias* Coleman, buried 11 December.

589   John Andrewes, buried 16 January.

1591/2

590   John Pierson, buried 12 April.

591   Helena, or Eleanor, Ailes, buried 26 April.

592   Alice Foster, buried 30 April.

593   Elizabeth Wandsborrough, buried 1 May.

1592/3

594   Edith Thresher, buried 13 May.

595   Elizabeth Coleman, buried 4 September.

596   Agnes Ingram, buried 20 January.

597   Susan Wansborrough, buried 21 January.

1593/4

598   Richard Ingram, buried[1] 27 April.

---

1   *sepultus fuit* is repeated

599 Margaret Eyles, buried 3 August.

600 Elizabeth Snelgar, buried 2 September.

601 John Wallis, buried 21 October.

602 Philip Bennet, buried 16 November.

1594/5

603 John Hoskins, buried 6 September.

604 Elizabeth Morrice, buried 28 November.

605 Thomas Rives, buried 29 December.

606 Edward Bennet, buried 29 February.[1]

1595/6

607 Henry Snelgar of Bapton, husbandman, buried 14 May.

608 Joan Rawlins, buried 18 May.

1596/7

609 Richard Rawlins, buried 29 June.

610 Philip Williams, a native of Wales,[2] by profession a clerk, vicar of the church in this place, father of many children, and who had achieved old age,[3] buried 4 August. His successor was Joel Doughtey, clerk, etc.

611 Agnes Eiles, daughter of Henry Eyles, *alias* Hicks, of Bapton, husbandman, buried 11 September.

612 Alice Wansborrough, wife of John Wandsborrough of Bapton, husbandman, buried 29 December.

1   *sic*
2   *patria Cambro-Britannus*
3   *senilem aetatem assecutus*

613 John Doughtey, son of Joel Doughtey, clerk, vicar of this church, buried 29 January.

614 Edward Hoskins of Bapton, yeoman, head of a household, buried 11 March.

615 Agnes Merriot, wife of John Merriot, buried 15 March.

616 John Merriot, labourer, husband of this Agnes Merriot, head of a household, buried 22 March.

1597/8

617 Joan Pierson, *alias* Vargeis, widow, buried 4 April.

618 Joan Bowles, wife of John Bowles, labourer, buried 15 April.

619 John Bowles, labourer, husband of this Joan, buried 16 April.

620 Thomas Frie, labourer, of Bapton, head of a household, buried 14 May.

621 Mary Wandsborrough, sister of William Wandsborrough the elder, buried 10 June.

622 John Loadfield, formerly of Codford, buried 2 July.

623 Stephen Hulet of Fisherton, husbandman, head of a household, buried 8 September.

624 A certain traveller, unknown,[1] buried 24 October.

625 Peter Farret, labourer, who at the time was parish clerk, was snatched by death suddenly while in the church on church business,[2] also buried 24 October.

626 Agnes Andrewes, a little infant, buried 25 October.

1   *viator quidam, ignotus*
2   *in facte eccl'ie*: the reading is uncertain and the meaning unclear

627   Honor Farret, daughter of the forementioned Peter Farret, died suddenly and was buried 2 November.

628   Joan Andrewes, widow, of Fisherton, buried 6 November.

629   George Smyth, husbandman and head of a household, buried 21 December.

630   Joan Smyth, widow, buried 19 January.

631   William Forster of Bapton, head of a household, buried 26 February.

632   John Fry, son of Thomas Frye who had recently died, buried 7 March.

633   Agnes Forster, widow, the relict of — Forster,[1] formerly of Bapton, buried 10 March.

1598/9

634   Margaret Smyth, daughter of Christopher Smyth, labourer, buried 29 March.

635   John Andrewes, shoemaker,[2] buried 14 June.

636   Thomas Rebeck of Bapton, husbandman, head of a household, buried 29 October.

637   Richard Adams, an unknown traveller, buried 30 November.

638   Jordan Slade, son of John Slade of Fisherton, husbandman, buried 6 January.

639   Reginald Eyles *alias* Hicks, an extremely elderly man, of Fisherton, husbandman, buried 25 February.

---

1   a space is left for the forename
2   *sutor calcareus*

1599/1600

640   Agnes Eyles *alias* Hicks, widow, buried 2 April.

641   Elizabeth Soppe, daughter of John Soppe of Fisherton, shepherd, buried 21 April.

642   Mary Moore, daughter of a certain John Moore, buried 22 July.

643   John Turner, head of a household, buried 15 October.

1600/1

644   George Mascoll, labourer, head of a household, buried 31 July.

645   William Norton of West Cranmore[1] in Somerset, husbandman, head of a household, buried in Fisherton churchyard 16 August.

646   William Munday, a certain elderly man, buried 14 October.

1601/2

647   Edward Eyles, son of Henry Eyles *alias* Hicks of Bapton, husbandman and head of a household, buried 13 October.

1602/3

648   William Tincker, a certain elderly man, buried 14 September.

1603/4

649   Elizabeth Head, daughter of Richard Head of Fisherton, yeoman, at that time farmer of the rectory, buried 20 April.

650   Christopher the illegitimate son of Alice Passion, buried 26 April.

651   Henry Grey, buried 15 June.

652   John Wallis, buried 16 February.

1   *Cranmer occidentali*

653 William Andrewes, son of John Andrewes, husbandman of Fisherton, buried 9 March.

1604/5

654 John Lidyard a certain head of a household, buried 10 March.

1605/6

655 Henry Eyles *alias* Hicks, of Bapton, husbandman, head of a household, almost in his seventies, made a will on 15 March 1604, died on Easter Sunday, 31 March, buried the next day, that is, Monday in Easter week, 1 April, 1605.

656 Agnes Forster, daughter of Philip Forster of Bapton, husbandman, and of Agnes his wife, buried 13 April.

657 Henry Court son of Alice Court, a poor widow of Fisherton, buried 17 April.

1606/7

658 Reginald Eyles *alias* Hicks, a youth, son of William Eyles *alias* Hicks, and of Margaret his wife, buried 31 October.

1607/8

659 George Hodder of Bapton a husbandman there, but actually a tailor by trade, head of a household, a married man 60 years old, buried 5 August.

1608/9

660 Thomas Forster of Bapton, husbandman, head of a household, almost in his seventies, and twice married, buried 8 May.

661 Henry Walleis, a youth, son of John Walleis, formerly of Fisherton, labourer, deceased, buried 5 January.

1609/10

662   Agnes Eyles, a poor widow, relict of Mark Eyles *alias* Hicks formerly of Fisherton, labourer, deceased, buried 20 May.

663   John Eastman *alias* Easton, of Bapton, labourer, head of a household, a poor man in his sixties, buried 29 November.

1610/11

664   William Passion of Fisherton, husbandman, a very elderly man, almost one hundred years old, head of a household, buried 22 May.

665   John Wandsborrough of Bapton, by occupation a husbandman there, though in fact by skill a butcher,[1] head of a household, an elderly man at least 80 years old, buried 13 January.

1611/12

666   Thomas Ingram, young infant son of John Ingram the elder of Bapton by Lippe-yate, husbandman, and of Amy his wife, buried 2 June.

667   Edmund Goodridge, a certain elderly labourer of Bapton, buried 19 June.

668   Joan Flemming, young infant daughter of Nicholas Flemming of Fisherton, and of Joan his wife, buried 16 September.

669   Agnes Pierson, an unmarried girl of almost nineteen years, daughter of John Pierson *alias* Vargeis of Bapton husbandman, and of [*left blank*] his wife, buried 26 November.

1612/13

670   William Wandsborrowgh of Bapton, husbandman, head of a household, a married man more or less 60 years old, buried 9 September.

671   Agnes Bennet, head of her household, almost 60 years old, second wife of Thomas Bennet of Fisherton, husbandman, buried 20 October.

---

1   *arte vero lanius*

672 Eleanor Hayter, a woman more or less 18 years old, wife of Thomas Hayter of Bapton, but from Wishford, husbandman; she was in fact the daughter of Henry Eyles, formerly of Bapton, husbandman, deceased, and of Margaret his wife; and mother of one son, called Robert; buried 25 October.

673 Henry Dibble, young infant son of Henry Dibble of Bapton, labourer, and of Susan his wife, buried 31 October.

674 Elizabeth Hevell, widow, relict of William Hevell of Fisherton, husbandman, deceased, a woman more or less 60 years old, buried 2 March.

1613/14

675 Edmund Snelgar of Bapton, unmarried labourer, almost 60 years old, buried 5 July.

676 Joan Hibbard, the very ancient head of a household, mother of many children, and distinguished by diverse plaudits of womanly virtues, she was descended from a once freeholding family, the Eyles of Fisherton; twice widowed, she was the relict first of Edward Hoskins, yeoman, the freehold farmer of Bapton manor, then of the deceased Stephen Hibbard of Barford, yeoman. She died at Bapton 10 July, buried 11 July, almost seventy years old.

677 John Bowles, a young unmarried labourer, descended from the labouring family of Bowles of Bapton, a household servant of Henry Hoskins, buried 10 August.

678 Joan Steevens, little infant daughter of Josiah Steevens of Fisherton, from Chilmark, weaver, and of [left blank] his wife, buried 2 October.

679 Joel Doughtey, clerk, vicar of this church. It is asserted from the evidence with scarcely any doubt that these have been the stages of his life and death. Birth – a native of Kent, from the town or street of Marden, of freeholder parents; childhood – at school in Peterborough; youth – in the University of Cambridge, where he laboured to achieve the degree of Bachelor. Taking leave of the university he moved to Southampton,[1] where he lived for some time at a school as an assistant teacher without payment, and became engaged to be married. Leaving the school he entered the ministry and was admitted to the retinue of the Honourable William, Marquis of Winchester; through whose generosity he obtained this vicarage, which he held for almost 17 years, not without hardship. Commending his soul to God, his body to the earth, his money to those nearest him, and his place to his successor, he expired peacefully 19 October, and was buried in the choir of his church 1 November.

680 I, Thomas Crockford, have been his next successor to this vicarage. I am a native of Berkshire; of freeholding parents; and I was born and baptised in Wargrave, a not unknown village close to the Thames almost four miles from Reading, at the end of October 1580. I am the last and only surviving son of Richard Crockford, husbandman, a descendant of the Crockfords of Rotherfield Peppard,[2] and of Elizabeth his only wife descended from the Denleys or Nashes of Basildon.[3] In boyhood and early adolescence I thoroughly learnt discipline and grammar in the choir of my village church[4] under the tutelage of the scholarly Thomas Baker, Bachelor of Arts, a learned man and my close friend, who is now Reverend vicar of Eton Dorney in Buckinghamshire.[5] When I was in my fifteenth year my most beloved mother was taken away by disease and death, to my utter sorrow. The next year I was received into the household of the children of a man of happy memory, John Mochett, best of gentlemen and most prudent in matters of justice and fairness, who was initially lord of the manor of Scarlets in Wargrave, by right of his wife, and then of Crowsley in Shiplake, in his own right. After I had been in this situation for almost two years, having attended faithfully to my household duties, and inclining towards the diligent study of the liberal arts, eventually by the efforts and no little expense of my lord and patron I was admitted to Oxford, with favourable omens,[6] and took my place at the most illustrious Magdalen College, among the lesser pupils of that house, beginning in spring 1597. For almost five years I worked as chamber-servant and under the charge of a man in every way most highly adorned with the greatest

1   *Australem Hamtoniam*
2   *Pepperensium*
3   *Bassendoniensibus*, probably Basildon (Berks), north-west of Reading
4   *in chore temple patrii*
5   *Dorneyensis . . .prope Eaton*
6   *faustis auspiciis*

piety, the dearly loved Isaac Pocock, Master of Arts and Fellow of the college.

In May 1602, when a sufficiently ample payment was offered me, I made the move from the academy to the countryside, the land of Oxfordshire for that of Wiltshire, and my college for a school. In the same year, when I was 22, my elderly father died, completely worn down by years and cares (for he had indeed seen 70 summers), and was buried at Wargrave not long before I came to Stockton to take charge of the school for boys,[1] where I laboured diligently for almost 14 years.[2] For the first five or six years I lived in the house of the reverend theologian John Terry, rector of the church, as his lodger. Under him I took on the role of novice, just as Elizeus did under Elias,[3] Paul under Gamaliel,[4] or Timothy under Paul himself.[5] I never entered into conversation with him without learning something, or at the least I would leave his company wiser through his prudence. We certainly had many deep discussions, and I have committed to memory many of his brief and apt sayings. I will never ever be ungrateful to him, and I must honestly confess that I would not have progressed but for this man alone.[6]

It was principally his doing that I obtained the friendship of the gentry, Topp and Potticary of Stockton, and gradually the society of many other eminent people in this neighbourhood.[7] It was in 1603 that I attained first the degree of arts and second truly of service, through the generosity of the scholars at Oxford in the one instance, and of the reverend father in Christ, Henry Cotton, bishop of Salisbury, in the other.[8] Once I had achieved the rank of minister I served as curate the neighbouring parishes

1 *curam paedagogicam filii*
2 If Crockford is correct, this would be until 1615 or 1616, suggesting that the register was written up retrospectively, since this autobiography is headed 1613
3 *Ecclesiasticus* 48, v. 12
4 *Acts* 22, v. 3
5 *Acts* 16, v. 1–4
6 *ut non ingenue fatear per quem fere unum profecerim.* The sentiment, if not the literal meaning, seems clear.
7 *Ipsius praesertim ope Generosos nactus sum Amicos Toppum et Potticarum Stocktoniae, quorum Gratia multis etiam aliis, in hoc tractu praeclaris paulatim int'otiu'.* The precise syntax and meaning of this and the following sentence are somewhat obscure.
8 *Gradu' Artis unu' ministerique vere duos; illu' Academicoru' Oxoniensiu' hos autem Reverendi in Christo Patris Henrico Cottonii, Saru' Episcopi, benignitate attigi utru'qu' A'o 1603*

– Stockton, Codford, Wylye, Wishford – and I devoted my labour out of friendship to this Fisherton and the other churches with pleasure; and I held this position, by both commission and proclamation, and also through the influence by his word and authority of the foresaid bishop.[1]

On 12 January 1612[2] I married my wife, who was of the best gentry lineage, and I and she both became involved very quickly in domestic affairs, so that I had almost nothing else definite[3] except my friends at Stockton. And it was with their help and testimonials that through grace I approached that honourable man William, marquis of Winchester, so that I was presented, through his gracious gift, instituted by the pastoral authority of the foresaid bishop, and on the written instruction of the venerable archdeacon Pichaver[4] I was finally legally inducted into this church, this care of souls, this slender vicarage, at the hands of the aforesaid John Terry, ever to be remembered, rector of Stockton, on 19 November in the foresaid year 1613, in the 34th year of my age.

Thus far I have passed through the separate periods of my life and fortune, which at this point it does not seem unreasonable to narrate starkly and in outline,[5] and to bring together in writing in my own hands. What may happen to me in future is not for me to predict – it is the determination of God and perhaps the judgement of men. God has so ordered it that I have obtained here by his grace this Sparta, that I may be able to honour, by institutes, studies, precepts and examples, those to whom I am in debt, to His glory, to the service of the church, and in the discharge of my duties; and ultimately to our shared salvation through Jesus Christ on the last day. Amen.

681   Henry Dibble, son[6] of Henry Dibble of Bapton, labourer, and of Susan his wife, was born and baptised 24 December 1613, as is seen in the baptisms, and buried 5 January.

1   *Ministerii ordines adeptus, Curis Circumvicinis subinde inservii, Stocktonia, Codfordiae, Wiliae, Wishfordiae Curatus dictus; Fishertoniae huic meae, et aliis ecclesiis ad placitum, nomine amicitiae, operam dedi, tam legendo, quam praedicando, cujus etiam facultatem verbo, et authoritate episcopi antedicti benigne concessa habui*

2   i.e. 1613

3   *certi*: Crockford appears to mean that he had no other means of support to call on

4   Ralph Pickhaver, archdeacon of Salisbury (CCEd)

5   *nude tantum et jejune enarrare.* Crockford's meaning could be expressed in modern jargon as 'the bare bones of a narrative'

6   The number 2 is interlined, presumably indicating the second son

682   Elizabeth Ingram, widow, head of her household, an ancient woman almost 80 years old, relict of Richard Ingram of Bapton at Lippeyate, husbandman, deceased, died and was buried 1 March.

1614/15

683   Thomas Ingram, unmarried labourer, more than 40 years old, son of Richard Ingram, formerly of Bapton at Lippeyate, husbandman, and of Elizabeth his wife, lately deceased, died 23 January and buried 24 January.

684   John Ingram the elder, husbandman, married head of his household, almost 50 years old, eldest brother of the said Thomas, born of the same mother.[1] Either because of the debilitating effect of jaundice, or through a longstanding sickness of his body, he was known as Angry John, at first as a joke but later in earnest, and habitually as a distinguishing nickname; a decidedly honourable man; he died and was buried 2 February.

685   Thomas Rider, a young servant[2] and nephew of Elizabeth Doughtey, widow, descended from the Riders of Romsey,[3] died 6 May and buried 7 May 1614.[4]

1615/16

686   Tamsin Knight, a woman almost in her fifties, second wife of William Knight, an old man of Fisherton, but from Stockton, ploughwright, died in childbirth, buried 30 July.

687   Dorothy Hevell, a woman in the flower of her youth, wife of Francis Hevell of Fisherton, labourer or shepherd, died while giving birth to twins, buried 20 August.

688   Henry Peareman, almost a youth, son of a certain Peareman of Motcombe in Dorset, a shepherd, also a servant of Phillip Hulett of Bapton, also a shepherd, died and buried 6 September.

---

1   *germanus pariter et uterinus*
2   *adolescens famulus*
3   *Rumsey*
4   This entry, headed '*postscriptum 1614*,' is out of sequence

689 John Ingram the elder, of Bapton street, husbandman, more or less 60 years old, head of a well-known family of some importance,[1] father of many children and husband of one wife, generous to his place, his neighbours and those close to him, well disposed to anyone who was honest, and unsparingly endowed with other qualities regarding the management of local affairs.[2] He died 28 October and buried 29 October.

690 Alice Eyles, commonly known as Alice Markes, because she was the daughter of Mark Eyles (*alias* Hicks) formerly of Fisherton. She was a poor unmarried woman, though a descendant of the Eyles family of Fisherton, formerly freeholders. She died 11 December, and buried 12 December.

1616/17

691 — Rose, who was a labourer on Fisherton manor, but originated in North Bradley (it is thought), and had been taken on as an incomer for harvest work. He died and was buried at the end of August or beginning of September. Precise details of the month and day have now been lost to us, but exist accurately in the transcript of our register for this year sent to Salisbury according to canon law.

692 Joan Flemming, wife of Nicholas Flemming, a labourer of Fisherton, but from Stockton, mother of many children, a woman 40 years old, died 13 January, buried 14 January.

693 John Gullyford, a young unmarried labourer, who was living and died at Deptford, was buried in our cemetery at Fisherton on 5 February. The reason for this burial was the floodwaters which around this time closed off the road to Wylye.

1617/18

694 Eleanor Easton or Eastman of Bapton, a poor elderly woman, widow of John Easton or Eastman, likewise formerly of Bapton, labourer, died 5 April and buried 6 April.

695 Edward Hoskins, a little infant, the fourth son of Henry Hoskins of

1   *potioris*
2   *(pro loco) aeconomiam*

Bapton, yeoman, and of Joan his wife, died 26 November and buried 27 November.

696 John Gherish, a young man, unmarried, son of a certain John Gherish once of Melksham, yeoman, deceased, and of Joan his widow, who married secondly Henry Hoskins, farmer[1] of Bapton, died at Bapton 30 November, and buried in Fisherton churchyard[2] 1 December.

697 Christopher Hoskins, a little boy, not yet four years old, the third son of the same Henry Hoskins, farmer of Bapton, and of Joan his wife, died 1 December and buried 2 December.

698 Elizabeth Doughtey, a matron almost sixty years old, the widow of Joel Doughtey, clerk, formerly the vicar of this church, deceased. She was head of her household, a most painstaking[3] and experienced manager of labour, descended from the freeholding Rider family from near Southampton. She leaves behind her a numerous enough progeny of both sexes, and died 13 December, buried 14 December.

699 Elizabeth Pierson *alias* Vargeis the elder, an unmarried woman, daughter of John Pierson *alias* Vargeis, formerly of Bapton, husbandman, and of Catherine his wife. She suffered from epilepsy for a long time,[4] and eventually died on 16 December, and was buried 17 December.

700 Edmund Ingram, a young unmarried husbandman, eldest[5] son of the deceased John Ingram, formerly of Bapton street, husbandman, and of Joan his wife. He deserved praise for his honesty, self-restraint, even-handedness and modesty of every kind; he was obedient to his parents, kind to his relatives, accommodating to his neighbours, hurtful to no-one, and loved by all. He died 18 December, and buried 21 December.

701 Elizabeth Pierson *alias* Vargeis the younger, another of the daughters of the same John Pierson *alias* Vargeis, formerly of Bapton, husbandman, and of Catherine his wife. She was a girl deceived in the hope of marriage by the blandishments of a man named Durham, a good-for-nothing

1 *firmario*
2 an abbreviation, presumably signifying 'churchyard' or 'church'
3 *aerumnosa*
4 *morbo comitiali diu*
5 *natu maximus*

liar who was married[1] but pretended that he was single. Robbed of her chastity, and following the pain of childbirth, she loudly expressed her repentance (so it is reported), but went into a gradual decline and died and was buried on the feast of Our Lord's birth, 25 December.

702 George Pierson *alias* Vargeis, the said Elizabeth's illegitimate son, very much a young infant, died and was buried 31 December.

1618/19

703 Agnes Hodder of Bapton, twice widowed, firstly by Thomas Rebbecke formerly of Bapton, husbandman, deceased, and secondly by George Hodder also of Bapton, husbandman and tailor, deceased. She was the head of her household, industrious and honest, mother of two sons by Rebbecke,[2] a woman about 70 years old, more or less. She died 31 May, and was buried 1 June.

704 Joan Snelgar, who was also of Bapton, and likewise twice widowed. Her first husbamd was — Takle of Stoke St Michael, Somerset, smith,[3] and her second was Henry Snelgar, formerly of Bapton, husbandman, deceased. She was the head of her household, highly praised for her honesty, benevolence, generosity, and all kinds of charity; she was pious towards God, making herself ready for church, where she was attentive to the words;[4] she treated the minister with respect, her relatives with concern, her neighbours with generosity, the poor with aid, and everyone in whatever place with calmness.[5] As a woman she had no offspring of her own, but acted almost as a mother to many of her relatives' children. She is believed to have reached the age of sixty, more or less, and bearing witness to her faith, hope of salvation, and life-enhancing consolation,[6] she bequeathed her truly Christian soul to heaven, her body to the earth, and her possessions to her nearest relatives. She fell asleep peacefully in Christ, and died on 21 August, buried 24 August.

705 Edward Dew, a young unmarried labourer, son of a certain Dew

1   *perjuri nebulonis et conjugati*
2   *e Rebecco*
3   space left for forename; *Stoake Lane*; 'smith' is written 'Smyth' in English
4   *in deum pia in eccl'iam parata, in verba'* attenta
5   ?*serenitate*, but the reading is uncertain
6   ?*vivacem solatiu'*

of Gomeldon.[1] He was the servant of Christopher Smyth yeoman, proprietor of the demesne mill of Fisherton, and died 17 October, buried 18 October.

1619/20

706 Margaret Dibble, little infant daughter of Henry Dibble of Bapton, labourer and of Susan his wife, died and buried on 22 May.

707 John Hoskins of Bapton, the elder, labourer. Although descended from the freeholding Hoskins family of Bapton manor, he was a poor man, head of his household, but reduced for various reasons to the misery of extreme poverty by divine dispensation. Begetter of many children, he had reached more than eighty years, and died 10 September, buried 11 September.

708 Joan Hoskins, also of Bapton, a poor elderly woman, widow of John Hoskins previously above written, and his only wife. She was descended from the freeholding Bysse family of Chicksgrove, and had reached more than sixty years, died on 28 September, and buried 29 September.

709 Henry Hoskins, also of Bapton, yeoman, freehold farmer of the manor of Bapton, son[2] of Edward Hoskins, also freehold farmer of the same manor (while he was alive), and of Joan his wife. Head of his household, he was endowed with very many outstanding virtues, pious, honest, faithful, a generous friend, compassionate, kind, affable, a most generous benefactor who kept his promises, steadfast in goodwill, careful to make peace and easily pacified, harsh to no-one for very long,[3] accommodating to everyone, dear, agreeable and beloved. He was the husband of one wife, whom he left surviving, and the legitimate father of four sons and two daughters. He was seized by a very severe burning fever[4] for about a week, suffering most gravely with a deteriorating mind and voice, and after some memorable testimony of Christian piety and hope he finally expired peacefully in the Lord on Friday 15 October at the hour of six or seven in the evening, and with solemn rite was buried in the church with

1   *Gummilton*: Gomeldon in Idmiston
2   Crockford has written *ingenitus filius*, perhaps in error for *unigenitus* 'only-begotten'. *Ingenitus* usually means 'unborn'.
3   *nemini diu peracerbus*
4   *casone sive febre ardentissima*

his ancestors on Sunday 17 October, shortly after the start of his 47th year.

710   Joan Stoakes of Bapton, a poor elderly unmarried woman, more than 60 years old and of honest life. She was weakened by a slight[1] fever and her old age, and died and was buried on Saturday[2] 16 October.

711   John Peirson alias Vargeis, likewise of Bapton, husbandman, brother by the same mother of the Joan Stoakes previously above written. He was a distressed[3] head of a household, husband of one wife, father of many children, who reached the age of sixty more or less, died on Friday 22 October, and buried on Saturday 23 October.

712   George Peirson alias Vargeis, also of Bapton, husbandman, son and heir of John previously above written, over thirty years old. Recently married, he was praised for his honesty, hard work, and frugality according to his station, the hope of his family, the helper of his mother and grandmother, the solace of his most sorrowful wife, esteemed by his neighbours and welcomed by everyone, he died on Wednesday 1 December, and buried Thursday 2 December.

713   Agnes Farret of Fisherton, a poor elderly woman, widow of Peter Farret, deceased, once a labourer here in Fisherton. She was descended from the Hullet family of husbandmen of Fisherton, a woman worn down by age, work and hardship, a fertile mother of children of each sex. Her life was innocent and her reputation unblemished, and she died on Wednesday 14 December, and buried on Thursday 16 December.

1620/1

714   Joan Othen, the wife of John Othen, labourer, an incomer engaged in rural work[4] on the manor of Fisherton. She was a woman more than thirty years old, mother of three children, who died and was buried on Tuesday 28 March.

715   Joan Easton *alias* Eastman of Bapton, a poor maiden[5] almost thirty

1   *innocuae*
2   *Sabbathi Judaici*
3   *aerumnosus*
4   *ad opus rusticu'*
5   *virgo*

years old, daughter of John Easton alias Eastman, formerly of Bapton, labourer, and of Eleanor his wife, both deceased. She was taken ill suddenly, and declined in an increasingly serious illness[1] so that in the space of an hour, more or less, she expired, and died on Wednesday 3 May, buried Thursday 4 May.

716 Henry Holloway, the elder, a poor labourer more or less seventy years old, once widowed. He was a very elderly and constantly faithful servant to his kindly master[2] Christopher Smyth, the proprietor of the lord's mill of Fisherton, but after a long period in the same place his age grew burdensome to him. He was a very dear foster-son,[3] of blameless life and unblemished reputation. He declined partly as a result of old age and partly from quartan fever, and died on the feast of St Paul, namely Thursday 25 January, buried on Friday 26 January.

1621/2

717 An unnamed[4] infant boy, the firstborn son of George Merriott of Bapton, labourer, and of Catherine his wife, was born prematurely[5] alive, however (as the women assisting at the birth are witness) within the space of one hour he expired, and was dead before reaching the water of baptism; he was buried on Tuesday 8 May.

718 Margery Hulett, the widow of Stephen Hulett, formerly of Fisherton, deceased husbandman, a woman (as is reported) 81 years old, descended from the farming family of Hevells of Fisherton. She was the nourishing mother[6] of children of each sex, a pious, honest and prudent matron, who, weakened equally by old age and by an illness, and having declared in outstanding fashion by calls and signs her joyful hope of heavenly life, she bid farewell to the world and clung[7] to heaven. She expired peacefully in Christ and died on Monday 14 May at Stockton; she was buried in Fisherton churchyard beside her husband, as she expressed in her vows, on Tuesday 15 May.

1   *repentino morbo correpta, malo in gravescente deficit*
2   *perbenigni d'ni perantiquus et perpetuo fidelis famulus*
3   *alumnus*: the word can also mean 'student'
4   *sine praenomine*
5   *abortivus*
6   *alma mater*
7   *adhaesit*

719   Catherine Pierson *alias* Vargeys of Bapton, widow of John Pierson alias Vargeys, formerly also of Bapton, deceased husbandman. She was a woman 60 years old, more or less, one of the daughters of — Benger, a Shrewton butcher while he was alive, the nourishing mother[1] of numerous children, a true and prudent matron, but troubled.[2] Weakened by a fatal sickness, she commended herself to God repeatedly and frequently with prayer and lamentations,[3] and finally fell asleep in Christ. She died on Thursday 27 September, and buried on Friday 28 September.

1622/3

720   William Wandsborrough and his twin brother, who was born before him without being named. They were the firstborn infant sons of William Wandsborrough of Bapton the younger, husbandman, and of Joan his wife. Brought into the light by premature birth on Friday 26 April, one was dead, the other alive but mute; one was blessed by baptism, but the other lacking it, and both were buried in the same grave on Saturday 27 April.

721   An unnamed infant boy, the firstborn son of Thomas Crockford, clerk, vicar of this church, and of Joan his wife, was stillborn, also to the great danger of his mother, on Saturday between the hours of eleven and twelve in the night and buried in the churchyard among the other little infants sleeping there, on the following Sunday, 1 September.[4]

722   James Hoskins, a little infant boy recently born and baptised, the firstborn son of Edward Hoskins of Bapton, tailor, and of Elizabeth his wife, died on Monday 18 November, and buried on Tuesday 19 November.

723   Arminella Maurice, assuredly[5] the wife of an old man, John Maurice of Fisherton, weaver. She was descended from a farming family,

---

1   *alma mater*
2   *aerumnosa*
3   *ejaculationibus*
4   Against this entry is a marginal note in English: NB Compare this entry with a very singular monument in the outside wall of the chancel about 7 or 8 feet high near the north east corner. [in a later hand:]. This monument was placed in the church, May 22nd 1902.
5   *admodum*

the Gardiners of Stockton; a wretched woman, the sole wife of a sole husband, nourishing mother of two sons and two daughters, she was worn out by old age and illnesss, and had completed, (so it is reported) more than sixty eight years. With piety and in peace she fell dead on Wednesday 4 December, and buried on Thursday 5 December.

724 Phillip Andrews of Fisherton, an unmarried labourer, 36 years and a little over 8 months old, descended from a farming family of this neighbourhood. After wasting away for a long time with a paralysing fatal illness, oppressed and defeated at last he suddenly grew weaker. He searched within himself,[1] and as witness to the appropriate hope of a Christian man he moderately and peacefully expired. He died on Thursday 12 December, and was buried on Friday 13 December.

725 William Bushell, a poor young man, the son of William Bushell formerly of Stockbridge in Hampshire, the man responsible for loading[2] a mill (as it is reported). He was the nephew of the sister of Edward Jennings, shepherd of the manor of Fisherton, and he died and was buried on Monday the feast of St Mathias in Lent 24 February.

1623/4

726 Thomas Spenser, a young man of more or less 24 years, recently married to a wife, who was born and had his dwelling in the small village of Motcombe in Dorset. His trade was that of a tailor, but having come to these parts of Wiltshire for harvest labour (as many strangers are accustomed to do) and carrying out his work satisfactorily as a hireling, according to the strong opinion here in Fisherton,[3] he suddenly succumbed to a deadly illness, which rendered him senseless and speechless, and after almost two days had elapsed, with sighs. groans and pitiable wailing[4] he finally deteriorated and died on Monday 18 August, and was buried on Tuesday 19 August.

---

1   *depetit penitus*

2   *oneratoris*

3   *satis ut videbatur, validis Fishertoniae nostra, operam conductivam peracturus.* The implication of '*validus*' seems to be literally 'to those persons of authority' but the translation tries to preserve the basic meaning of strength.

4   *quo ad vocis usque deliquum, stupefactus post biduam fere, suspiriis, gemitibus, et planctibus miserandis transactu'*

727   A little young infant unnamed, the second son of John Hoskins, a Fisherton labourer from Bapton, and of Margaret his wife. He was stillborn (very severely endangering his mother) and was buried as quickly as was appropriate on the same day that he was born,[1] which was Friday 19 December.

728   Margaret Hoskins wife of the same John Hoskins, and mother of this stillborn young infant. She was descended from the labouring family of Faretts of Fisherton, and had almost reached the age of 43 years, the troubled mother of two sons and three daughters. She was still suffering from her last childbirth and was unable to recuperate; a swelling grew worse day by day so that she gradually grew faint, declined and expired. She was buried on Sunday 4 January.

1624/5

729   Susan Ayles *alias* Hicks, a poor elderly woman from Bapton, widow of a certain Anthony Ayles *alias* Hicks, who while he lived was a tailor from Deptford. She descended from the Wandsborroughs, a family of husbandmen from Bapton, and was a woman more or less 70 years old. Troubled by old age, and suffering from a wasting disease, she confessed her Christian faith and fell asleep. She died and was buried on the Saturday before Pentecost, 15 May.

730   Alice Crockford, a young infant girl, little more than two months old, the third daughter of Thomas Crockford, clerk, the vicar of this Church, and of Joan his wife. She died at Teffont Magna,[2] at the house of Purchase, a wet nurse, and was then promptly brought to this Fisherton to be buried in the churchyard alongside and close to her unnamed brother, among the other young children of the parish on Wednesday 26 May.

731   Sarah Smyth, wife of an eminent man, Christopher Smyth, yeoman, [tenant] by right of a bond[3] of Fisherton mill. She was descended from the freehold family of Jolleys of Harnham and from the same noble[4] family of

---

1   *quantu' par erat, expedite, ipso nativitatis sua die*
2   *Teffontiae superiori*
3   The words *jure ligatorio d'ni* are followed by an abbreviation, interpreted here to signify that Smyth was the tenant, but *ligatorius* is a curious word to use in this context
4   *patricia*

the city of Salisbury, Wife of one husband and a very respected matron, she was the most loving mother of children of either sex, a prudent head of her household, a neighbour accommodating to her neighbours, kind to many, harmful to no one; in short she was blessed in praiseworthy fashion with the feminine virtues.[1] She was often worn down by repeated bouts of ill health, and at last contracted a fatal illness; she languished, declined, and returned her soul to God, dying at Fisherton on Friday 8 October. She was taken to Salisbury, and received solemn burial in the cathedral church beside the body of her mother (in her lifetime a revered matron), under one and the same tomb as her elder sister, the wife of Lawes of Hale, who had died at almost the same hour on the same day (a circumstance on account of its rarity not unworthy of mention). Burial was on Sunday 10 October, and it is said that she was over 40 years old.

732 Thomas Meriot, a very delicate[2] young infant, not yet four days alive, the second son of George Meriot of Bapton, labourer, and Catherine his wife, died and was buried on Tuesday 2 November.

733 John Rogers, a certain young man from an ordinary[3] family from Frome[4] in Somerset (as is reported in letters of testimonial), who had been sent out by public authority into the army. He was making his way on foot, with legitimate permission to return, and very much struggling under an illness, when he fell mortally ill, and died at our Fisherton in the care of his commander and supervisor.[5] At the expense of the parish he had a fitting burial in the churchyard on Friday 18 February.

734 Eleanor Andrews, the wife of John Andrews of Fisherton, husbandman, descended from the Gillingham family from the parish of Cattistock[6] in Dorset. She was the wife of one husband, mother of one daughter, a woman of unblemished reputation, more or less 50 years old, weakened[7] by chronic infirmities she finally contracted a fatal illness. She called to witness her Christian faith and hope, and in piety and calmness she fell asleep, died and was buried on Friday 18 March.

1   *faemineis sum'atim virtutibus laudate aucta*
2   *tenerrimus*
3   *plebeia*
4   *Froome Sel-Wood*
5   *decurionis et supervisor' cura*
6   *Catstoke*
7   *elanguescens*

735   Henry Eyles, second son of Robert Eyles *alias* Hicks of Fisherton, husbandman, and of Elizabeth his wife, a youth of fourteen years. Having endured a year of atrophy with a chronic wasting disease, he weakened and expired in the piety of Christ, and died and was buried on Saturday 19 March.

1625/6

736   William Eyles *alias* Hicks of Fisherton, husbandman, was descended from a family there of freeholding[1] farmers, and formerly enjoyed the rank of freeholder himself.[2] He was the second husband of one woman, and the father of three sons., who having endured the changing inconstancy of the world, and worn out[3] by his labours and old age, he was at length weakened by wretched illnesses. He testified to his faith very many and expired peacefully in Christ, died and was buried on Thursday 23 June, nearly 87 years old.

737   Elizabeth Moore, an elderly matron, very grave,[4] the wife of old Thomas Moore of Bapton, a yeoman. She was more than 80 years old, and descended from a family of equal status,[5] the Patients of Westbury. She was a woman equipped with the appropriate[6] virtues who, after leading a commendable life, was exhausted by various longstanding infirmities of old age, and eventually weakened by illness. Bearing witness to her Christian faith she commended her soul to God, her body to the cemetery, and she died and was buried on Tuesday 16 August.

738   Anne Merriot, a very delicate young infant, the second daughter of George Merriot, labourer, and of Catherine his wife. She died on Sunday the feast of Christ's nativity, and was buried on Monday the feast of St Stephen the first martyr, 26 December.

---

1   *libertino.* Crockford's use of this term, in contrast to *ingenuus* in the next line, may imply that the family had attained freehold status, whereas William Eyles was born into the rank of freeholder.
2   *ordine vivens olim ingenue*
3   *attritus* (interlined)
4   *gravissima.* It is unclear whether this is meant as a compliment (venerable) or a criticism (severe).
5   *e parilis,* i.e. also of yeoman rank
6   *idoneis*

1626/7

739 Joan and Elizabeth Doughtie, premature young infant twins and first and second daughters of John Doughtie of Fisherton, yeoman, and of Joan his wife, were born and baptised, died and were buried on Tuesday 4 April.

740 William Young formerly of Sherrington mill, an unmarried load-carrier,[1] more than 30 years old. He was descended from an ordinary[2] family of [gap] near Fordingbridge who, becoming ill, transferred himself to Bapton where it is said that he had found a wife for himself. He died there and received Christian[3] burial here in Fisherton churchyard on the Tuesday of Easter week, 11 April.

741 Margaret Eyles alias Hicks of Fisherton, widow, descended from the freehold [family] of Marks of Steeple Ashton,[4] an elderly matron. She was twice widowed, firstly by William Imber formerly of Chitterne, yeoman, deceased, and secondly by William Eyles alias Hicks formerly of Fisherton, yeoman, also deceased. She was the caring mother to an equal number of children from both Imber and Eyles, and a woman who experienced the varying instability[5] of the world. Weakened by old age and a wretched illness, and bearing witness to her Christian faith, she returned her soul peacefully to God on Tuesday 18 April, and was buried in our cemetery, close to her former husband, on Wednesday 19 April, 88 years old (as is reported).

742 Joan Ingram of Bapton, widow, descended from the freehold family of Potticary of Wylye, an elderly matron, widow of John Ingram formerly also of Bapton street, yeoman, deceased. She was the caring mother of three sons and three daughters, a woman, particularly honest, bountiful and generous. After a longstanding infirmity of her body at length she weakened, she declared her will when appropriate, and returned her soul as a Christian to God. She died on Monday 12 February and buried close

1 *onerarius*
2 *plebeia*
3 Above the word *sepulturam* are interlined the words *fide Christ'*, or similar, but very crowded and indistinct
4 *Stepul Achton*
5 *labilem*

to her former husband on Wednesday 14 February, 70 years old (as is reported).

1627/8

743   Amy Ingram of Bapton by the field gate,[1] widow, descended from the labouring family of Farrett of Fisherton, a little elderly woman, relict of John Ingram the elder, formerly of Bapton by the same gate, husbandman, deceased. She was the unfortunate[2] mother of one daughter, who is dead; her life was harmless, and at last she perished gradually from an odious wasting disease, dying on Thursday 26 April, and buried on Friday 27 August, 57 years old.

744   Elizabeth Wallice of Fisherton, a poor elderly widow, descended from the labouring Fish family formerly of Fisherton. She was the widow of John Wallice formerly of Fisherton, labourer, deceased; the troubled mother of several children, an honest hardworking woman, wild in her old age[3] and worn out by illness. She died on Monday the last day of April, and was buried on Tuesday 1 May, 80 years old (as is agreed).

745   A young infant unnamed, the — daughter[4] of Henry Dibble of Bapton, labourer and of Susan his wife, was stillborn, prematurely, and buried on Sunday 3 June.

746   Ralph Bennett of Bapton street, but from Fisherton, husbandman, the last-born son[5] of John Bennett of Fisherton, yeoman, husband of one wife and father of one little daughter. Much loved for his kindness, so far as he could, he gave the best hope of generosity out of the ordinary.[6] He was seized by a burning fever, and died in Christ and was buried on Tuesday 5 June, 31 years old.

747   Emma Mascall the wife of Phillip Mascall of Fisherton, who is

---

1   *agrariam portam*
2   *infaelix*
3   *fera senio*
4   Crockford has written, after *filia*, the letter *s* followed by a space, as if
      intending to write *secunda*
5   *filius natu minimus*
6   *plusquam vulgaris*

sometimes a weaver, sometimes a labourer. She was a little woman[1] almost 40 years old, the troubled mother of four children, who was descended from the shepherding family of Willis of East Codford.[2] She suffered from chronic dropsy and succumbed at last, falling asleep in Christ; she died and was buried on Tuesday 11 March.

1628/9

748   Joan Pierson *alias* Vargeis, an unmarried woman almost 30 years old, who was descended from a farming family from Bapton. She died at Codford on Friday 18 April, and was buried in Fisherton churchyard (as it is said that she had wished to be)[3] on Saturday 19 April.

749   John Maurice of Fisherton, a weaver, an extremely elderly man, a widower, the father of two sons and as many daughters, by one wife, Arminella, deceased. He was a painstaking craftsman, as was fitting,[4] pious honest, frugal and hard working. Weakened by his age and health, he was overcome by a fatal illness, and having made preparation to return his soul to God, he found his rest in Christ, on the day of peace for Christians, the Lord's day of course,[5] 5 October. He was buried in Fisherton churchyard close to his former wife on Monday 6 October, 96 years old (as we have accepted by his own calculation).[6]

1629/30 [no entries]

1630/1

750   Thomas Guilbert, young infant, almost two months old, the second son of John Guilbert of Fisherton, husbandman, and of Eleanor his wife. He died on the Wednesday of Easter week, 31 March, and was buried on Thursday 1 April.

751   Alice Court, a poor elderly widowed almswoman,[7] of Fisherton,

1   *muliercula*
2   *Codford orientali*, i.e Codford St Mary
3   *ut in votis habuisse dicitur*
4   *aerumnosus artifex (ut par fuit)*
5   *die nimiru' dominico*, i.e. Sunday
6   The age is written, as if for emphasis, in both roman and arabic numerals
7   *eleemosynaria*

descended from the ordinary[1] family of Smyth of Deptford. She was the widow of a certain Thomas Court, who had deserted her, etc,[2] and she died on Thursday 20 May, and was buried on Friday 21 May, 60 years old (as is conjectured).

752 Alexander Ingram of Bapton, an unmarried young husbandman, the second son of Henry Ingram also of Bapton street, yeoman, and of Mary his wife. He was standing in for his usual master, so far as is ascertained,[3] and at Shaftesbury, as a result of an unfortunate fall into a pit for draining away water, although it was not deep, he unexpectedly suffered an injury and choked.[4] It is said that he died on Friday 29 May, and he was buried, so it is asserted, in the church of St James, Shaftesbury, in Dorset.[5]

753 A young infant with no name, the first daughter of John Hoskins, now of Fisherton, labourer, and of Cecily, who is now his wife, and was formerly his mistress.[6] She was stillborn on Saturday 22 January and buried unbaptised on Sunday 23 January.

1631/2

754 Elizabeth Guilbert, a three-day old infant, the third daughter of John Guilbert of Fisherton, husbandman, and of Eleanor his wife. After a hasty baptism, but properly conducted with the due offices, Baptism had been carried out,[7] she gradually weakened and expired on Saturday 14 May, and was buried on Sunday 15 May.

755 Joan Snelgar, a little infant, recently born and baptised, the second daughter of John Snelgar the elder, husbandman, of Bapton and of Elizabeth his wife, died and buried on Tuesday 13 September.

756 William Patient of Fisherton, yeoman, and also descended from a

1 *plebeia*
2 *fugitivi hominis etc*
3 *m'ro solenni, quoad intentionem, proximus*
4 *casu infaelici puteum non altum, aquae desumendae, inexpecto contusus et suffocat'*
5 The register for St James records that he died of 'acsaddent fall' on 19th May and buried on 23 May
6 *nunc uxor' nuper amasiae*
7 *post baptisma expedita maturatione habita et debite ministratu'*

family of freeholders, the best of heads of households, the most trusted of neighbours, and the most beloved of grandfathers. He contracted a deadly disease and became weak, copiously[1] testifying to his faith in Christ; he piously fell asleep in Christ on Sunday[2] 3 March, and was buried in the churchyard close to his father on 6 March.[3] having first had a holy address by the most gifted man,[4] George Ditton, vicar of Chitterne.

1632/3

757 Joan Patient wife of Henry Patient of the manor of Deptford, yeoman, almost 47 years old, nourishing mother of eight children, and caring head of her family. Copiously[5] testifying to her faith in Christ she expired and died on Friday 6 July at Deptford[6] and was buried on Sunday 8 July at our Fisherton; having first had a holy address by the most gifted man[7] George Collier,[8] curate of Langford. She lies next to her mother Elizabeth Doughtie.

758 A little infant son of John Hoskins of Bapton, labourer and of Cecily his wife born on Wednesday 24 October, and buried 24 October.[9]

759 A little unnamed infant child, first daughter of William Wandborough of Bapton the younger, husbandman, and of Joan his wife, born Monday 16 December and buried on Tuesday 17 December.[10]

1 *abunde*
2 *die sabato Christiano*
3 Both dates have been overwritten and are unclear, but 3 March 1631/2 was a Sunday, and burial on 6 March is confirmed by the Bishop's Transcript
4 *habita prius sacra concione per ornatissimum virum*
5 *abunde*
6 *die veneris* is repeated
7 the passage is identical to that in the previous entry
8 Only '*Coll*' is legible, but members of the Collier family served as rectors of Steeple Langford 1607-1732 (*VCH Wilts*, xv, 191), and a George Collier was ordained by Bishop Davenant of Salisbury in 1624, becoming rector of Nunney and vicar of Shapwick (CCEd)
9 Some words in this entry are unclear, and the same date of birth and burial is repeated
10 Much of this entry is illegible

1633/4 [no entries][1]

1634/5

760   Thomas Crockford vicar of this church, died on Wednesday 26 March, in the year of our Lord 1634, and was buried on the following Wednesday 2 April.[2]

Entries in English continue to 1637 at the foot of the same page, but all subsequent pages of this register are missing.

---

1   Two entries for this year are recorded in the Bishop's Transcript: Henry Ingram buried on Monday 10 June; and Jane Heyter buried on 20 January.
2   This entry is written boldly in Latin.

STOCKTON

Registration Book

This is the register Book of public enactments in the Parish Church of Stockton by the ministers of the same; from the years of Our Lord 1589 and 1590, and successively. Beginning each and every year according to the reckoning of the Church of England, which is to say, from the Feast of the Annunciation of the Blessed Virgin Mary, which by the best authority is judged the beginning of the Incarnation of Our Saviour, Jesus Christ.

Faithfully copied out anew from the old, and original, book which was written by the venerable John Terrie, Master of Arts, rector of this Church, by Thomas Crockford, Bachelor of Arts, schoolmaster of the same; who came to take on the charge of youthful education in the aforesaid parish, on Tuesday 28 May, in the year of Our Lord one thousand, six hundred and two, in the three and fortieth Year of Queen Elizabeth's reign, which is to say, the last but one thereof.

Marriages Solemnly Contracted in the parish Church of Stockton, from the year of the Lord's Incarnation 1590, and successively.

1590/1

761   Jerome Potticary, clothier,[1] and Eleanor Fooks, married 26 June.

762   George Mascall and Joan Hinton, married 24 October.

1591/2

763   John Oliver, weaver, and Frideswide Powell, married 2 August.

764   John Farley, yeoman, and Dorothy Poulden, married 4 October.

765   Richard Chambers and Alice Saunders, married 30 October.

---

1   written in English (later instances are in Latin, generally *pannarius*)

1592/3

766   William Web and Alice Widowes, married 15 April.

767   John Crosse and Elizabeth Stockwell, married 12 June.

768   William Mascall and Agnes Hopkins, married 7 October.

769   Christopher Daniel, yeoman, and Jane Maton, married 23 February.

1593/4

770   Andrew Gennings and Anne Woort, married 28 January.

1594/5

771   John Hilman and Melior Exden, married 8 April.

772   Edward James, *alias* Mason, and Emma Taylor, *alias* Piffin, married 18 April.

773   John Furnell and Mary Ham, married 13 October.

1595/6

774   Henry Batten and Mary Goff, married 19 May.

1596/7

775   Thomas Sanders and Ada Surman, married 16 August.

776   John Sly, woolworker, and Elizabeth Oliver, married 8 November.

1597/8

777   William Cooke, clerk, and Martha White, daughter of John White of Stanton St John in Oxfordshire, gentleman, married 27 April.[1]

---

1   John Terrie, then Rector of Stockton, was married to one of the same family

778   Ambrose Cockerell, husbandman, and Elizabeth Hooper, daughter of John Hooper, husbandman, married 10 January, the same year.

779   William Colborne, gentleman, and Mary Toppe, daughter of John Topp, gentleman, deceased, married 15 of the same January, the same year.

1598/9

780   Ellis[1] Hopkins, husbandman, and Joan Sparow, married 2 October.

781   Thomas Maton of Enford, yeoman, and Agnes Maton, daughter of Nicholas Maton of Stockton, yeoman, married 6 December.

1599/1600

782   Nicholas Keloe and Joan Maton, married 3 May.

783   William Sheepheard and Margaret Chruch,[2] married 22 January.

1600/1

784   Abraham Langley, labourer, and Eleanor Rodney, married 13 October.

785   Richard White, weaver, and Cecily Mascall, married 16 January, the same year.

786   John Bentley, labourer, and Joan Crosse, widow, married 26 January, the same year.

787   Thomas Macy *alias* Banstone of Chilmark, labourer, and Joan Cockerell, elder daughter of Nicholas Cockerell of Stockton, husbandman, married 29 January, the same year.

788   William Goodinough and Warbora Rocksborrow, married 3 February, the same year.

---

1   *Elizeus*
2   Chruch, *sic* altered from Church, and presumably representing the local name Crooch.

1601/2 [no entries]

1602/3

789   John Skydmore, shepherd, and Tamsin White, married 18 May.

790   John London, labourer, and Jane Skydmore, married 3 July.

791   John Goodridge, blacksmith, and Agnes Cockerell, daughter of Edward Cockerell, blacksmith, married 25 October.

1603/4

792   Walter Withers of Codford St Mary, husbandman, and Mary Bennet, daughter of Edward Bennet of Stockton, husbandman, deceased, married 20 June.

793   George Hobbs, weaver, and Joan Vincent, married 1 August.

794   Thomas Rydgedale, weaver, and Dorothy Hill, married 5 October.

795   Thomas Willett of East Stour,[1] Dorset, yeoman, and Frideswide Oliver, widow, relict of John Oliver of Stockton, weaver, married 15 January.

796   William Web, labourer, and Anne Barter, married 16 January.

1604/5

797   Edmund Taylor *alias* Piffin, carpenter, youngest son of Thomas Taylor *alias* Piffin, carpenter, and Anne Hill, married 25 June.

1605/6

798   John Greene, labourer, and Eleanor Edridge, married 8 April.

799   Joel Gyrdler of Wylye, clothier, and Alice Maton, daughter of Nicholas Maton of Stockton, yeoman, married 29 April.

1   *Stowr estowre*

800 John Curteys of Shaftesbury,[1] labourer, and Mary Lewes, married 3 June.

1606/7

801 Stephen Sherelock, husbandman, native of Long Sutton,[2] Hampshire, and Grace Alford, daughter of Thomas Alford of Mere, clothier, married 16 June.

802 Jerome Cockerell, labourer, son of Nicholas Cockerell, husbandman, deceased, and Joan Fry, married 7 July.

803 William White, labourer, and Joan Stacy, married 29 September.

1607/8

804 Thomas Macy *alias* Bandstone, labourer, widower, and Kinbury Yokeney, of Warminster, married 19 July.

805 John Maton, yeoman, third son of Nicholas Maton, and Warbora Ryly, gentlewoman, widow, relict of John Ryly, gentleman, deceased, late of Upton Lovell, married 13 August.

1608/9

806 Jeffery Davies, blacksmith, formerly of Codford St Peter, and Jane Hailestone, married 4 April.

807 Henry Greenehill, gentleman, eldest son of John Greenehill of Steeple Ashton, gentleman, and Amy Poticary, daughter of Jerome Potticary, late of Stockton, clothier, deceased, married 8 August.

808 George Bennet, weaver, youngest son of Edward Bennet, husbandman, deceased, and Eleanor Whitaker, formerly of Westbury, married 5 February.

---

1 *Shaston*
2 *Sutton, near Odyam*

1609/10

809   Thomas Taylor, *alias* Piffin, carpenter, eldest son of Thomas Taylor, *alias* Piffin, deceased, and Elizabeth Scut formerly of Codford St Mary, married 9 October.

1610/11 [no entries]

1611/12

810   Thomas Ridgdale, weaver, widower, and Joan Cockerell, a woman not previously, married, younger daughter of Nicholas Cockerell, deceased, married 25 November.

1612/13

811   Thomas Crockford, clerk, schoolmaster[1] of this parish; son of Richard Crockford, yeoman, sometime of Wargrave, Berks, deceased; Bachelor of Arts from Magdalen College, Oxford; and Joan Alford, youngest daughter of Thomas Alford, late of Mere, freeholder and clothier, married 13 January.[2]

812   Christopher Gardner, of King's Sombourne,[3] Hampshire, gentleman; and Mary Whitaker, gentlewoman, widow, relict of Nash Whitaker, gentleman, in his lifetime a clothier of Tinhead, Wiltshire; she was also the eldest daughter of Jerome Potticarie of Stockton, gentleman, clothier, deceased;, married 15 March.

1613/14

813   James Hooper, gentleman, third son of Edward Hooper of Boveridge, in Cranborne parish, Dorset, esquire; and Penelope Whitaker, sixth daughter of Jeffery Whitaker, late of Tinhead, in Edington parish, Wiltshire, in his lifetime gentleman and clothier;, married Tuesday, 14 September.

---

1   *ludim[agister]*
2   Marginal note in English in a later hand: 'n.b. — 1613 inducted to the Vicarage of Fisherton Dallomer'
3   *Sumboorne Regis*

814   John Bayley, of Pensford, a town in Somerset, dyer,[1] and Frances Alfoord, ninth daughter of Thomas Alford, late of Mere, clothier, married 9 November.

1614/15

815   Thomas Vincent, labourer, son of John Vincent, labourer, deceased; and Eda, otherwise Edith, Frie, daughter of John Frie of Sutton Veny,[2] husbandman, deceased, married 18 July.

816   Thomas Ridgedale, a weaver twice widowed; and Dionise Foster, widow and relict of Robert Foster, late of Warminster, travelling merchant,[3] married 19 September.

817   Robert Greene, husbandman, son of Robert Greene, late of Heytesbury, husbandman, deceased; and Elizabeth Cockerell, widow and relict of Ambrose Cockerell, husbandman, married 8 November.

818   John Tanner, labourer, widower, son of Robert Tanner of Stockton, labourer; and Joan Idney, a woman not before married, a native of Deptford,[4] married 28 November.

1615/16 [no entries]

1616/17

819   Thomas Hobbes, a poor weaver, son of Robert Hobbes, deceased; and Warbora Dibble, a poor woman who before marriage was his mistress, married 22 April.

820   Thomas Bennet, husbandman, a bachelor in his forties, son of Edward Bennet, husbandman, sometime of Stockton, deceased, and Joan his wife; and Susan Steevens, the fourth daughter of Richard Steevens, late of Chilmark, yeoman, deceased, a woman not previously, married, and of unblemished reputation, married 1 July.

---

1   *coccarius*, presumably referring to *coccum*, a berry yielding a scarlet dye
2   *Venie Sutton*
3   *mercator' circumforanei*
4   *Detford*, i.e. Deptford in Wylye

821   Thomas Daniel, yeoman, a bachelor aged about 36 years, eldest son of Christopher Daniel of Norridge in Upton Scudamore[1] parish, yeoman; and Eleanor Maton, the youngest daughter of Nicholas Maton, sometime freeholding farmer of Stockton demesne,[2] deceased, married 27th January.

1617/18

822   James Chalke, of Ashton Gifford in Codford St Peter parish, a poor labourer once widowed; and Amy Surman, a poor woman also once widowed, relict of John Surman, sometime of this Stockton, a poor labourer, married 28 April.

1618/19

823   Nicholas Hart, bachelor, a young labourer; and Anne Surman, a woman not before, married, daughter of John Surman, sometime of Stockton, a poor labourer, deceased, and of Amy his wife, married 24 August.

824   Richard Sheepeheard, bachelor, a young labourer, servant of John Piercy of Stockton, husbandman; and Margery Golding, daughter of Richard Golding of Stockton, weaver, a woman previously unmarried, married 5 November.

825   Timothy Cooper, bachelor, a young carpenter, lately apprentice to Thomas Tayler of Stockton, carpenter, descended from the Coopers of Salterton;[3] and Jane Hevell, widow, relict of one John Hevell, sometime of Edington, tailor,[4] and herself the daughter of a Rodney of Stockton; married 26 October.[5]

1619/20

826   John Snelgar, of Bapton, husbandman, a bachelor more than 50 years of age, son of Henry Snelgar, sometime of Bapton, husbandman,

---

1   *Skydmore*
2   *ingenui Stocktoniensis praedii olim firmarii*
3   i.e. Salterton in Durnford
4   *sutor vestiarii*, literally a stitcher of clothes
5   This and the previous entries are prefixed 1, 3, 2, to signify that they are out of order

and of Elizabeth his wife, both deceased, John being the elder of two brothers of the same name; and Elizabeth Belton, a woman not previously married almost 23 years old, daughter of Robert Belton of Westbury, merchant, and of Mary his wife, married 2 August.

827 Jerome Goffe of Stockton, husbandman, a man once widowed; and Grace Sherelock, once widowed, relict of Stephen Sherelock, sometime of Stockton, husbandman, deceased; married at St Thomas's Church, Salisbury, by the hands of Master Albright, curate there, on Monday, 7 September.

1620/1

828 Thomas Eyles, of Stockton, a husbandman once widowed, and an old man almost 70 years old; and Mary Molmes, a maiden about 30 years old, descended from the family of Molmes, husbandmen of Ditchampton,[1] married in Wilton church on Monday, 23 October.

829 Edward Flower, of West Lavington,[2] Wiltshire, by birth a freeholder, but by occupation a clothier, more than 40 years old, a man once widowed and the father, thus far, of three children; and Michaela Hooper, a maiden almost 32 years old, daughter of John Hooper, sometime of Stockton, husbandman, and of Elizabeth, his second wife; for long she was a servant of Christopher Potticary, clothier, and his wife Mary; where she was engaged faithfully and commendably for the most part working with wool;[3] married in Stockton church on Monday, 27 November.

1621/2

830 George Crooch, of Stockton, formerly of Upton Lovell, an unmarried labourer about 30 years old; and Joan Butler, likewise unmarried, about 36 years old, of the labouring family of Butler of West Knoyle,[4] both having been until now, or else lately, servants in the household of Thomas Bennet of Stockton, husbandman, married Monday, 4 June.

---

1 Ditchampton in Wilton
2 *Lavington episcopi*
3 *in opere ut plurimum lanario fideliter et laudate' versata*
4 *Knahill occidentali*

831   Thomas Battin, of Stockton, formerly of Netherhampton[1] near Wilton, labourer, an unmarried man about 28 years old; and Edith Sparey, likewise unmarried, and about 30 years old, by birth of the labouring family of Sparey of Hindon, both being household servants of John Toppe, esquire, married on Monday, 12 November.

1622/3

832   John Mervin, a young gentleman in the very flower of his youth, and a bachelor about 24 years old, the first-born son of George Mervin of Upton in [East] Knoyle[2] parish, gentleman, and of Elizabeth his wife; heir to his father by right of birth, and heir also to his uncle, Thomas Mervin, of Pertwood, esquire, by right of adoption; and Anne Toppe, a young woman of no less gentle birth, and likewise in the flower of her youth, being a maiden almost 19 years old, the firstborn daughter of John Toppe of this Stockton, esquire, and of Mary who was once his wife, married on Wednesday, 18 September.

833   Jeffery Hart, a young unmarried labourer about 25 years old, descended from a labouring family of Coulston; and Joan Pennie, a woman likewise unmarried, about 40 years old, by birth from a family of equal status, and both being in the domestic service of John Maton of this Stockton, freeholding farmer, and of Warbora his wife, married on Monday, 7 October.

1623/4 [no entries]

1624/5

834   Timothy Cooper, carpenter, a man once widowed, aged about 30 years, the father of one son of the same name; and Joan Gibbs, by birth of a tailoring family of Boyton,[3] a young woman near to the same age, and one of the wool-working employees[4] of Christopher Potticarie, clothier, and of Mary his wife, married on Monday, 5 April, the morrow of Low Sunday.

1   *Netherington*
2   *Kna-hill*
3   *sutoria Boytoniae familia: sutorius* does, properly, mean 'of a shoemaker', and may mean that here; but at this time it seems to be used mostly to refer to a *sutor vestiarii*, tailor
4   *lanario famulitio*

835 Richard Dowdale, tailor, an unmarried man about 40 years old, now of Stockton, but previously of Stop,[1] by birth of a tailoring family of Boyton; and Elizabeth Drewett, a young woman about 30 years old, by birth of a family of husbandmen from Tinhead, and in the private service[2] of Christopher Potticarie and of Mary his wife aforesaid;, married on Monday, 26 April, the morrow of St Mark.

836 Christopher Golding, weaver, an unmarried young man about thirty-five years old, etc; and Margaret Philipps, an unmarried woman not much the younger, from Ridge[3] near Warminster, married on Monday, 31 January.

1625/6

837 Thomas Moore of Bapton, yeoman, an old man once widowed, and nearly 80 years old, etc; and Alice Laurence, an unmarried woman not yet 30 years old, by birth of a humble[4] family from Dinton, and the servant of William Acrigge of this Stockton, merchant, etc;, married on Tuesday, 11th October.

838 Abel Rosewell, a young unmarried clothier about 26 years old, descended from a gentry family of Steeple Langford, and lately released from his apprenticeship in the clothmaking workforce of Christopher Potticarie; and Martha Crooch, a servant of about the same age, descended from a freeholding family of Orcheston, and in the same service; married on Monday, 21 November.

1626/7

839 Timothy Cooper, carpenter, a man twice widowed, etc; and Elizabeth Martin, a servant almost 30 years old, in the household service of Thomas Hawker, of Heytesbury, esquire, but by birth (it is claimed) of a family of clothiers formerly of Croscombe[5] near Wells in Somerset; married on Monday, 27 November.

1 in Fonthill Gifford
2 *ex interiore famulitio*
3 This could be Rudge (Somerset), Ridge in Chilmark, or possibly Norridge in Upton Scudamore
4 *plebeia*
5 *Coscombe*

1627/8

840   William Moonday, now of Stockton, husbandman, a bachelor nearly 44 years old, by birth of a family of husbandmen formerly of Rollestone,[1] etc; and Christian Hooper, a young woman a little over 16 years old, the only daughter of John Hooper of Stockton, husbandman, and of —[2] his former wife, who was by birth of the Fosters of Bapton, etc;, married on Monday, 26 November.

841   John Toppe, a young gentleman, second son of John Toppe of this Stockton, esquire, and of Mary his sometime wife, deceased, and the younger son bearing his father's name, aged a little above 28 years, etc; and Elizabeth Swayne, a young gentlewoman almost 17 years old, the only daughter of John Swayne formerly of [Tarrant] Gunville in Dorset, esquire, and of — his deceased wife, married in Gunville parish church aforesaid on Thursday, 17 January.

1628/9

842   Richard Golding, a young unmarried labourer, almost 30 years old, fourth son of Richard Golding, weaver, and of Elizabeth his former wife; and Honor Surman, a woman not before, married, almost 23 years old, the second daughter of John Surman formerly of this Stockton, labourer, deceased, and of Amy his wife, married on Monday, 10 November.[3]

1629/30

843   Thomas Hancocke, a young gentleman, son of —[4] Hancock, of the city of Salisbury, nobleman,[5] etc; and Mary Mussell, a maiden

---

1   *Rolston*
2   Alice, buried in 1613 according to the burial register (see **1185**).
3   The names of the rector, curate and churchwardens are appended to the entries at the end of this and the two subsequent years. In 1628 they are Christopher Greene, Dr. of Theology, etc, Rector; William Greene, Artium [?MA], Curate; and besides, Richard Taylor and John Hooper, Wardens. In 1629 and 1630 wardens are John Maton, gentleman and William Acrig, merchant. See below, **1068, 1072, 1079**.
4   Probably Thomas Hancock, mayor of Salisbury, 1605/6
5   *viri patricii*

gentlewoman, daughter of Tristram Mussell, late of Steeple Langford, gentleman, deceased, etc, and of Anellada, once his wife, married on Saturday, 1 August.

844 Henry Knight, a young unmarried ploughwright, fourth son of William Knight the elder of this Stockton, ploughwright, etc; and Sarah Barnes, a servant, long in the service of the rector, Rector Greene, by birth of respectable[1] parents in the Isle of Wight, married on Monday, 5 October.

845 Edward Potticarie, of Boyton, a young weaver, and son of a weaver from that place, now deceased; and Philippa Hayward, a woman in the household of Christopher Potticarie of this Stockton, and by birth from a respectable household of Wilton, married on the same day, Monday, 5 October.

846 Edward Fowles, a young labourer and servant of John Toppe, esquire, engaged in outdoors work,[2] by birth of a humble household of' — in the neighbourhood near Wells; and Grace Gardener, a woman not before, married, 27 years old, — daughter of John Gardener, formerly of this Stockton, tailor, now deceased, and of Agnes his wife, now his widow, married on Saturday, 28 November.

1630/1

847 Edward Italie, *alias* Iterie, a young unmarried labourer, etc; and Tamsin Skydmore, daughter of John Skydmore, etc, married on Monday, 8 November.[3]

848 John Lukeson, unmarried labourer, and Jane Maton, daughter of Thomas Maton, yeoman, and of Jane his Wife, married on Monday, 15 October.[4]

Entries continue in this register in Latin until 1709.

---

1 *honesta*
2 *ad opus rusticu'*
3 Although still in Crockford's hand, the writing of this and the next entry has noticeably deteriorated
4 This is the last entry in Crockford's hand

Baptisms celebrated publicly in the parish church of Stockton from the year of the Lord's Incarnation 1589 inclusively, and thereafter.

1589/90

849 Geoffrey Hobbs, son of Robert Hobbs, weaver, baptised 2 June.

850 Mary Maton, daughter of Nicholas Maton, yeoman, baptised 4 June.

851 Michaela Hooper, daughter of John Hooper, husbandman, baptised 15 June.

852 Thomas Cooles, son of John Cooles, baptised 27 July.

853 Christopher Oliver, son of John Oliver, weaver, baptised 8 October.

854 Anne Potticary, daughter of Jerome Potticary, gentleman clothier, baptised 30 November.

855 Anne Heath, daughter of Nicholas Heath, gentleman, baptised 23 February.

1590/1

856 Agnes Eyles, daughter of Thomas Eyles, husbandman, baptised 18 June.

857 John Golding, son of Richard Golding, weaver, baptised 18 July.

858 John Knight, son of William Knight, ploughwright, baptised 7 December.

859 George Gardner, son of John Gardner, tailor, baptised 22 January.

1591/2

860 Elizabeth Potticary, daughter of Jerome Potticary, gentleman clothier, baptised 16 December.

861 John Goffe, son of Richard Goffe, husbandman, baptised 16 February.

862 Joan Hooper, daughter of John Hooper, husbandman, baptised 5 March.

1592/3

863 Eleanor Maton, daughter of Nicholas Maton, yeoman, baptised 25 April.

864 Mary Golding, daughter of Richard Golding, weaver, baptised 27 May.

865 William Cockerell, son of William Cockerell, labourer, baptised 2 June.

866 Stephen Terry, son of John Terry, rector of this parish, baptised 20 August.

867 Susan Potticary, daughter of Jerome,[1] gentleman clothier, baptised 23 January.

1593/4

868 Jane Cockerell, daughter of William Cockerell, labourer, baptised 30 August.

869 John Terry, son of John Terry, rector of this church, baptised 1 November.

870 John Knight, son of William Knight, ploughwright, baptised 11 December.

---

1   the surname, Potticary, has been omitted

871   Alice Goff, daughter of Richard Goff, husbandman, baptised 11 March.

872   Margery Golding, daughter of Richard Golding, weaver, baptised 24 March.

1594/5

873   John Oliver, son of John Oliver, weaver, baptised 2 April.

874   John James, *alias* Mason, son of Edward James, *alias* Mason, blacksmith, baptised 18 August.

875   Jerome Potticary, second son of Jerome Potticary, gentleman clothier, baptised 19 August.

876   John Genings, son of Andrew Genings, baptised 6 October.

877   John Hobbs, son of Robert Hobbs, weaver, baptised 18 February.

878   John Bysse, son of James Bysse, labourer, baptised 7 March.

1595/6

879   Henry Crosse, son of John Crosse, labourer, baptised 18 June.

880   Ambrose Mascall, son of William Mascall, husbandman, baptised 20 June.

881   Samuel Terry, son of John Terry, rector of this church, baptised 6 July.

882   Ambrose Gardner, son of John Gardner, tailor, also baptised 6 July.

1596/7

883   Abraham Golding, son of Richard Golding, weaver, baptised 16 April.

884   John Potticary, posthumous third son of Jerome Potticary, gentleman clothier, deceased, baptised 12 September.

885 Edward Cockerell, son of Anne Cockerell, baptised 13 October.

886 John Topp, firstborn son of John Topp, gentleman, born 14 November, baptised 22 November.

887 Jerome Hooper, son of John Hooper, husbandman, baptised 10 November.

888 Agnes Mascall, daughter of William Mascall, husbandman, baptised 8 March.

889 Dorothy Crosse, daughter of John Crosse, labourer, baptised 20 March.

1597/8

890 John Terry, son of John Terry, rector of this church, baptised 25 May.

891 Henry Knight, son of William Knight, ploughwright, baptised 18 February.

1598/9

892 William Gardner, son of John Gardner, tailor, baptised 13 May.

893 Jerome Batten, son of Henry Batten, labourer, baptised 18 September.

894 Richard Golding, son of Richard Golding, weaver, baptised 31 January.

1599/1600

895 Thomas Hopkins, son of Ellis Hopkins, husbandman, baptised 13 June.

896 Joan Mascall, daughter of William Mascall, husbandman, baptised 12 August.

897   Martha Bechin, daughter of William Bechin, master builder,[1] baptised 10 September.

898   Christopher Maton, son of Thomas Maton, yeoman, baptised 3 October.

899   Nathaniel Terry, son of John Terry, rector of this church, baptised 11 November.

1600/1

900   Ellis Surman, son of John Surman, labourer, baptised 7 April.

901   George Batten, son of Henry Batten, labourer, baptised 9 April.

902   Elizabeth White, daughter of Richard White, weaver, baptised 23 November.

903   John Hopkins, son of Ellis Hopkins, husbandman, baptised 20 January.

1601/2

904   Elizabeth Golding, daughter of Richard Golding, weaver, baptised 10 May.

905   Jane Maton, daughter of Thomas Maton, yeoman, baptised 21 June.

906   Jane Macy, daughter of Thomas Macy, *alias* Bandstone, labourer, baptised 25 July.

907   Mary Langley, daughter of Abraham Langley, labourer, baptised 22 September.

908   Ambrose Cockerell, son of Ambrose Cockerell, husbandman, baptised 4 November.

---

1   *architecti*

909 Phyllis Bentley, daughter of John Bentley, labourer, baptised 22 November.

910 Grace Knight, daughter of William Knight, ploughwright, baptised 3 January.

911 Stephen Hopkins, son of Ellis Hopkins, husbandman, baptised 12 March.

912 Mary Batten, daughter of Henry Batten, labourer, baptised 21 March.

1602/3

913 Grace Gardner, daughter of John Gardner, tailor, baptised 21 August.

914 William Macy, son of Thomas Macy *alias* Bandstone, labourer, 28 November.

915 Stephen Maton, son of Thomas Maton, yeoman, baptised 26 December.

916 Michaela White, daughter of Richard White, weaver, baptised 1 February.

1603/4

917 Frideswide Mascall, daughter of William Mascall, husbandman, baptised 25 March.

918 Anthony Golding, son of Richard Golding, weaver, baptised 8 June.

919 Dorothy Surman, daughter of John Surman, labourer, baptised 26 June.

920 Mary Mabell, daughter of Joan Mabell, baptised 10 September.

921 Jane Langley, daughter of Abraham Langley, labourer, baptised 9 October.

922   Eleanor Ridgedale, daughter of Thomas Ridgedale, weaver, baptised 13 January.

923   Tamsin Skydmore, daughter of John Skydmore, shepherd, baptised 17 January.

924   Richard Bentley, son of John Bentley, labourer, baptised 20 January.

925   Jerome Potticary, firstborn son of Christopher Potticary, gentleman, clothier, born 24 February, and baptised 2 March.

926   Elizabeth Batten, daughter of Henry Batten, labourer, baptised 10 March.

1604/5

927   Leonard Fleming, son of Nicholas Fleming, labourer, baptised 29 March.

928   George Withers, son of Walter Withers of Codford St Mary, husbandman, baptised 9 April.

929   Mary Rockesborough, daughter of Richard Rocksborrough, labourer, baptised 3 June.

930   Susan Goodridge, daughter of John Goodridge, blacksmith, baptised 27 June.

931   Elizabeth Cockerell, daughter of Ambrose Cockerell, husbandman, baptised 25 September.

932   Alice Hopkins, daughter of Ellis Hopkins, husbandman, baptised 11 October.

933   Eleanor Edwardes, *alias* Web, daughter of William Edwardes, *alias* Web, labourer, baptised 27 October.

1605/6

934   Tamsin Macy, daughter of Thomas Macy *alias* Bandstone, labourer, baptised 2 June.

935 William Mascall, son of William Mascall, husbandman, baptised 25 July.

936 Martha Langley, daughter of Abraham Langley, labourer, baptised 4 September.

937 Jeffery Potticary, second son of Christopher Potticary, gentleman, clothier, born 8 September, and baptised 12 September.

938 Honor Surman, daughter of John Surman, labourer, baptised 6 October.

939 Thomas Gardner, son of John Gardner, tailor, baptised 17 November.

940 Anne Goodridge, daughter of John Goodridge, blacksmith, baptised 2 January.

941 Jane Batten, daughter of Henry Batten, labourer, baptised 14 February.

942 Agnes Fleming, daughter of Nicholas Fleming, labourer, baptised 28 February.

943 Thomas Ridgdale, son of Thomas Ridgdale, weaver, baptised 13th March.

1606/7

944 Joan Hobbs, daughter of George Hobbs, weaver, baptised 29 May.

945 Mary Skydmore, daughter of Robert Skydmore, shepherd, baptised 8 August.

946 Amy Agre, daughter of Richard Agre, labourer, baptised 8 November.

947   John White, son of Richard White, weaver, baptised 26 November.

948   Christopher Potticary, third son of Christopher Potticary, gentleman, clothier, baptised 30 November.

1607/8

949   Frances Fleming, daughter of Nicholas Fleming, labourer, baptised 19 April.

950   Jerome Cockerell, son of Jerome Cockerell, shepherd, baptised 26 April.

951   Grace Sherelock, daughter of Stephen Sherelock, husbandman, baptised 24 August.

952   Mary Cockerell, daughter of Ambrose Cockerell, husbandman, baptised 11 September.

953   George Golding, son of Richard Golding, weaver, baptised 16 September.

954   John Skydmore, son of Robert Skydmore, shepherd, was also baptised 16 September.

955   James Hopkins, son of Ellis Hopkins, husbandman, baptised 21 October.

956   Mary Toppe, second daughter of John Toppe, gentleman, born 25 November, and baptised 16 December.

957   John White, son of John White, clerk, rector of Dorchester, in Dorset, born 21 December, and baptised 27 December.

958   Eleanor Langley, daughter of Abraham Langley, labourer, baptised 13 January.

959   Anne Batten, daughter of Henry Batten, labourer, baptised 2 March.

960 Frances Edwards, *alias* Web, daughter of William Edwards, *alias* Web, was also baptised 2 March.

1608/9

961 Another Stephen Terry, who was the sixth son of John Terry, rector of this church, born 25 August, and baptised 31 August; whose name was given in memory of an earlier Stephen, a young man of most excellent hope and very diligent nature, who died at Oxford on 28 July of this year, having barely attained the age of 16.

962 George and Ambrose Ridgedale, twin brothers, sons of Thomas Ridgdale, weaver, baptised 4 September.

963 Thomas Fleming, son of Nicholas Fleming, labourer, baptised 25 January.

964 Elizabeth Davies, daughter of Jeffery Davies, blacksmith, baptised 19 February.

1609/10

965 Salem[1] Toppe, daughter of Alexander Topp, gentleman, born 30 April, and baptised 24 May.

966 Thomas Macy, *alias* Bandstone, son of Thomas Macy, *alias* Bandstone, labourer, baptised 2 June.

967 Anne Cockerell, daughter of Jerome Cockerell, shepherd, baptised 13 March.

1610/11

968 Joan Skydmore, daughter of Robert Skydmore, shepherd, baptised 31 March.

969 Agnes Ridgedale, daughter of Thomas Ridgedale, weaver, was also baptised 31 March.

1 *Salema*

970   Lucy Batten, daughter of Henry Batten, labourer, baptised 17 May.

971   Mary Gardner, daughter of Thomas Gardner, of Stanton St John, in Oxfordshire, gentleman, born 10 June, and baptised 24 June.

972   Elizabeth Toppe, daughter of John Toppe, gentleman, born 18 August, and baptised 3 September.

973   John Cockerell, posthumous son of Ambrose Cockerell, husbandman, lately deceased, baptised 5 October.

974   Winifred Tanner, daughter of John Tanner, labourer, baptised 3 November.

975   Anne Davies, daughter of Jeffery Davies, blacksmith, baptised 18 November.

976   Richard Rocksborrough, son of Richard Rocksborough, labourer, baptised 25 November.

977   Thomas Tanner, son of Mary Tanner, the daughter of Robert, labourer, baptised 22 February.

1611/12

978   Penelope Langley, daughter of Abraham Langley, labourer, born 17 August, and baptised 18 August.

979   Frances Sherelock, daughter of Stephen Sherelocke, husbandman, born 2 October, and baptised 20 October.

980   Christian Hooper, daughter of John Hooper, husbandman, born 19 October, and baptised 23 October.

981   Christopher Nash, son of John Nash, a poor man from Cranbourne near Winchester,[1] in Hampshire, baptised 7 March.

---

1   *Cranboorne prope Winton.* Cranbourne is north of Winchester, near Sutton Scotney.

1612/13

982   Nicholas Maton, son of Thomas Maton, yeoman, born 3 April, and baptised 5 April.

983   Eleanor Aplin, daughter of Thomas Aplin, of Iwerne Minster,[1] in Dorset, born and baptised 12 April.[2]

984   Elizabeth Potticarie, firstborn daughter of Christopher Potticarie, gentleman clothier, born at daybreak on Friday 17 July, and baptised on Sunday, 26 July; whose name was given in memory of Elizabeth, her paternal grandmother, a lady of the highest praise, by birth of the gentry family of Sandsborrough[3] of Upton Scudamore.[4]

985   Tamsin Skydmore, daughter of Robert Skydmore, shepherd, born 6 October, and baptised 7 October.

986   Anthony Cockerell, son of Jerome Cockerell, shepherd, born 8 November, and baptised 10 November.

987   Jane Davies, daughter of Jeffery Davies, blacksmith, born 11 December, and baptised 13 December.

1613/14

988   Henry Battin, son of Henry Battin, labourer, born 16 June, and baptised 18 June.

989   Edward Toppe, third son of John Toppe, esquire, born Thursday 12 August, and baptised Monday 13 September.

990   Arthur Tanner, son of Mary Tanner, the daughter of Robert Tanner, labourer, born 15 March, and baptised 18 March.

1   *Yuron Minstrell*
2   *sic*, but cf. **1176**
3   *Sandsborraeoru'*
4   *Skydmore*

1614/15

991 Another Christopher Potticarie, fourth son of Christopher Potticarie, gentleman and clothier, born 3 July about two o'clock of the afternoon, and baptised 17 July; whose name was given firstly out of regard for and as a consolation to his father, and also in memory of and as successor[1] to an earlier Christopher, a most pleasing little boy, who by fate died prematurely, in the fourth year of his age.

992 John King, firstborn son of John King, yeoman, the son of Richard King of Sedgehill, yeoman, born 24 December, and baptised 11 January.

993 Another Anne Goffe, second daughter of Jerome Goffe, husbandman, born 11 January, and baptised 23 January.

994 Joan Hooper, second daughter of John Hooper, husbandman, that is to say, his first daughter by his second wife, born 22 February, and baptised 26 February.

1615/16

995 Grace Vincent, firstborn daughter of Thomas Vincent, labourer, born 30 March, and baptised 5 April.

996 Thomas Cockerell, son of Jerome Cockerell, shepherd, born 12 April, and baptised 16 April.

997 Dionise Greene, firstborn daughter of Robert Greene, husbandman, born 5 June and baptised 10 June.

998 Susan Dibble, daughter of Warbora Dibble, a poor unmarried woman, born 14 November, and baptised 20 November.

999 Philip Knight, firstborn son of William Knight, ploughwright, who was himself son of William Knight, ploughwright, born and baptised 31[2] December.

---

1   the word is faint and unclear, but appears to be a form of *superstes*, literally survivor

2   *ult*

1000 Stephen Sherelocke, first-born son of Stephen Sherelocke, husbandman, born 3 March, and baptised 18 March.

1616/17

1001 Joan Langley, daughter of Abraham Langley, labourer, by his second wife, Joan Scammell, formerly of Donhead, born 5 April, and baptised 6 April.

1002 Thomas Vincent, son of Thomas Vincent, labourer, born 14 November, and baptised 1 December.

1003 Christopher Hobbs, son of Thomas Hobbs, a poor weaver, born 14 February, and baptised 16 February.

1004 Richard Potticarie, fifth son of Christopher Potticarie, gentleman and clothier, born Wednesday 19 February, between eight and nine o'clock in the evening, and baptised also on Wednesday, 26 February; whose name was given in memory of his paternal great-grandfather, Richard Potticarie, etc.

1005 Jeffery Davies, son of Jeffery Davies, blacksmith, by Jane his wife, born 7 March, and baptised on Sunday 9 March.

1617/18

1006 Mary Rede, illegitimate daughter of Bridget Reade, a maidservant of the servile class,[1] who was the daughter of one Ralph Reade formerly of Downton, deceased, born and baptised 25 March, that is, the first day of 1617.

1007 Mary Acrigg, daughter of William Acrigge, merchant, and of Susan his wife, born 3 July, and baptised 6 July.

1008 Anne Eyles, daughter of James Eyles, *alias* Hicks, of Fisherton Delamere, husbandman, and of Mary his wife, born 1 August, and baptised 3 August.

---

1 *servilis conditionis ancilla*

1009 Elizabeth Knight, daughter of William,[1] ploughwright, born 9 December, and baptised 14 December.

1010 Mary Bennett, firstborn daughter of Thomas Bennett, husbandman, and of Susan his wife, born 12 February, and baptised 15 February.

1011 Eleanor Vincent, daughter of Thomas Vincent, labourer, and of Ada his wife, born 3 March, and baptised 8 March.

1618/19

1012 Joan Green, second daughter of Robert Greene, husbandman, and of Elizabeth his wife, born 21 April, and baptised 26 April.

1013 Jerome Goffe, son of Jerome Goffe, husbandman, and of Agnes his wife, born 9 June, and baptised 14 June.

1014 Joan Hobbs, daughter of Thomas Hobbs, a poor labourer, and of Warbora his wife, born 3 September, and baptised 6 September.

1015 Mary Piercy, firstborn daughter of John Piercy, husbandman, and of Margaret his wife, born 11 September, and baptised 13 September.

1619/20

1016 Henry Flemming, son of Nicholas Flemming, labourer, and of Margaret his wife, born 22 April, and baptised 25 April.

1017 Richard and Rebecca Acrigge, twins, son and daughter of William Acrigge, merchant, and of Susan his wife, born just before the end of 7 May, that is, a little before the twelfth hour of the night, first the boy, and then the girl; and baptised 9 May.

1018 Ellis Davies, son of Jeffery Davies, blacksmith, and of Jane his wife, born 16 June, and baptised 18 June.

1019 Grace Goffe, daughter of Jerome Goffe, husbandman, and of Agnes his wife (Agnes, the child's mother, died not many days after this birth), born 12 July, and baptised 17 July; and immediately after the baptism of

---

1   K has been interlined, to denote that the surname was omitted

the child, the mother was buried.

1020 Susan Bennet, daughter of Thomas Bennet, husbandman, and of Susan his wife, born 19 July, and baptised 22 July.

1021 Richard Mowday, son of Thomas Mowday, husbandman, and of Agnes his wife, born 25 August, and baptised on Friday, 27 August.

1022 Catherine Potticarie, second daughter of Christopher Potticarie, gentleman and clothier, and of Mary his wife, born Friday, 10 September about nine o'clock at night, and baptised Wednesday, 15 September; whose name was given in memory of a lady revered (while she lived), the child's maternal grandmother, Catherine Whitaker, wife of an eminent man, Jeffery Whitaker, formerly of Tinhead, gentleman and clothier, who was descended from the freeholding Grant family of Bradford.

1023 Susan Knight, second daughter of William Knight the younger, ploughwright, and of Elizabeth his wife, born Thursday 13 January, and baptised on Sunday 16 January.

1024 Timothy Cooper, firstborn son of Timothy Cooper, carpenter, and of Jane his wife, born Saturday, 15 January, and baptised on Sunday, 16 January.

1025 Thomas Vincent, second son of Thomas Vincent, labourer, and of Ada his wife, born Monday, 6 March, and baptised on Wednesday 8 March.

1620/1

1026 Jerome Goffe, firstborn son of Jerome Goffe, husbandman, and of Grace his wife, born Thursday, 13 July, a little before the twelfth hour of the night, and baptised on Sunday, 16 July.

1027 Susan Greene, third daughter of Robert Greene, husbandman, and of Elizabeth his wife, born Friday 15 September, and baptised on Saturday, 16 September.

1028 Abraham Langley, firstborn son of Abraham Langley, labourer, and of Joan his wife, born Friday, 17 November, and baptised on Sunday, 19 November.

1029 Mary Potticarie, third daughter of Christopher Potticarie, gentleman and clothier, and of Mary his wife, born Tuesday 13 March at about the fifth hour before dawn, and baptised on Wednesday, 21 March; whose name was given chiefly out of regard for her mother, etc.

1621/2

1030 An unnamed infant, firstborn son of James Eyles of Stockton, formerly of Fisherton, husbandman, and of Edith his wife, born Tuesday, 16 May; he lived (as the midwives testified, for a short time)[1] and rapidly died from his infirmity, as was expected; and the holy water of the font[2] did not touch him; he died on the same day as his birth, and was buried (inasmuch as he was the son of Christian parents) with solemn rites, on the following day, Wednesday 17 May.

1031 Jerome Piercy, firstborn son of John Piercy, husbandman, and of Margaret his wife, born Sunday 27 May, and baptised the following Thursday, 31, the last day of May.

1032 Christopher Moodie, second son of Thomas Moodie, husbandman, and of Agnes his wife, born Sunday 1 July, and baptised on Wednesday, 4 July.

1033 Catherine Knight, third daughter of William Knight the younger, ploughwright, and of Elizabeth his wife, born Sunday 25 November and baptised the same day.

1034 Alice Goffe, illegitimate daughter of Alice Goffe, the daughter of Richard Goffe, husbandman, and of Agnes his wife, old people of an assuredly[3] honourable household, born Sunday 9 December, and baptised on Friday, 14 December.

1035 William, illegitimate son of Werburga, commonly Warbora, Hobbs, a poor widow, relict of Thomas Hobbes, deceased, born and baptised 2 February.

1   The writing is cramped, but appears to read: (*ut testamur obstetrices ad exiguu' temporis*)
2   *lavacru'*
3   *nimirum*

1622/3

1036 Anthony Davies, fourth son of Jeffery Davies, blacksmith, and of Jane his wife, born Tuesday, 28 May, and baptised on the Feast of the Ascension, Thursday, 30 May.

1037 Alice Eyles, daughter of James Eyles, husbandman, and of Edith his wife, also born Tuesday, 28 May, and baptised on the same feast day, at the same baptism.

1038 Nathaniel Acrigge, fourth son of William Acrigge, merchant, and of Susan his wife, born Tuesday, 20 August, and baptised on Thursday, 22 August.

1039 Joan Vincent, third daughter of Thomas Vincent, labourer, and of Eda, otherwise Edith, his wife, born Monday, 23 December, and baptised on the Feast of St Stephen, Thursday, 26 December.

1040 John Piercie, second son of John Piercie, husbandman, and of Margaret his wife, born Friday, 14 February, and baptised on Saturday, 15 February.

1623/4

1041 Thomas Potticarie, sixth son of Christopher Potticarie, gentleman and clothier, and of Mary his wife, born on Good Friday,[1] 11 April, and baptised on the Tuesday in Easter week, 15 April; whose name was given out of regard for his great-uncle, an elderly man of venerable dignity, and one filled most full of the more humane studies of every sort, Thomas Potticarie, Bachelor of Laws, sometime Fellow of St John's College, Oxford, and presently headmaster of a renowned school in the city of Salisbury, etc.

1042 Susan Gardiner, daughter and firstborn child of John Gardiner, husbandman, and of Elizabeth his wife, born Friday, 2 May, and baptised Saturday, 3 May.

1043 John Perrie, firstborn son of John Perrie, shepherd, and of Jane his wife, born and baptised on the feast of St Peter, Sunday, 29 June.

1   *die dom'cae passionis*

1044 Jerome Davies, fifth son of Jeffery Davies, blacksmith, and of Jane his wife, born Friday, 26 September, and baptised on Sunday, 28 September.

1045 Thomas Goffe, second son of Jerome Goffe, husbandman, and of Grace his wife, born Thursday, 3 October, and baptised on Saturday, 5 October.

1046 John Helme, firstborn son of John Helme, husbandman, and of Eleanor his wife, born Thursday, 4 December, and baptised on Saturday, 6 December.

1047 Edward Greene, firstborn son of Robert Greene, husbandman, and of Elizabeth his wife, born Sunday, 1 February, and baptised the Monday next following, the Feast of the Purification of the Virgin, also of the Presentation of Our Lord, 2 February.

1624/5

1048 Mary Knight, fourth daughter of William Knight the younger, ploughwright, and of Elizabeth his wife, born the Tuesday of Whit week, 18 May, and baptised on Saturday, the Eve of Trinity, 22 May.

1049 John Gardiner, firstborn son of John Gardiner, now a labourer, and of Elizabeth his wife, was born and baptised on the eleventh Sunday after Trinity, 8 August.

1050 Abel Cooper, second son of Timothy Cooper, carpenter, being his first son by Joan, his second wife; born Tuesday, 22 February, and baptised on the Sunday in Shrovetide called Quinquagesima, 27 February.

1051 John Vincent, third son of Thomas Vincent, labourer, and of Edith, otherwise Ada, his wife, born Saturday 5 March, and baptised on Sunday, the first Sunday in Lent, 6 March.

1625/6

1052 William Flemming, third son of Nicholas Fleming, labourer, and of Margaret his wife, born Saturday 5 November, and baptised on

Wednesday, 9 November.

1053 A third Christopher Potticarie, seventh son and tenth child of Christopher Potticarie, gentleman and clothier, and of Mary his wife, born Sunday 8 January, and baptised on Friday, 13 January; whose name was given by his principal godfather,[1] Dr Christopher Greene, the rector, for a consolation to the child's father, and in memory of his two brothers of the same name, deceased.

1054 William Gardener, second son of John Gardener, labourer, and of Elizabeth his wife, born Saturday 14 January, and baptised on Sunday, 15 January.

1626/7

1055 Margaret Helme, firstborn daughter of John Helme, husbandman, and of Eleanor his wife, born Thursday 20 July, and baptised on Saturday, 22 July.

1056 Thomas Knight, second son of William Knight, ploughwright, and of Elizabeth his wife, born Wednesday 17 January, and baptised on Friday, 19 January.

1057 Bartholomew Mussell, first son of Bartholomew Mussell, labourer, and of Frideswide, now his wife, previously his mistress, born Thursday, 8 February, and baptised Saturday, 10 February.

1058 Philippa Sprite, illegitimate daughter of Jane Sprite, a maidservant of the servile class, born Friday 16 February, and baptised on Sunday 18 February.

1627/8

1059 George Gardener, second son of John Gardener, labourer, and of Elizabeth his wife, born Monday, 8 October, and baptised on Friday, 12 October.

---

1   *susceptore*

1628/9

1060 John Bundy, firstborn son of William Bundy, labourer, and of Joan his wife, born Tuesday 25 March, and baptised on Wednesday 26 March.

1061 Nicholas Maton, firstborn son of Stephen Maton, labourer, and of Mary his wife, born Tuesday 30 September, and baptised on Sunday, 5 October.

1062 Anne Mussell, first daughter of Bartholomew Mussell, and of Frideswide his wife, born Friday 9 January, and baptised Saturday 10 January.

1063 Joan Helme, second daughter of John Helme, yeoman, and of Eleanor his wife, born Saturday 17 January, baptised on Sunday, 18 January.

1064 Jane Vincent, fourth daughter of Thomas Vincent, labourer, and of Edith his wife, born Thursday 19 February, and baptised on Saturday, 21 February.

1065 Elizabeth Toppe, firstborn daughter of John Toppe the younger, gentleman, and of Elizabeth his wife, born Wednesday, 4 March, about the third hour before dawn, and baptised the Sunday following, 8 March.

1066 Mary Dowdale, firstborn daughter of Richard Dowdale, yeoman and tailor, and of Elizabeth his wife, born on the fourth Sunday in Lent, and baptised the Wednesday next following, 18 March.

1067 Anne Knight, fifth daughter of William Knight the younger, ploughwright, and of Elizabeth his wife, born Tuesday, 17 March, and baptised likewise on Wednesday, 18 March.[1]

1068 [register signed by] Christopher Greene, Doctor of Theology, rector; William Greene, Arts, curate; Richard Taylor, carpenter,[2] and John Hooper, husbandman, churchwardens.

---

1   This, and subsequent years to 1630, give the names of rector, curate and churchwardens, as marriages: Richard Taylour, and John Hooper are wardens

2   *carp'*

1629/30

1069 Frances Goffe, second illegitimate daughter of Alice Goffe, a prostitute,[1] etc., born Friday, 5 June, and baptised on Saturday, 6 June.

1070 Mary Golding, firstborn daughter of Richard Golding, labourer, and of Honor his wife, born Wednesday, 12 August, and baptised on Saturday, 15 August.

1071 Elizabeth Moonday, firstborn daughter of William Moonday, husbandman, and of Christian his wife, born Thursday, 18 March, and baptised on Saturday, 20 March.

1072 [register signed by] Christopher Greene, Doctor of Theology, rector; William Greene, curate; John Maton, gentleman, and William Acrig, merchant, churchwardens.

1630/1

1073 Lydia Bentley, daughter of John Bentley, labourer, and of Joan, his second wife, born Wednesday, 16 June, and baptised on Friday, 18 June.[2]

1074 Joan Gardiner, daughter of John Gardiner, labourer, and of Elizabeth his wife, born on the Feast of Peter, and baptised on the Sunday following, 4 July.

1075 Warbora Fowles, first daughter of Edward Fowles, labourer, and of Grace his wife, born Sunday, 22 August, and baptised on the Feast of Bartholomew,[3] etc.

1076 Alice Helme, third daughter of John Helme, yeoman, and of Eleanor his wife, born Friday 24 September, and baptised on Sunday, 26 September.

1077 Thomas Pierson, first son of Henry Pierson, *alias* Vargeis, husbandman, and of Joan his wife, born Thursday 7 October, and baptised on Sunday, 9 October.

1   *mericula*, not found, but cf. *meretricula*, **1664**
2   From this entry on the writing deteriorates
3   24 August

1078 Elizabeth Dowdale, second daughter of Richard Dowdale, tailor, and of Elizabeth his wife, born Friday 11 February, and baptised on Sunday, 13 February.[1]

1079 [register signed by] Christopher Greene, Doctor of Theology, rector; William Greene, curate; John Maton, gentleman, and William Acrig, merchant, churchwardens.

Entries continue in this register in Latin until 1709.

1   This is the last entry in Crockford's hand

Funerals celebrated and transacted in the parish church of Stockton[1] from the year of the Lord's Incarnation, according to the reckoning of the English church, 1589 and thereafter.

1589/90

1080 Margaret Oliver, wife of John Oliver, weaver, buried 3 October.

1081 George Howell, labourer, buried 25 October.

1082 Anne Heath, gentlewoman, wife of Nicholas Heath, gentleman, buried 12 March.

1590/1

1083 Elizabeth Potticary, gentlewoman, wife of Jerome Potticary, gentleman clothier, died 9 April and buried 11 April.

1084 Christopher Oliver, son of John Oliver, weaver, buried 26 February.

1591/2

1085 John Mascall, husbandman, buried 10 April.

1086 Elizabeth Baker, widow, buried 19 October.

1087 Cecily Merriot, widow, buried 21 November.

1592/3

1088 Joan Andrewes, widow, buried 31 August.

1089 Joan Widowes, daughter of Alice Widowes, 20 March.

1   *Stocton*

1593/4

1090 Dionise Rownsey, widow, buried 17 January.

1091 John Goffe, son of Richard Goffe, husbandman, buried 28 October.

1092 John Bishopp, labourer, buried 30 October.

1093 Mary Hooper, wife of Anthony Hooper, yeoman, buried 22 March.

1094 In addition[1] Joan Surman, wife of Thomas Surman, labourer, buried 16 April in the same year.

1095 John Crosse, son of John Crosse, labourer, buried 8 October in the same year.

1594/5

1096 Magdalena[2] Mowday, widow, buried 28 October.

1097 Edward Bennett, husbandman, buried 21 November.

1098 Anne Eyles, daughter of Thomas Eyles, husbandman, buried 27 May of the previous year.[3]

1595/6

1099 Ambrose Mascall, son of William Mascall, husbandman, buried 20 June.

1100 Thomas Surman the elder, labourer, buried 11 February.

1596/7

1101 Elizabeth Hunt, widow, buried 17 April.

1102 Joan Saunders, wife of Thomas Saunders, husbandman, buried 19

1   *insuper* to denote that this and the following entry are out of chronological order
2   *Motlina*, probably intended to render Magdalena into Latin
3   *praecedentis hoc anno*

April.

1103 Jerome Potticary, gentleman, while he lived a famous clothier, died 3 May, buried 10 May, in the 52nd year of his age.

1104 William Mascall the elder, husbandman, buried 4 June, almost in the 100th year of his age.

1597/8

1105 Nicholas Cockerell, husbandman, buried 24 May.

1106 William Cockerell, labourer, buried 4 September.

1107 Avice Wall, wife of Robert Wall, tailor, buried 25 September.

1108 John Cockerell, a young man, son of Ambrose Cockerell, husbandman, buried 2 October.

1109 Elizabeth Cockerell, wife of the same Ambrose Cockerell, buried 24 October.

1110 Joan Rocksborrough, daughter of Thomas Rocksborrough, shepherd, buried 27 October.

1111 Thomas Rodney, tailor, buried 6 December.

1112 Robert Hobbes,[1] weaver, buried 24 January.

1113 Geoffrey Minety, labourer, buried 29 January.

1114 Agnes Cocke, widow, buried 30 January.

1598/9 [no entries]

1599/1600

1115 John Cockerell, son of Edward Cockerell, blacksmith, buried 11 November.

1   written *Hobbs*, but with a mark of contraction

1600/1

1116 Robert Dibbins, labourer, buried 11 April.

1117 John Hopkins, son of Ellis Hopkins, husbandman, buried 22 January.

1118 Elizabeth Surman, widow, buried 25 January.

1119 Robert Wall, elderly tailor, buried 22 February.

1601/2

1120 John Hobbs, son of Robert Hobbs, deceased weaver, buried 29 April.

1121 Jane Macy, daughter of Thomas Macy, *alias* Bandstone, labourer, buried 21 September.

1602/3

1122 Christian Hooper, elderly widow, buried 25 March.

1123 Agnes Howell, poor elderly widow, buried 14 August.

1124 John Oliver, weaver, buried 10 October, more than 80 years old.

1125 Elizabeth Mascall, widow, relict of William Mascall the elder, deceased, also buried 10 October, in almost the 100th year of her age.

1126 Nicholas West, labourer, buried 28 October.

1603/4

1127 Alice Vincent, wife of John Vincent, labourer, buried 31 May, almost 60 years old.

1128 Alice Edwards, *alias* Webb, wife of William Edwards, *alias* Web, buried 25 June.

1129 Dorothy Surman, daughter of John Surman, labourer, buried 30 June.

1130 George Lacock, a young man, servant of Richard Golding, weaver, buried 10 August.

1131 Warbora Mascall, widow and relict of John Mascall, husbandman, deceased, buried 22 September.

1132 Elizabeth Golding, wife of Richard Golding, weaver, buried 9 October.

1133 Mary Mabell, illegitimate[1] daughter of Joan Mabell, buried 12 October.

1134 Richard Bentley, son of John Bently, labourer, buried 27 January.

1135 Joan Potticary, a very elderly matron, and by birth of the gentry family of Toppe, the widow and relict of Richard Potticary, a freeholder and while he lived a clothier, who was descended from the Potticarys of Wilton; she died at Wylye, and was interred in the choir of this church at Stockton on 1 March; she was 80 years old, or more.

1136 Thomas Skydmore, shepherd, almost 80 years old, buried 27 March.

1137 Thomas Tayler, *alias* Piffin, carpenter, almost 70 years old, buried 22 September.

1138 Robert Mascall, labourer, almost 70 years old, buried 29 November.

1139 Richard Goff, aged near 28 years, kitchen clerk[2] to the Lady Marchioness of Northampton, wife of Sir Thomas Gorges, knight; he was the son of Richard Goff of Stockton, husbandman, and was buried at Longford[3] near Salisbury, 8 November.

1   *spuria*
2   *clericus culinae*
3   *Langfordiae* (but there is no church at Longford, so Britford or Nunton may
        be intended. Lady Northampton (born Helena Snakenborg), of East

1140 Agnes Mascall, a poor widow, almost 80 years old, buried 8 February.

1606/7

1141 Agnes Fleming, little daughter of Nicholas Fleming, labourer, buried 17 May.

1142 Mary Skydmore, little daughter of Robert Skydmore, shepherd, buried 20 September.

1143 Elizabeth Batten, little daughter of Henry Batten, labourer, buried 18 October.

1607/8

1144 Joan Macy, wife of Thomas Macy, *alias* Bandstone, labourer, buried 10 April.

1145 Frances Fleming, little infant daughter of Nicholas Fleming, labourer. buried 29 April.

1146 Michaela Hopkins, a widow almost 80 years old, relict of William Hopkins, husbandman, buried 25 June.

1147 John White, little infant son of Richard White, weaver, buried 19 July.

1608/9

1148 Richard Idney, a young man, servant of Christopher Potticary, gentleman, clothier, buried 12 September.

1149 Ambrose Ridgdale, little infant son of Thomas Ridgedale, weaver, buried 13 September.

1150 George Ridgdale, a child, another little infant son of the same Thomas Ridgdale, buried 21 September.

Gothland, Sweden, was the sister-in-law of Queen Katherine Parr

1151 John Hooper the elder, husbandman, almost 70 years old, buried 8 January.

1152 Nicholas Maton, yeoman, elderly head of a household and freeholding steward of Stockton manor,[1] buried 20 January, almost 70 years old.

1153 Agnes Mascall, almost 40 years old, wife of William Mascall, husbandman. buried 3 March.

1154 Anne Batten, little infant daughter of Henry Batten, labourer, buried 15 March.

1609/10

1155 Joan Goare, a poor widow, relict of one Nicholas Goare of London, buried 6 July.

1156 John Piercy, yeoman, almost 70 years old, buried 6 December.

1157 Joan White, a widow almost 80 years old, buried 24 March.

1610/11

1158 Alice White, wife of Jeffery White, carpenter, almost 50 years old. buried 31 March.

1159 Jeffery White, a young tailor, son of William White of Fovant, labourer, nephew and brother of the elder Jeffery aforesaid,[2] buried 2 April.

1160 Ambrose Cockerell, husbandman, almost 70 years old, descended from a gentry family, the Cockerells from the North, by a famous scion,[3] Walter Cockerell, of whom the older people of Stockton now remember

---

1   *praedii Stocktoniensis ingenuus villicus*
2   The meaning seems to be that the deceased Jeffery was the nephew, and William the brother, of the elder Jeffery. His death was presumably the result of the fire described in the memorandum below.
3   the reading seems to be *allium* (literally garlic)

nothing, but of whom in the church both the windows and the walls even now show some evidence; died 7 April, buried 8 April.[1]

1161 Joan Hobs, a little girl, daughter of George Hobs, weaver, buried 7 May.

1162 George Hobbs, weaver, son of Robert, deceased, and father of the aforesaid Joan, buried 23 July.

1163 Christopher Potticarie, a little boy nearly four years old, third son of Christopher Potticarie, gentleman clothier, died 1 September, and was buried 2 September, in the choir near his great-grandfather and great-grandmother, Richard and Joan Potticarie.

1164 Elizabeth Davis, the little daughter of Jeffery Davies, blacksmith, buried 21 November.

1165 Winifred Tanner, the little daughter of John Tanner, labourer, buried 24 November.

1166 Joan Taylor *alias* Piffin, the widow and relict of Thomas Taylor *alias* Piffin, 70 years old or thereabouts, died 20 January, and buried 21 January.

1167 Memorandum that on 29 June 1609 the house of Thomas Hooper, yeoman, and on 2 April 1610 the house of Jeffery White, carpenter, were destroyed by fire, but the other dwelling houses of the parish (by the grace of God) were untouched.

1611/12

1168 Mary Hobs, daughter of Robert Hobs, weaver, deceased, an unmarried woman, 22 years old or thereabouts, buried 19 April.

1169 Elizabeth Hooper, widow and relict of John Hooper, husbandman, a woman 60 years old or thereabouts, buried 1 June.

1170 Dorothy Ridgdale, wife of Thomas Ridgdale, weaver, a woman 30 years old or thereabouts, died and buried 13 July.

---

1   a manicule (small marginal drawing of a hand) points to this entry

1171 Agnes Ridgedale, little infant daughter of the same Thomas Ridgedale, died 6 August, buried 7 August.

1172 Alice Howell, a poor woman nearly 50 years old, daughter of George Howell and Agnes his wife, both deceased, died the last day of September, buried 1 October.

1173 Eleanor Potticary, daughter of John Potticary of Wylye, gentleman, by occupation[1] a clothier; a maiden nearly 17 years old or more, died 25 October, buried 26 October.

1174 John Rodney, tailor, son of Thomas Rodney, deceased, died and buried the last day of October, 30 years old or a little more.

1175 Margaret Deadman, infant daughter of John Deadman of Warminster, buried 2 February.

1612/13

1176 Eleanor Aplin, a very small child, daughter of Thomas Aplin of Iwerne Minster[2] in Dorset, husbandman, was born and baptised 22 April, buried the 24 of the same April.

1177 John Skydmore, a little boy four years old, son of Robert Skydmore, shepherd, died and buried 7 May.

1178 Mary Knight, a woman in her fifties, wife of William Knight, ploughwright, died and buried 10 August.

1179 John Vincent, labourer, an old man in his eighties, died and buried 8 January.

1180 Alice Cockerell, a little old woman in her eighties, widow and relict of Nicholas Cockerell, while he lived a husbandman, died 8 March, buried 9 March.

1181 John Kent, gentleman, firstborn son of John Kent of Devizes,

---

1 *facultate*, perhaps with the inference of prosperity or success
2 *yuron Minstrell*; the birthdate is given as 22 April, but cf. **984**.

gentleman, and clerk of the peace[1] for Wiltshire; a young man 25 years old or thereabouts, died at Stockton of a burning fever 18 March, and buried at Devizes, the town of his birth, 21 of the same month of March.

1613/14

1182 Penelope Langley, infant daughter of Abraham Langley, labourer, died 13 April, buried 14 April.

1183 Eleanor Langley, wife of the same Abraham Langley, and mother of the same little girl, a woman nearly 40 years old, and daughter of Thomas Rodney, tailor, deceased; died 14 April, buried 15 April.

1184 Joan Acrigge, a widow 60 years old, relict of William Acrigge, late of the city of Salisbury,[2] clothier and linen-draper;[3] by birth of the freeholding family of Helme of Chilmark, a dame of commended integrity[4] and the mother of ten children, died 3 September, buried 5 September.

1185 Alice Hooper, wife of John Hooper, husbandman, a woman 30 years old, daughter of Thomas Foster formerly of Bapton, husbandman, died 23 December, buried 25 December.

1186 Anne Goffe, infant daughter of Jerome Goffe, husbandman, died and buried 5 January.

1187 Joan Ridgdale, wife of Thomas Ridgedale, weaver; of the Cockerell family, a woman 40 years old, died 12 January, buried 13 January.

1188 Phyllis Bentley, daughter of John Bentley, labourer, a girl 12 years old, died and buried 25 February.

1614/15

1189 Robert Frost, labourer, by birth from Pilton near Barnstaple[5] in

---

1 *clerici ad pacem*
2 *novae Saru'*
3 *lintearii*, or linen-weaver
4 *laudatae probitatis matrona*
5 *Barstable*

Devon, an incomer living in this parish, 40 years old, died and buried 9 April.

1190 John Surman, labourer, nearly 60 years old, died 27 May, buried 28 May.

1191 Martha Langley, third daughter of Abraham Langley, labourer, died and buried 25 August, having almost reached nine years old.

1192 Christopher Potticary, little infant boy, fourth son of Christopher Potticary, gentleman and clothier, died 31 December, buried 1 January.

1193 John King, little infant boy, firstborn son of John King, yeoman, born 24 December, baptised 11 January, died and buried 20 January.

1194 Joan Hill, a poor little old woman who never married, died and buried 7 February.

1615/16

1195 Thomas Sanders, husbandman, very much (as the years bear this out) an old man, inasmuch as having attained the age of one hundred years and more, by natural causes, or else worn out by old age itself, came to his end, died and buried 21 September.

1196 Alice Skydmore, a poor little old woman in her nineties, widow and relict of Thomas Skydmore, a shepherd while he lived, died and buried 2 January.

1197 Sibyl Rockesborrough, a poor little old woman more than 90 years old, wife of Thomas Rockesborrough, an old man and a shepherd, died and buried 17 February.

1616/17

1198 Joan Bennet, a widow in her eighties, of the family of Goffe, husbandmen, and relict also of a husbandman, Edward Bennet, deceased, died 21 May, buried 23 May.

1199 Thomas Vincent, firstborn son of Thomas Vincent, labourer, a little boy, died and buried 22 January.

1200 John Gardner, an old man nearly 70 years old, husbandman and tailor, and one of the two churchwardens for this year, died and buried 29 January.

1617/18

1201 Mary Read, illegitimate daughter of Bridget Read, a maidservant of the servile class, etc, born 25 March, died and buried 29 March.

1202 Mary Toppe, truly a gentlewoman, wife of the distinguished John Toppe, esquire, lord of the chief manor of Stockton, and eldest daughter of a worshipful old man, Edward Hooper, of the hamlet of Boveridge, in the larger parish of Cranborne in Dorset, esquire, and of Dorothy, his worshipful lady wife. She was a daughter most obedient towards her parents, a consort most complaisant towards her husband, the best of mothers to her children, a most skilled wife and mother, a most kindly mistress to her household, a neighbour most generous to her neighbours, of the greatest liberality to the poor, of the greatest friendship to the good, one and all. She was a lady most dignified, most sweet, most courteous, most diligent of peaceful fairness, most observant of Christian duty, and lastly most excellent of all character, grace, and endowments. When she reached the age of 43 years, suffering from a long-term wasting disease, she became weak from dysenteric morbidity, but asserting true knowledge, unshaken faith, living hope, unimpaired charity, and unconquerable endurance; ardently desiring Christ, willingly taking leave of the world, most wisely counselling, most dutifully admonishing, and most devoutly praying for her family and friends. At the beginning of the Christian Sabbath, that is to say, about the sixth hour of Sunday, 6 April, she came calmly to her end, and most peacefully fell asleep in the Lord; beginning, beyond all doubt, a Sabbath journey, following close on certain of her near prophetic discourses uttered a little before death, to take possession of a Heavenly dwelling-place in the company of God and his holy Saints, in everlasting peace. She leaves behind her, surviving, her only husband, and six children, that is, three sons: John the elder, a young man, John the younger, a youth, and Edward, a small boy; likewise three daughters, Anne, Mary, and Elizabeth, most pleasant girls; also both parents, venerable by age as by their virtues; three brothers, Thomas the elder, Thomas the younger, and James, most distinguished men; four sisters, Catherine,

Dorothy, Martha, and Honor; and very many other kindred by blood and by marriage, all most deeply grieving together their common loss. She had her interment, attended by very many, in this church of Stockton, and a funeral in accordance with her worth; and before this there was a holy address by a divine on all sides venerable, John Terry, Master of Arts, rector of this church; and following this a very great gift of alms was announced to the poor, on the Wednesday in Easter Week, 23 April 1617.

1203 Christopher Hobbs, infant son of Thomas Hobbes, a poor weaver, died 24 April, buried 25 April.

1204 Mary Eyles, wife of James Eyles of Fisherton Delamere, husbandman, and daughter of Thomas Eyles of Stockton, husbandman, 36 years old, or thereabouts, being still weak from childbirth and lying sick in her bed, the eighth day after the birth of her firstborn little daughter Anne, she died peacefully and went to God, and was buried in Stockton churchyard 11 August.

1205 Thomas Rocksborrough, shepherd, an old man in his eighties, died and buried 7 November.

1206 Philip Knight, a little boy almost three years old, son of William Knight the younger, ploughwright, and of Elizabeth his wife, died and buried 18 February.

1618/19

1207 Jerome Goffe, little infant son of Jerome Goffe, husbandman, and of Agnes his wife, was born 9 June, baptised 14 June, died 20 June, and buried 21 June.

1208 Stephen Sherelock, husbandman, an old man in his sixties, descended from a family of husbandmen, the Sherlocks of Sutton[1] near Odiham in Hampshire; he was for many years in the service, as steward to his household, to the Reverend Master John Terrie, rector of this church, and his lord and fellow countryman;[2] he was honourably married into the freeholding Alford family, and afterwards obtained a tenement in the manor of Stockton, working on which he grew old; he died 28 July, buried 29 July.

1   Long Sutton, where Revd. Terrie was born
2   *domino et populari suo*

1209 Joan Hobbs, little infant daughter of Thomas Hobs, formerly a weaver but now a poor labourer, and of Warbora his wife, was born 3 September, baptised 6 September, died 15 September, and buried 16 September.

1210 Elizabeth Hill, a poor little old widow in her sixties, relict of a certain Hill, formerly of Stockton, husbandman, deceased; died 13 October, buried 14 October.

1211 Sibyl Surman, a poor little old woman, wife of Thomas Surman, an elderly labourer, died and buried 20 November.

1619/20

1212 Warbora Eyles, wife of Thomas Eyles of Stockton, husbandman, herself by birth of the family of Mascall of Stockton, husbandmen, a dame long afflicted by hardships and sicknesses, the mother of only one single daughter, and a woman about 60 years old, died Monday 17 May, buried Tuesday, 18 May, in Whit Week.

1213 Richard Acrigge, a little infant boy, third son of William Acrigge, merchant, and of Susan his wife, one of twins lately born and baptised (as is to be seen in its place),[1] growing gradually weaker by a wasting disease, died and buried 22 May.

1214 Agnes Goffe, wife of Jerome Goffe, husbandman, herself by birth of the family of Withers of Codford St Mary,[2] husbandmen, a woman about 40 years old and the mother of one son and three daughters; labouring too strenuously in her last childbirth, on 12 July she gave birth to a daughter, died 16 July, buried 17 July.

1215 Thomas Hobbes, a poor weaver, head of a household, one of the Hobbes family of Stockton, weavers, father of one daughter, a man nearly 40 years old, died Tuesday, 9 November, buried Wednesday, 10 November.

1216 Elizabeth Skydmore, wife of Robert Skydmore, a poor shepherd,

---

1   *ut suo loco videre est*, presumably a reference to the entry in the baptism register
2   *Codfordensiu' orientalium*

a woman full of hardships, long afflicted by quinsy,[1] and carried off at last by starvation; she was about 40 years old, died Monday, 29 November, buried Tuesday, 30 November.

1620/1

1217 Eleanor Rocksborrough, daughter of John Rocksborrough, shepherd, and of Elizabeth his wife, a girl about fifteen years old, died Thursday, 23 November, buried Friday, 24 November.

1218 Eleanor Reeves, daughter of one Robert Reeves late of Westbury in Wiltshire, and of Mary his wife, a girl nearly 16 years old; she was descended, through her mother, from the freeholder family of Whitaker of Westbury, and employed in the wool-working business of Christopher Potticary and of Mary his wife, died and was buried Friday, 24 November.

1219 Mary Colboorne, a young gentlewoman about 22 years old, firstborn and only daughter of William Colboorne of Bruton in Somerset, gentleman, and of Mary his first wife, who was by birth of the gentry family of Topp of Stockton; died on Saturday, 10 March and buried in Stockton churchyard, near the north corner of the church, on Monday, 12 March.

1621/2

1220 George James, *alias* Mason, third son of Edward James, *alias* Mason, of Bapton, blacksmith, and of Emma his wife, a young man a little over 21 years old, the nephew, through a sister, of Thomas Tayler of Stockton, carpenter, and one also devoted to this same woodworking craft, and especially dear to his uncle; receiving, as is asserted, a wound on the head, he contracted a deadly sickness, from which he certainly died, and buried at Stockton on Tuesday, 27 March.

1221 Mary Potticarie, a very frail little infant girl, third daughter of Christopher Potticarie, gentleman and clothier, and of Mary his wife; when she had unexpectedly lived for one month, falling asleep at the house of the nurse, wife of William Wandsborow, at Bapton, she expired, dying on Wednesday, 11 April; and was interred in the choir of Stockton church, close to her great-grandparents Potticary, on Thursday, 12 April.

1   *morbo gutterino*

1222 Jerome Piercy, a very frail little infant boy, firstborn son of John Piercy, husbandman, and of Margaret his wife, lately born, he was baptised (as his condition clearly warranted), died and buried Monday, 4 June.

1223 Joan Rodney, a poor little elderly widow, relict of Thomas Rodney sometime of this Stockton, tailor, deceased; a woman about 80 years old, the mother, full of hardships, of two sons and two daughters, after a long sickness calmly borne with Christian endurance, at last she failed, and peacefully expired in Christ. She died on Sunday, 17 June, and was buried on Monday, 18 June.

1224 Ursula Rogers, little infant daughter, as is asserted, of one Thomas Rogers, a poor man of Romsey in Hampshire, and of Alice his wife, lately born near Charlton Musgrove in Somerset, died and buried at Stockton on Monday, 19 November.

1622/3

1225 William, little infant illegitimate son of Warbora Hobs, a poor widow, died and buried Wednesday, 15 May.

1226 A little unnamed girl, the first daughter of Jerome Goffe, husbandman, and of Grace his wife, was stillborn on Friday, 14 June; she had no baptism, but was given a church burial, inasmuch as she was born of faithful parents, Saturday, 15 June.

1227 Mary Piercie, a little girl nearly four years old, firstborn daughter of John Piercie, husbandman, and of Margaret his wife, died and buried Friday, 28 June.

1228 Anthony Davies, a little infant boy not yet two months old, fourth son of Jeffery Davies, blacksmith, and of Jane his wife, died and buried Friday, 12 July.

1229 Rebecca Acrigge, a little girl and one of twins, a little over three years old, fourth daughter of William Acrigge, merchant, and of Susan his wife, died Tuesday 27 August, buried Wednesday, 28 August.

1230 A little unnamed boy, firstborn son of George Crooch, labourer, and of Joan his wife, was stillborn and buried on Tuesday, 15 October.

1231 Joan Maton, widow and relict of an elderly man much respected in his lifetime, Nicholas Maton, sometime freeholding farmer of Stockton demesne;[1] she was by birth of the gentry family of May of Chilmark, a dutiful and prudent lady, the only wife to an only husband, the kindly mother of numerous offspring; having experienced repeatedly the fickleness of fortune, by hardships, by age, and by sicknesses, gradually she failed, and peacefully fell asleep in Christ, on Thursday, 17 October. She was buried on Saturday, 19 October, age 72.

1232 Jane Cooper, wife of Timothy Cooper, carpenter, and herself by birth of the Rodney family of tailors, a woman about 40 years old, the lawful wife of two men, the kindly mother by the first husband of a daughter, and by the second of a son,[2] died Wednesday, 18 December, buried Thursday, 19 December.

1623/4

1233 Robert Tanner, a poor elderly labourer, thought to be 90 years old, the only husband of his one elderly wife, the troubled father of several children, common oxherd of the parish, etc,[3] died Wednesday, 12 November, buried Thursday, 13 November.

1234 Jerome Davies, an infant almost four months old, fifth Son of Jeffery Davies, blacksmith, and of Jane his wife, died and buried Wednesday, 13 January.

1624/5

1235 Mary Battin, wife of Henry Battin, labourer, and herself by birth of the husbandmen family of Goff, of this Stockton, a woman about 50 years old, until now the only wife of her one husband, the troubled mother of many children; after the long endurance of a debilitating illness,[4] at last she died, and returned her soul to God, on Wednesday, 27 October. She was buried on Thursday, 28 October, the feast of Simon and Jude, the apostles.

1   *praedii Stocktoniensis ingenui olim firmarii*
2   A word appears to have been erased brfore *filii*
3   *parochiae communis bubulcus*, etc
4   *morbi conterentis*

1236 Abell Cooper, a very frail little infant boy, second son of Timothy Cooper, carpenter, but his first son by Joan, his second wife; died the first Sunday in Lent and buried the following day, Monday, 14 March.

1625/6

1237 Robert Skydmore, a poor labourer once widowed, and almost 60 years old, the only husband of his one wife, deceased, the troubled father of several children, etc, died on Easter Sunday and buried the Monday in Easter week, 18 April.

1238 Agnes Scammell, a widow nearly 70 years old, relict of John Scammell, sometime of Donhead St Mary,[1] yeoman, mother of several children, etc, died the Tuesday in Easter week and buried in our churchyard, the Thursday of the same week, 21 April.

1239 Reverend John Terrie, most worthy rector of this church, of most blessed memory. Of his life it has been possible to distinguish these stages with certainty. He was born, in the year of Christ 1555, of an outstanding freeholding family, in the manor of the rural hamlet of Sutton,[2] near Odiham in Hampshire. He was the firstborn among six brothers, and led a very steady boyhood and delicate youth, as a pupil of Winchester School. From there in due time he moved on to Oxford; where he was admitted a member of Wykeham College,[3] and he gave outstanding proofs of a diligent application to his studies, and took the two degrees in arts, then gained both the orders of divinity, by the hands of the Reverend then Bishop of Salisbury, John Pierce. Not very long afterwards Thomas Cooper, the Reverend then Bishop of Winchester, calling him from the academy, he left his college and went to the bishop's palace in the position of Chaplain. It was not then long before (on the death of Simnell, the priest)[4] he obtained, by the entirely free gift of his lord, this rectory of Stockton, in the year of Christ 1590. Then first he came to think of taking a wife, and entered upon a marriage which did honour to Christ: he took a maiden dutifully and excellently raised, Mary White, of a comparable family, of Stanton St John, near Oxford. By this one and only consort he got six sons, Stephen, John,

1   *Donet superiori*
2   Long Sutton, south of Odiham; it is in fact an ancient parish
3   i.e. New College
4   *Simnello sacrificulo defuncto.* He was John Simnell (CCEd).

Samuel, Josiah, Nathaniel, and another Stephen. All of these, with their mother, he left behind him surviving, except the first, who died at Oxford.

He was a man most upright, most excellent, most learned, most lettered, most wise, most dignified, most good, and most holy. He was a father most loving, a husband most chaste, a householder most generous, a rector most mild, a pastor most watchful, a preacher most painstaking, a neighbour most kind-hearted, and, as to the measure of his wealth distributed to the poor, one most generously devoted to the needy; a friend most sure, to a good man, whoever it may be, most kind;[1] and so, in a word, equipped with all the divine and humane virtues.

When, labouring so long with weaknesses of the body at such an admirable course of life; and after expounding the word of God honestly, diligently, earnestly, and to good effect; and after pondering the truth in four books[2] with studied and mature judgement, most deeply, most dutifully, and most fully; and after expounding the same analysis in the epistle to the Romans (which for a long time in Sunday lessons he made known to his flock); at last, alas, he met with a fatal illness, growing weak by a wasting disease, which he bore, for longer than was looked for, with unceasingly Christian endurance. Feeling himself from day to day failing, in good time he set in order his household and wrote a will; in which he committed his soul to God, his body to the churchyard, his worldly goods to his nearest kin. These things thus completed, repeatedly, with faithful cries many times uttered, in a voice which, old as he was, was feeble, he prayed prophetically for the tranquillity of the Church, the happiness of the King, everlasting duration to the Gospel, the peace of the homeland, the loyalty of the people to the great and the nobles, for charity to parishioners, neighbours, and fellow countrymen, and, finally, for a blessing upon all.

Little by little he failed utterly; and religiously, peacefully, in his Christ he died. Having deceased on Tuesday, 10 May, at the — hour of the evening, he was buried, in accordance with an instruction he had given, in the churchyard, near the house that had been his, and alongside the ordinary people of the parish,[3] by the hands of his most sorrowing pupil in theology, Thomas Crockford, presently vicar of the church of Fisherton; and before this there was given a sound and holy address, by a divine instructed among the foremost, John Antram, the reverend the pastor of

1 *bono cuivis benignissim'*
2 *The Triall of Truth,* (3 parts, 1600-25); *The Reasonablenesse of Wise and Holy Truth* (1617)
3 *vulgares parochianos*

Little Langford, on Friday, 13 May; in the 70th year of his age, the 35th of his incumbency as rector, and the first of King Charles.

1240 William Webbe, a poor elderly labourer, etc, more than 70 years old, so it is thought, following after his Lord, died a Christian on Saturday, 14 May, buried Sunday, 15 May.

1241 Joan Cooper, second wife of Timothy Cooper, carpenter, about 30 years old, the mother of one infant boy who recently died, by birth of a tailoring family from Boyton, etc, died Thursday, 19 May, buried Friday, 20 May.

1242 The Venerable Christopher Greene, Doctor of Sacred Theology, of Corpus Christi College, Oxford, a native of Bristol, and of gentry parentage, etc, was inducted into this rectory of Stockton by the hands of the Reverend John Lee, Bachelor of Sacred Theology, on Saturday 16 [July],[1] and on the following day, the [fifth][2] Sunday after Trinity, he gave publicly in the same church, according to law, his full assent to the articles of religion established at the Synod of London in the Year 1562.

1243 William Flemming, a little infant boy, very recently born, third son of Nicholas Flemming, labourer, and of Margaret his wife, died and buried on Thursday, 10 November.

1244 Jeffery Whitaker, a young gentleman, firstborn son of Nash Whitaker, gentleman, and (while he lived) clothier, formerly of Tinhead, deceased, a man adorned with many titles of dutiful virtue, and of Mary his wife, a lady no less excellent, etc. As a boy he occupied himself faithfully with the study of his letters, and in young manhood with the cloth trade; modestly obedient to his parents, guardians, teachers, and instructors, by duty and by honesty he achieved very much, and high hopes were entertained for him. But he was stricken by a deadly and fatal sickness, and died before his time on Saturday, 10 December. He was interred in the choir of this church, next to his great-grandparents Potticary and others of his mother's kindred, on Monday, 12 December, near to the end of the 21st year of his age.

---

1   The month is left blank, but may be inferred from the day and date
2   Left blank, but may be inferred

1626/7

1245 Joan Bentley, wife of John Bentley, labourer, a woman about 60 years old, more or less, the wife in turn of two husbands, the troubled mother of three children, etc, died and was buried on Sunday, 17 September.

1246 Richard Goffe, an elderly man, sometime a husbandman, lately a poor labourer, husband of one wife, the troubled father of three sons and three daughters; almost 90 years old, and worn out by a disease of old age, he died as a Christian on Saturday 18 November, and was buried Sunday, 19 November.

1247 A little infant girl, firstborn daughter of George Crooch, labourer, and of Joan his wife, was stillborn on Monday, 22 January, and buried Tuesday, 23 January.

1248 John Rocksborrough, almost a young man, nearly 21 years old, the first son of John Rocksborrough, shepherd, and of Elizabeth his wife, etc, died Thursday, 1 March, and buried Saturday, 3 March.

1627/8

1249 Thomas Eyles of Stockton, formerly of Bapton, husbandman, an elderly man more than 70 years old, husband, in turn, of two wives, father of one daughter, deceased, and the troubled grandfather, by that daughter, of one granddaughter; a man tested by fortune of both kinds, unexpectedly he failed, and died on Wednesday, 23 January. He was buried on Thursday, 24 January.

1250 Elizabeth Tanner, a poor little elderly widow, relict of Robert Tanner, late a labourer, etc, the troubled mother of several children, died and was buried Friday, 22 February, having reached the age, so it is claimed, of almost 100.

1628/9

1251 John Bundy, a little infant boy, son of — Bundy, etc, was buried.[1]

1252 Eleanor Langley, a young woman nearly 20 years old, fourth

1   Inserted in a cramped space above the following entry

daughter of Abraham Langley of Stockton, labourer, and of Eleanor his former wife, died Wednesday, 7 January, buried Thursday, 8 January.[1]

1629/30

1253 Cecily White, a poor woman in her sixties, wife of Richard White, a poor weaver, died Saturday, 29 August, and buried Sunday, 30 August.

1254 Edward Reynes, a young man, a labourer and farm servant to John Maton of Stockton demesne, gentleman, died Saturday, 30 January, and buried Sunday, 31 January.

1630/1

1255 John Gardener, a little boy nearly six years old, firstborn son of John Gardener, labourer, and of Elizabeth his wife; by a lamentable misfortune he was scalded[2] by hot water, little by little fell sick, weakened, and died on Wednesday, 7 April; buried Thursday, 8 April.

1256 Alice Helme, a little infant girl, third daughter of John Helme, yeoman, and of Eleanor his wife, died Wednesday, 7 October, buried Thursday, 8 October.[3]

1257 Thomas Pierson. a little infant boy, the first son of Henry Pierson *alias* Vargeyse, husbandman, and of Joan his wife, died Thursday, 21 October, buried Friday, 22 October.

1258 Agnes Goffe, a poor little elderly widow, relict of Richard Goffe, sometime of this Stockton, husbandman, deceased, the troubled mother of many children, nearly 80 years old, etc, died Sunday, 31 October, buried Monday, 1 November.

1259 Agnes Webbe, a poor little elderly widow more than 60 years old, relict of William Webbe, *alias* Edwards, in his lifetime a labourer, deceased, the troubled mother of two daughters, etc, died Saturday, 12 February,

1   This, and the entries for 1629 and 1630, are followed by the names of the rector, curate and churchwardens, as for marriages and baptisms; see above, **1068**, **1072**, **1079**.
2   *liquefactus*
3   Either the dates or days in this entry are wrong.

buried Sunday, 13 February.

1260 Elizabeth Dowdale, wife of Richard Dowdale, yeoman and tailor, a woman more than 40 years old, died the same Sunday, buried Monday, 14 February.[1]

Entries continue in this register in Latin until 1712.

---

1 This is the last entry in Crockford's hand.

WYLYE

Register of the parish church of Wylye in the county of Wiltshire

that is, a book chronological, topological[1] and tropological[2] of parochial
affairs, chiefly ecclesiastical, so far as can be truly and completely established
to have taken place there, from imperfect original texts not so accurately
written, and derived from the memory of trustworthy men still alive,
beginning in the year of the Incarnation of Lord Christ 1581.[3]

Marriages held and celebrated in the parish church of Wylye, Wiltshire,
from the year of the Lord's Incarnation 1581, and thereafter.

1581/2

1261 William Meryweather and Joan Pierson, married 30 July.

1262 William Potham[4] and Christian Newman, married 15 March.

1582/3 [no entries]

---

1   The English word 'topology', first recorded in 1659, denotes the science of
    locations (cf. topography); its Latin adjectival equivalent, *topologicus*, has
    not hitherto been recorded.
2   The equivalent English word 'tropological' was used to describe a moral
    discourse based on scripture; its Latin equivalent, *tropologicus*, means
    figurative.
3   This portion of text is in poor condition and partly illegible. The Latin
    appears to be: *Liber chronologicus, topologicus, et tropologicus [rerum?] parochialiu'
    praecipue ecclesiasticaru' ibidem [gestarum?] quam vere et perfecti constare iam
    possunt tam imperfectis archetypis ante hac non ita acurati [. . .] ex hominum fide
    dignorum adhuc viv[entium?] memoria, incipiens, ab anno incarnationis [Domin?]
    Christi, 1581.* This reconstruction is based in part on the similar preamble
    to the Fisherton register.
4   the initial P is uncertain

1583/4

1263 Richard Taylor and Christian Oliver, married 17 October.

1264 Edward Smyth the elder and Elizabeth Moonday, married 2 September.

1265 William Poticarie and Joan Bower, married 23 September.

1266 Edward Smith the younger and Joan Perfect, married 1 November.

1267 Robert Locke and Joan Harderwere, married 29 January.

1584/5

1268 Thomas Hillman and Elizabeth Amor, married 28 June.

1269 Morgan Spenser and Alice Oliver, married 26 November.

1270 John Hughes, *alias* Clearke, and Mary Newman, married 28 November.

1585/6

1271 John Moonday and Tamsin Baker, married 29 June.

1586/7 [no entries]

1587/8

1272 John Ingram of Bapton street, husbandman, and Joan Potticarie of Wylye, married 2 February.

1273 Robert Saintsbury and Joan Clearke, also married on 2 February.

1588/9 [no entries]

1589/90

1274 Rawlin[1] Piercy and Alice Thacham, married 10 April.

1275 Robert Farnell and Mary Smyth, married 2 May.

1276 John Potticarie, clothier, and Eleanor Woodford, married 8 May.

1277 William Tuckey of Deptford, yeoman, and Maud Woort, married 26 August.

1278 Edward Clearke and Margaret Smyth, married 20 November.

1279 William Baker and Elizabeth Woollyweare,[2] married 10 December.

1590/1 [no entries]

1591/2

1280 John Ayles, *alias* Hicks, and Alice Barnes, married 20 October.

1592/3 [no entries]

1593/4

1281 Alexander Cooke and Margery Bishop, married 10 October.

1594/5

1282 Richard Meateyard and Joan Baker, married 25 April.

1595/6

1283 John Harries and Mary Webbe, married 10 November.

1596/7

1284 John Eustace and Alice Bowery,[3] married 27 September.

---

1   *Rawlinus*
2   the name is blotched and uncertain
3   the name is rubbed and uncertain

1597/8

1285 Thomas Surman of Stockton, labourer, and Sibyl Taylour, married 24 May.

1598/9

1286 John Marsh and Susan Hillman, married 13 June.

1599/1600

1287 John Crutchel and Alice Lock.[1]

1288 Richard Joanes and Joan Hillman.[2]

1289 Richard Rockborrough of Stockton, labourer, and Christian Idney of Deptford.[3]

1600/1

1290 Matthew Aymor, labourer, and Catherine Woodland, married on Trinity Sunday[4] — in May.

1291 Thomas Bellie of Wylye, husbandman, and Agnes Ivy-may, married 29 August.

1292 Ambrose Aldridge and Alice Bond, married 20 October.

1601, 1602 [no entries]

1603/4

1293 Christopher Randoll, yeoman, and Maud Wandsborrough, widow, married 2 July.

1294 Thomas Weeks and Margery Barnes, married 23 January.

1   no date is given
2   no date is given
3   no date is given
4   a space is left for the date; Trinity Sunday was 18 May

1295 Thomas Candy, yeoman, and Catherine Crotchett, married 30 January.

1604/5

1296 William Potticarie of Wylye, yeoman, once widowed, and Julian[1] Cowley, married 22 May.

1297 Matthew Poole and Tamsin Moonday, married 23 May.

1298 Richard Kent, husbandman, and Susan Smyth, daughter of S Smyth of Wylye, husbandman, married 14 October.

1299 William Webbe and Eleanor Taylor, married 4 November.

1605/6

1300 Richard Bristowe and Mary Cowdrey, married 1 April.

1301 William Swift of Trudoxhill,[2] Somerset, butcher, and Bridget Hillman, daughter of Thomas Hillman of our Wylye, parish clerk, married 6 February.

1606/7

1302 John Baker of Wylye and Elizabeth Furnell, daughter of Humphrey etc, married 26 June.

1303 Matthew Amor and Elizabeth —,[3] his second wife, married 28 November.

1607/8 [no entries]

1608/9

1304 William Hill, tailor of Wylye, and Grace Smyth, daughter of Edward

1   *Juliana*
2   *Truttocks-hill*
3   a space left, and no surname given

Smyth, likewise of Wylye, husbandman, married 14 November.

1609/10

1305 Robert Grace and Elizabeth Harries, married 22 October.

1306 Thomas Hobbs of Wylye, labourer, and Alice Taylour, daughter of Richard Taylour of Wylye, husbandman, married 25 October.

1307 John Blunt and Lucy Hobbes, married 22 January.

1610/11

1308 Jeffery White of Stockton, carpenter,[1] and Mary Fleming, married 9 August.

1309 George Gowen of Wylye, blacksmith, and Honor Potticarie, daughter of William Potticarie of Wylye, yeoman, etc, married 29 November.

1611, 1612, 1613 [no entries]

1614/15

1310 William Lake and Catherine Line, married 9 August.

1615, 1616, 1617 [no entries]

1618/19

1311 Robert Baker *alias* Chate, woodworker, once widowed, descended from the Bakers of Wylye, etc; and Mary Willies, a woman hitherto unmarried, raised in Steeple Langford, married 10 May.

1312 John Ward, a young unmarried husbandman, raised in Orcheston St George, and Anne Locke, a woman hitherto unmarried, descended from the Wylye family of the Lockes, husbandmen, married 29 June.

---

1   *carpenter*: this is written as English, 'carpenter', rather than Latin *carpentarius,* cartwright.

1313 Robert Locke, a young unmarried labourer, son of Robert Locke formerly of Wylye, husbandman, deceased, etc; and Jane Brian, a woman hitherto unmarried, son[1] of John Brian of Little Langford, labourer, etc, married 23 July.

1314 Hugh Henwood, a young unmarried blacksmith, son of a certain Henwood of Amesbury,[2] labourer; and Maud Sebrey, a woman hitherto unmarried, descended from the Sebreys in or close to[3] Cranborne, domestic servant of the master rector, married 10 January.

1315 These were celebrated in the aforesaid year 1618 by Thomas Bower, rector; Thomas Crockford, assistant; Richard Kent, William Hoskins, Nicholas Potticary, churchwardens.

1619/20

1316 John Hillman, a young unmarried tailor, the lawful and only son of Thomas Hillman of Wylye, husbandman, clerk of the parish church, etc; and Edith Rowden, a young widow, the relict of Alan Rowden of Hanging Langford, an elderly husbandman deceased, married Monday 29 March.

1317 John Dewe, a young unmarried blacksmith, raised in Gomeldon,[4] etc, and Honor Gowen, a widow, relict of George Gowen late of Wylye, also a blacksmith, deceased, married Sunday 6 June.

1318 John Seale *alias* Bullie of Wylye, an unmarried man of full age,[5] fuller, etc, and Joan Oliver, twice widowed, relict of John Oliver, an elderly husbandman of Wylye, recently deceased, married Monday 14 June.

1319 These were celebrated in the aforesaid year 1619 By John Lee, Bachelor of Divinity, rector; Thomas Crockford, Bachelor of Arts, assistant, vicar of Fisherton Delamere; George Ditton Scholar of Oxford, curate; John Locke of Wylye, married, and William Clearke of Wylye, unmarried, husbandmen, churchwardens.

1 *filius*, although *filia*, daughter, must be intended
2 *Ambsburie*
3 *infra, vel p'pe*
4 *Gumilton*
5 *aetate integra*

1620/1

1320 Christopher Smyth of Deptford, butcher, once widowed, more than 50 years old, etc, and Christian Edridge, a woman hitherto unmarried, about 30 years old, descended from a family of husbandmen of Sherrington, married Monday 16 October.

1321 Humphrey Furnell of Wylye, husbandman, once widowed, almost 80 years old, etc, and Elizabeth Baker *alias* Chate, twice widowed, almost 60 years old, married Monday 23 October.[1]

1322 Henry Minety of Erlestoke,[2] husbandman, widower, more or less 40 years old, and Susan Ayles *alias* Hicks of Wylye, a maid[3] a little more than 30 years old, married Saturday, the feast of Saint Matthias the Apostle, 24 February.

1323 These were celebrated in the aforesaid year 1620
By John Lee, Bachelor of Divinity, rector; Thomas Crockford, vicar of Fisherton Delamere, assistant; John Lee the younger, Bachelor of Arts, curate;[4] Richard Eyles *alias* Hickes of Deptford, married, and John Locke of Wylye, unmarried, husbandmen, churchwardens.

1621/2

1324 William Hughes *alias* Clearke of Wylye, a young unmarried man who is a skilful husbandman but also a tailor, etc; and Joan Whitehart *alias* Thring, etc, married Monday 26 August.

1325 Stephen Nash of Edington, an unmarried tailor, etc, and Christian Larkeham of Wylye, widow, etc, married —[5] the feast of all Saints, 1 November.

---

1   a large manicule has been written in the margin to point up this unusual marriage.
2   *Stoake Com'*
3   *Puella*: the word is underlined and there is a manicule and 'of 30' in the margin against it, presumably to express surprise that a woman of that age might be described as *puella*.
4   interlined
5   a space has been left for the day of the week

1326 David Spring *alias* Kent of Wylye, a young unmarried labourer, etc, and Christian Starre *alias* Stranton *alias* Chate, also of Wylye, an illegitimate young woman,[1] married Monday 26 November.

1327 Thomas Wadland of Wylye, a young unmarried labourer, etc, and Edith Abell of Langford, a woman hitherto unmarried, of full age, married Thursday 14 February.

1328 These were celebrated in the aforesaid year 1621
By John Lee, Bachelor of Divinity, rector; Thomas Crockford, vicar of Fisherton Delamere, assistant; John Selwood of Deptford, married, and John Locke of Wylye, unmarried, again, husbandmen, churchwardens.

1622/3

1329 In this year 1622 no wedding at all was celebrated in the aforesaid church,
By John Lee, Bachelor of Divinity, prebendary and canon of the cathedral church of Sarum, rector; John Lee the younger, Bachelor of Arts, curate; Thomas Kent of Deptford, yeoman, and John Taylor of Wylye street, brewer,[2] churchwardens.

1623/4

1330 John Sutton of Shrewton, a young unmarried ploughwright, etc, and Susan Locke, a woman also unmarried, one of the daughters of Martin Locke, formerly of this Wylye, weaver, deceased, and of Joan his wife, married Monday 19 January.

1331 Only this one marriage was celebrated in the aforesaid church this year 1623
By John Lee, Bachelor of Divinity, prebendary and canon of the cathedral church of Sarum, rector; John Lee the younger, Bachelor of Arts, curate; Joel Gyrdler of Wylye mill, clothier, and John Hillman of Wylye, tailor, churchwardens.

1624/5

1   *puella notha*
2   *cervisiario*

1332 No Wedding at all was celebrated in this Year 1624.
By John Lee, Bachelor of Divinity, prebendary and canon of the cathedral church of Sarum, rector; John Lee the younger, Bachelor of Arts, curate; Edward Smyth the elder, and John Barnes, both of Wylye, husbandmen, churchwardens.

1625/6

1333 No Wedding at all was celebrated in this Year 1625.
By John Lee, Bachelor of Divinity, etc, rector; John Lee the younger, Bachelor of Arts, curate; John White, priest,[1] curate; William Locke and Thomas Potticary, both of Wylye, husbandmen, churchwardens.

1626/7

1334 Thomas Scammell of Deptford, but from Wylye, an unmarried labourer, almost 40 years old, and Mary Marshman, a woman hitherto unmarried, of a family of labourers also of Deptford, almost 30 years old, married Monday 10 July.

1335 By John Lee, Bachelor of Divinity, etc, rector; John White, priest, curate; Thomas Crockford, Bachelor of Arts, priest, assistant; James Rebeck of Wylye, but from Bapton, and William Hill of Wylye manor, husbandmen, churchwardens.

1627/8

1336 John Foord of Chicklade, a young man, by occupation a limeburner,[2] but now a husbandman, almost[3] — years old, and Grace Locke, a young woman 23 years old, the first daughter of William Locke of Wylye, husbandman and brewer, and of Agnes his wife, married Monday 6 August.

1337 Nicholas Potticary of Wylye, an unmarried freeholder, descended from a gentry family, now master of one of the hostels,[4] 38 years old; and

---

1   *presbytero*
2   *calciarius praxi*
3   a space has been left for the age
4   *nunc unius ex hospitiis dominus*

Bridget Everley, the first daughter of Guy Everley now of Wylye, yeoman, and of Olive his wife, etc, a young woman a little more or less than 17 years old; married on Monday in the week before Lent,[1] — February.

1338 By John Lee, Bachelor of Divinity, etc, rector; John White, priest, curate; Thomas Crockford, priest, of Arts, etc, assistant; Anthony Ballard of Wylye, but from Bapton, and Henry Patient of Deptford manor, yeomen, churchwardens.

1628/9

1339 Richard Tilley of Erlestoke,[2] tailor, a young unmarried man about twenty 26 years old, etc, and Mary Patient, the first daughter of Henry Patient of Deptford manor, yeoman, and of Joan his wife, a woman hitherto unmarried, about 19 years old, married in our church on Monday 28 April.

1340 William Potticarie of Wylye, a young unmarried husbandman, 22 years old, etc, the first son of William Potticarie formerly of this Wylye, yeoman, deceased, by his second wife Julian, now a widow, etc; and Eleanor Rendall of Hanging Langford, yeoman,[3] and of Elizabeth his wife, married (as it is stated) in Steeple Langford[4] church, on Sunday 19 October.

1341 By John Lee, Bachelor of Divinity, etc, rector; John White, priest, curate; Thomas Crockford, Bachelor of Arts, priest, etc, assistant; Guy Potticarie and John Barnet of Wylye, yeomen, churchwardens.

Subsequent marriage entries in this register are in different hands, in English 1629-33, and in Latin 1636-43, when the sequence ends.

---

1 *die lunae in carnisprivio*, followed by a space left for the date, *recte 25*
2 *Stoake Com'*
3 the father's name is omitted, but there is no space
4 *Langford Magn'*

Baptisms

Infants lawfully admitted to the list of Christian people through the holy sacrament of baptism in Wylye church[1] in the county of Wiltshire, from the year of the Incarnation 1581, and thereafter.

1581/2

1342 Joan Potticarie, baptised 7 April.

1343 John Locke, son of Martin Locke, baptised 20 April.

1344 John Selin, baptised 28 December.

1345 John Selin, brother of the foresaid John, also baptised 28 December.[2]

1346 John Carde,[3] baptised 14 February.

1347 Edmund Taylor, also baptised 14 February.

1348 Agnes Hewet, baptised 18 February.

1349 Alice Gullyford, baptised 24 March.

1582/3

1350 Susan Wastefeeld, baptised 14 June.

1351 Susan Ayles, baptised 24 August.

1352 John Taylour, also baptised 24 August.

---

1   *infantes in album hominum Christianorum legitime admissi, per venerabile sacramentum baptismi in eccl'ia de Wiley*

2   This and the previous entry are rubbed and indistinct, but the reading is confirmed by the burial of both two months later, below **1683-4**

3   Badly rubbed, and reading uncertain

1353 Mary Longynough, baptised 24 September.

1354 Susan Mabil, baptised 30 September.

1355 Christian Locke, baptised 11 February.

1356 Mary Smyth, baptised 12 February.

1357 Jane Harries, baptised 13 October in this same year.[1]

1583/4

1358 Henry Spring, baptised 8 April.

1359 Agnes Woods, baptised 25 April.

1360 John Taylour, baptised 14 September.

1361 William Baker, baptised 27 December.

1584/5

1362 John Baker, baptised 14 June.

1363 Alexander Smyth, baptised 19 July.

1364 John Barnes, baptised 25 July.

1365 Mary Moonday, baptised 14 August.

1366 Thomas Wastefield, baptised 6 October.

1367 Tamsin Longynough, baptised 9 October.

1368 John Lock, baptised 24 October.

1369 Dorothy Taylour, baptised 29 January.

1370 Susan Smyth, also baptised 29 January.

1   added, because out of order

1585/6

1371 Elizabeth Locke, baptised 3 April.

1372 Joan Taylour, also baptised 3 April.

1373 Thomas Reade, baptised 27 August.

1374 Grace Smyth, baptised 3 October.

1375 Alexander Carde, baptised 27 November.

1376 Guy Potticarie, son of William, baptised 27 December.

1377 John Moore, son of a certain traveller,[1] baptised 1 January.

1378 William Gullyford, baptised 7 February.

1379 Bridget Hillman, baptised 13 February.

1380 Philip Moonday, baptised 27 February.

1586/7

1381 Thomas Cleark, baptised 6 June, the only (baptism) this year.[2]

1587/8 [no entries]

1588/9

1382 John Kent, son of Thomas Kent of Deptford, yeoman, baptised 18 September.

1383 Agnes Barnes, baptised 2 January.

1384 Bridget Creede, baptised 4 January.

1   *peregrini cuiusd'*
2   four further entries wrongly ascribed to this year have been crossed through, and rewritten under 1588

1385 Maurice Gullyford, son of — Gullyford[1] of Deptford, baptised 7 March.

1589/90

1386 Robert Lock, son of — Lock[2] of Wylye, baptised 8 May.

1387 Thomas Tuckey, son of William Tuckey of Deptford, yeoman, etc, baptised 10 May.

1388 Mary Clearke, daughter of John Clearke of Wylye, baptised 7 September.

1389 Alice Taylour, daughter of Richard Taylour of Wylye, husbandman, etc, baptised 7 September.

1390 Honor Potticarie, daughter of William Potticarie of Wylye, yeoman, etc, baptised 9 September.

1391 Honor Bower, daughter of Thomas Bower, clerk, rector of this church, and of Elizabeth his wife, baptised 10 September.

1392 Roger Ford, baptised 10 January.

1590/1

1393 Thomas Locke, son of — Locke[3] of Wylye, baptised 8 April.

1591/2

1394 Margaret Locke, daughter of — Locke[4] of Wylye, baptised 8 October.

1395 Alice Taylor, daughter of — Taylor,[5] baptised 16 October.

1   a space is left for the forename
2   a space is left for the forename
3   a space is left for the forename
4   a space is left for the forename
5   a space is left for the forename

1396 Edward Baker, son of — Baker,[1] baptised 28 November.

1397 George Smyth, son of — Smyth,[2] baptised 20 December.

1398 Nicholas Potticarie, firstborn son of John Potticarie of Wylye, clothier, and of Eleanor his wife, baptised (as his nurse remembers) 7 March, although in the old book it is incorrectly written 7 April 1591.[3]

1592/3

1399 Thomas Longynough, son of David Longynough of Wylye, tiler, etc, baptised 25 March.

1400 Agnes Gullyford, daughter of — Gullyford[4] of Deptford, baptised 26 March.

1401 Agnes Kent, baptised 26 March.

1402 John Ayles, son of John Ayles, *alias* Hicks of Wylye, husbandman, etc, baptised 27 March.

1403 Catherine Cullimore, baptised 28 March.

1404 Agnes Smyth, baptised 29 March.

1405 Thomas Potticarie, son of William, baptised 10 April.

1406 William Barnes, son of — Barnes,[5] also baptised 10 April.

1407 Giles[6] Tuckey, son of William Tuckey of Deptford, yeoman, baptised 17 April.

---

1   spaces are left for the forename and place
2   spaces are left for the forename and place
3   *(ut in memoria nutricis) septimo Martii, licet in veteri libro imperfect' scribat'r 7 Aprilis, 1591*
4   a space is left for the forename
5   a space is left for the forename
6   *Aegidius*

1408 Walter Gullyford, baptised 10 June.

1409 Edward Smyth, son of — Smyth,[1] baptised 17 June.

1410 Mary Potticarie, daughter of John Potticarie of Wylye, clothier,[2] etc, baptised 30 July.

1411 – Lock,[3] daughter of Locke of Wylye, baptised 17 December.

1593/4[4]

1412 [. . .] Spring [. . .] 23 April?

1413 George? Taylour, son of Richard Taylour of Wylye, husbandman, [. . .]

1414 Elizabeth [. . .], daughter of [. . .] of Wylye, labourer, baptised [. . .] January.

1415 Thomas [. . .]le, son of [. . .]

1416 Richard Whyte? son of [. . .], baptised 24 October.

1594/5[5]

1417 Elizabeth Kent [. . .]

1418 Elizabeth [. . .]

1419 Joan Coll[. . .]

---

1   spaces are left for the forename and place
2   written in English, thus
3   the page is badly rubbed, so that the forename, if ever written, has been erased; a space is left for the father's forename
4   The page is badly rubbed and most entries for this year are largely illegible or uncertain
5   The page is badly rubbed and most entries for this year, are largely illegible or uncertain

1420 John Hillman, son of — Hillman,[1] baptised 3 July.

1421 William Pearse?, son of John[2] Pearse?, [. . .]

1422 George? Harries?, son of — Harries,[3] baptised 15 September.

1423 Matthew Lock, son of — Lock,[4] baptised 22 December.

1424 Francis Baker, son of — Baker,[5] baptised 30 December?

1425 Eleanor Potticarie, daughter of Robert? Potticarie of Wylye, clothier, and of Eleanor his wife, 2 October.

1426 John Hillman, son of — Hillman,[6] baptised 3 January.

1427 Fortune Ayles, daughter of John Ayles of Wylye, husbandman, also baptised 3 January.

1595/6

1428 John and Susan Smyth, twin son and daughter of — Smyth,[7] baptised 14 May.

1429 Guy Cullimore, son of — Cullimore,[8] baptised 8 January.

1430 Avice Longynough, daughter of David Longynough of Wylye, tiler, baptised 22 June.

1431 Richard Potticarie, son of William Potticarie of Wylye, yeoman, baptised 6 July.

1 spaces appear to be left for the forename and place
2 The name John (in English, not *Johannes*), has been overwritten in a bold
   17th-century? hand (not Crockford's) suggesting that the page was already
   faded from an early date
3 spaces appear to be left for the forename and place
4 spaces appear to be left for the forename and place
5 spaces appear to be left for the forename and place
6 spaces appear to be left for the forename and place
7 spaces are left for the forename and place
8 spaces are left for the forename and place

1432 John Barnes, son of — Barnes,[1] baptised 7 September.

1433 John Harries, son of — Harries,[2] baptised 10 November.

1434 Mary Webbe, daughter of — Webbe,[3] also baptised 10 November.

1435 Agnes Tuckey, daughter of William Tuckey of Deptford manor, yeoman, etc, baptised 9 November.

1436 Margery Wandsborrough, daughter of — Wandsborrough,[4] baptised 27 December.

1437 Elizabeth Hillman, daughter of — Hillman,[5] baptised 23 February.

1438 Maud Barnes, daughter of — Barnes,[6] baptised 23 March.

1596/7

1439 Joan Potticarie, daughter of John Potticarie of Wylye, clothier, and of Eleanor his wife, baptised 18 April.

1440 Agnes Ford, daughter of — Ford[7] of Wylye, also baptised 18 April.

1441 Julia Skire, daughter of — Skire,[8] baptised 8 May.

1442 Eleanor Kent, daughter of Thomas Kent of Deptford, yeoman, etc, baptised 5 November.

1443 John Perrie, son of Thomas Perrie of Hanging Langford,[9] baptised 13 November.

1 spaces are left for the forename and place
2 spaces are left for the forename and place
3 spaces are left for the forename and place
4 spaces are left for the forename and place
5 spaces are left for the forename and place
6 spaces are left for the forename and place
7 a space is left for the forename
8 spaces are left for the forename and place
9 *Langford pendent*

1444 Henry Cleark, son of — Cleark,[1] baptised 6 January.

1445 Roger Peareman and Alice Peareman, twin infants, children of — Peareman,[2] baptised 13 January.

1597/8

1446 John Harding, son of — Harding,[3] baptised 20 November.

1447 William Tuckie, son of William Tuckie of Deptford manor, yeoman, etc, baptised 27 November.

1448 Anne Potticarie, daughter of John Potticarie of Wylye, clothier, and of Eleanor his wife, baptised 11 December.

1449 Tamsin Potticarie, daughter of William Potticarie of Wylye, yeoman, and of Joan his wife, baptised 27 February.

1598/9

1450 Agnes Hillman, daughter of — Hillman,[4] baptised 18 June.

1451 Mary Beachin, daughter of William Beachin of Wylye, master builder,[5] baptised 23 July.

1452 Thomas Bysse, son of James Bysse, *alias* Best, of Wylye, labourer, baptised 20 December.

1453 John Barnes, son of William Barnes,[6] baptised 16 January.

1454 Thomas Spring, son of Henry Spring the younger of Wylye, husbandman, etc, baptised in this year[7] 21 September.

1   spaces are left for the forename and place
2   spaces are left for the forename and place
3   spaces are left for the forename and place
4   spaces are left for the forename and place
5   *architecti*
6   a space is left for the place
7   added because the entry is misplaced

1455 Thomas Wadland, son of Richard Wadland of Wylye, weaver, and of Elizabeth his wife, baptised 13 February.

1599/1600

1456 Joan Smyth, daughter of — Smyth, baptised —.[1]

1457 Alice Oliver, daughter of — Oliver, baptised —.

1458 William Crutchel, son of — Crutchel, baptised —.

1459 Mary Smyth, daughter of — Smyth, baptised 14 October.

1600/1 [no entries][2]

1601/2

1460 Henry Bellie, son of Thomas Bellie of Wylye, husbandman, etc, baptised 26 April.

1461 Margaret Clement, the illegitimate daughter of Tamsin Clement of — [3] baptised 2 May.

1462 Richard Smyth, son of Christopher Smyth of Deptford, butcher, baptised 13 June.

1463 Joan Barter, daughter of — Barter[4] of Wishford baptised 6 December.

1602/3

1464 Joan Wadland, daughter of Richard Wadland of Wylye, weaver, and of Elizabeth his wife, baptised 29 June.

---

1   this and the following two entries lack father's forename, place and date of baptism, and spaces have been left for each
2   a large space has been left as if anticipating that entries may be found
3   no place is given
4   a space is left for the forename

1465 John Dewe, son of John Dewe of Wylye, husbandman etc, baptised the fourth of July.

1466 Joan Starre, daughter of Thomas Starre *alias* Warminster, of Wylye, tailor etc, baptised 10 July.

1467 William Style, son of William Style of Wylye, load-carrier,[1] baptised 18 July.

1468 Susan Bacon, daughter of Thomas Bacon of —[2] baptised 23 July.

1469 Christian Oliver, daughter of John Oliver of Wylye the younger, husbandman etc, baptised 25 July.

1470 William Belly, son of Thomas Bellie of Wylye, husbandman etc, baptised 24 November.

1603/4

1471 Susan Style, daughter of William Style of Wylye, load-carrier, etc, baptised 20 November.

1472 Thomas Starre, son of Thomas Starre *alias* Warminster, of Wylye, tailor etc, baptised 8 January.

1473 Alice Barnes, daughter of William Barnes of —[3] baptised 21 January.

1474 John Smyth, son of Edward Smyth of Wylye, husbandman, and of his wife, baptised 25 January.

1475 Elizabeth Smyth, daughter of Christopher Smyth of Deptford, butcher, baptised at Fisherton Delamere,[4] 15 January.

1476 John Oliver, son of John Oliver of Wylye the younger, husbandman, baptised 13 February.

---

1   *onerar'*
2   no place is given
3   no place is given
4   *Dall*

1604/5

1477 Grace Locke, daughter of William Locke of Wylye, husbandman etc, baptised 3 June.

1478 Jerome Smyth, son of Jerome Smyth of Wylye, tailor, baptised 29 October.

1479 Elizabeth Bellie, daughter of Thomas Bellie of Wylye, husbandman etc, baptised 7 November.

1480 Catherine Hoskins, daughter of William of Wylye, but from Bapton manor, weaver, baptised 2 December.

1605/6

1481 Margery Moonday, daughter of John Moonday the elder of —[1] baptised 7 April.

1482 William Potticarie, son of William Potticarie of Wylye, yeoman, and of Julian his wife, baptised 9 September.

1483 Reginald Hoskins, son of William Hoskins of Wylye, weaver etc, baptised 17 February.

1484 Jane Sedgewike, daughter of Nicholas Sedgewik from Little Wishford, labourer, baptised 30 April.[2]

1606/7

1485 William Starre, son of Thomas Starre *alias* Warminster of Wylye, tailor, baptised 4 June.

1486 Alice Style, daughter of William Style of Wylye, load-carrier, baptised 11 June.

1487 Jane Ayles, daughter of William Ayles *alias* Hickes of Deptford, yeoman, baptised 21 October.

1 no place is given
2 placed under 1605 but unless out of sequence *recte* 1606

1488 Joan Baker, daughter of John Baker of Wylye, labourer, baptised 1 February.

1607/8

1489 Joan Locke, daughter of William Locke of Wylye, husbandman etc, baptised 12 April.

1490 John Smyth, son of Christopher Smyth of Deptford, butcher, baptised 4 May.

1491 Margaret Steevens, daughter of John Steevens of Deptford, baptised 24 June.

1492 Christopher Potticarie, son of William Potticarie of Wylye, yeoman, and of Julian his wife, baptised 16 September.

1608/9

1493 John Selwood, son of John Selwood of Deptford, husbandman and tailor, and of Jane his wife, baptised 8 May.

1494 William Baker, son of Robert Baker *alias* Chate of Wylye, woodworker, and of Elizabeth his wife, baptised 7 June.

1495 Jerome Payne, son of Charles[1] Payne of —[2] baptised 20 October.

1496 Julian Baker, daughter of John Baker of Wylye, labourer, etc, baptised 6 November.

1497 Margaret Potticarie, daughter of John Potticarie of Wylye, clothier, and of Eleanor his wife, baptised 14 December.

1498 John Imber, son of Edward Imber of Deptford, husbandman, etc, baptised 6 January.

1499 Susan Kent, daughter of Richard Kent of Wylye, husbandman, and

1   the forename *Caroli* appears to have been misspelled and not entirely corrected
2   no place is given

of Susan his wife, baptised 10 January.

1500 John Bacon, son of Thomas Bacon of Deptford, labourer etc, baptised 2 February.

1501 Elizabeth Starre, daughter of Thomas Starre of Wylye, tailor, baptised 22 February.

1502 Eleanor Swift, daughter of William Swift of Trudoxhill,[1] Somerset, butcher, and of his wife —,[2] baptised 26 February.

1609/10

1503 Christopher Smyth, son of Christopher Smyth of Deptford, butcher, baptised 18 April.

1504 Crescens[3] Moonday, son of John Moonday of Deptford, labourer, baptised 14 May.

1505 Roger Hill, son of William Hill of Wylye, tailor etc, baptised 5 August.

1506 Elizabeth Barter, daughter of Edward Barter of —[4] baptised 5 September.

1507 Dorothy Hobbes, daughter of Thomas Hobbes of Wylye, labourer etc, baptised 13 January.

1508 Joan Taylour, daughter of John Taylour of Wylye husbandman etc, baptised 25 February.

1509 William Marshman, son of William Marshman of Deptford, labourer, 16 March.

---

1   *Truttockshill*
2   a space is left for the forename
3   A Biblical name, companion of Paul: 2 Timothy 4. 10
4   no place is given

1610/11

1510 Nicholas Potticarie, son of William Potticarie of Wylye, yeoman, and of Julian his wife, baptised 25 April.

1511 John Steevens, son of John Steevens of Deptford, husbandman and shepherd etc, baptised 11 May.

1512 Josiah Imber, son of Edward Imber, deceased, lately of Deptford, etc, and of —[1] his wife, baptised 14 June.[2]

1513 Elizabeth Kent, daughter of Richard Kent of Wylye, husbandman, and of Susan his wife, baptised 15 July.

1514 Olive Locke, daughter of William Locke of Wylye, husbandman, and of Agnes his wife, baptised the same day, 15 July.

1515 Jane Selwood, daughter of John Selwood of Deptford, husbandman and tailor, and of Jane his wife, baptised 12 August.

1516 John Starre, son of Thomas Starre *alias* Warminster of Wylye, tailor, baptised 2 September.

1517 Jeremiah Selwood, son of Thomas Sellwood of Deptford, labourer, baptised 21 December.

1518 William Gowan, son of George Gowan of Wylye, blacksmith, and of Honor his wife, baptised 23 December.

1519 Eleanor Hill, daughter of William Hill of Wylye, tailor, baptised 12 January.

1520 Thomas Smyth, son of Henry Smith of Wylye, tailor and lodging-house keeper,[3] and of Susan his wife, baptised 23 January.

1521 William Philpot, illegitimate son of[4] Philpot of Wylye, of the

1   a space is left for the forename
2   the page is rubbed and the date uncertain (Hadow edn. reads 13 June)
3   *hospitii tenentis*
4   the forename is illegible, and could not be read by Hadow

condition of a servant, baptised 16 March.

1611/12

1522 David Dewe, illegitimate son of Susan Dewe of —[1] baptised 25 March.

1523 James Longynough, illegitimate son of Elizabeth Longynough of Wylye, baptised 6 April.

1524 Thomas Baker, son of John Baker of Wylye, labourer, and of Elizabeth his wife, baptised 14 April.

1525 Thomas Goldisbrough, son of William Goldisbrough of Deptford manor, a gentleman raised in Shrewton, and of —[2] his wife, born Thursday 27 June, and baptised the Sunday following, 30 June.

1526 John Gullyford, son of —[3] Gullyford of Deptford, labourer, baptised 2 October.

1527 Thomas Hobbes, son of Thomas Hobbes of Wylye, labourer, and of Alice his wife, baptised 14 February.

1528 James Moonday, son of John Moonday of Deptford labourer, and of —[4] his wife, baptised 9 March.

1612/13

1529 Agnes Taylour, daughter of John Taylour of Wylye, husbandman, and of Joan his wife, baptised 19 April.

1530 Joel Gyrdler, son of Joel Gyrdler of Wylye mill, clothier, and of Joan his wife, baptised 30 May.

1531 Frances Locke, daughter of William Locke of Wylye, husbandman, and of Agnes his wife, baptised 7 March.

1   no place is given
2   a space is left for the forename
3   a space is left for the forename
4   a space is left for the forename

1532 Christopher Joannes, son of J—[1] Joannes of —[2] baptised 12 March.

1613/14

1533 Anne Sellwood, daughter of John Sellwood of Deptford, husbandman and tailor, and of Jane his wife, baptised 18 April.

1534 John Pyle, son of John Pyle of Wylye, butcher etc, baptised 25 April.

1535 Grace Lambert, daughter of Richard Lambert, clerk, and of Susan his wife, baptised 29 April.

1536 John Baker, illegitimate son of Christabel Baker of Wylye a poor servingwoman[3] etc, baptised 30 April.

1537 Agnes Kent, daughter of Richard Kent of Wylye, husbandman, and of Susan his wife, baptised 2 May.

1538 Matthew Sams, son of Matthew Sams of[4] baptised 19 May.

1539 William Swift, son of William Swift of Trudoxhill,[5] Somerset, butcher etc, baptised 20 January.

1614/15

1540 Olive Taylour, daughter of John Taylour of Wylye, husbandman etc, and of Joan his wife, baptised 30 October.

1541 Nicholas Gowen, son of George Gowen of Wylye, blacksmith, and of Honor his,[6] baptised 6 December.

---

1   a space is left for the rest of the forename
2   no place is given
3   *ancilla paupercula*
4   no place is given
5   *Truttockshill*
6   'wife' is omitted, but no space

1542 John Locke, son of William[1] Locke of Wylye, baptised 3 February.

1615/16   [No entries]

1616/17

1543 John Selwood, third son of John Selwood of Deptford, husbandman and tailor, and of Jane his wife, born and baptised on the Tuesday of the Lord's Easter, 2 April.

1617/18   [No entries]

1618/19

1544 Dorothy[2] Gamlin, daughter of Nicholas Gamlin of Wylye, labourer, and of Mary his wife, born 21 and baptised 26 April.

1545 Richard Baker, son of John Baker of Wylye, labourer, and of Elizabeth his wife, born 30 April, baptised 3 May.

1546 Anne Girdler, second daughter of Joel Girdler, the master[3] etc of Wylye mill etc, and of Joan his wife, born 21 and baptised 25 May.

1547 Elizabeth Wayle, daughter of Richard Wayle of Wylye, sieve-maker[4] etc, and of Margaret his wife, born and baptised 26 May.

1548 Maurice Gullyford, son of William Gullyford of Deptford, labourer, and of Margaret his wife, born 19 and baptised 21 June.

1549 Joan Smyth, daughter of Edward Smyth the younger of Wylye, labourer, and of Alice his wife, born 6 and baptised 8 July.

1550 Lucretia Locke, daughter of Robert Locke of Wylye labourer and of Jane his wife, born 9 and baptised 14 October.

1   *Guilielmi* has been crossed out
2   Hadow reads *Jonathan* but *Dorothea* is clearly the correct reading
3   *domini*
4   *cribrarii*

1551 Susan East, daughter of Edward East, miller,[1] now an incomer living in Wylye, and of Elizabeth his wife, born and baptised 18 October.

1552 John Hill, son of William Hill, one of the keepers of the lodging-house at Wylye,[2] and of Grace his wife, born 1 and baptised 8 November.

1553 John Locke, son of John Locke of Wylye, labourer, and of Joan his wife, born 28 and baptised 30 November.

1554 Elizabeth Patient, daughter of Henry Patient *alias* Passion of Wylye, but from Fisherton, husbandman, and of Joan his wife, baptised 6 December.

1555 William Eyles, the firstborn son of Richard Eyles, *alias* Hicks, of Deptford, husbandman, and of Maud his wife, born 22 and baptised 23 January.

1556 Mary Furnell, daughter of William Furnell of Wylye, husbandman, and of Lettice his wife, born 18 and baptised 21 March.

1557 These thirteen baptisms were conducted in this year 1618.
By Thomas Bower, Master of Arts (as it is stated), rector to 23 February; Thomas Crockford, Bachelor of Arts, vicar of Fisherton, assistant for almost all the year; Richard Kent of Wylye husbandman, William Hoskins of Wylye, weaver, Nicholas Potticarie of Wylye, yeoman, churchwardens.

1619/20

1558 John Locke, firstborn son of William Locke of Wylye husbandman etc, and of Anne his wife, born on Easter Sunday, 28 March, baptised the following Sunday, 4 April.

1559 Philip Steevens, first son of John Steevens of Deptford, husbandman and shepherd, and of Eleanor his wife, born Wednesday 26, baptised Sunday 30 May.

1560 Mary Bush, third daughter of Philip Bush of Deptford, labourer, and of Margery his wife, born 9 September, baptised on Sunday 12

---

1   *molitoris*
2   *unius ex hospitiorum Wiliensium tenentibus*

September.

1561 Reginald Crosse, first son of Henry Crosse of Wylye, labourer, and of Dorothy his wife, born Thursday 21 and baptised Sunday 24 October.

1562 Winifred Starre, first daughter of William Starre *alias* Warminster of Wylye, tailor, and of Anne his wife, born Friday 7 January, baptised Sunday 9 January.

1563 John Wayle, first son of Richard Wayle of Wylye, sieve-maker, and of Margaret his wife, was born and baptised on that same 9 January.

1564 Thomas Hillman, firstborn son of John Hillman of Wylye, tailor, and of Edith his wife, born Friday 14 January, baptised Sunday 16 January.

1565 John Kent, second son of Richard Kent of Wylye, husbandman, and of Susan his wife, born Monday 14 February, baptised Sunday 5 March.

1566 These eight baptisms were conducted in this year 1619
By John Lee, Bachelor of Divinity, rector; Thomas Crockford, Bachelor of Arts etc, assistant; George Ditton, Scholar of Oxford, curate; John Locke of Wylye, married, husbandman and William Clearke of Wylye, unmarried, husbandman, churchwardens.

1620/1

1567 Henry Longynough, third illegitimate son of Elizabeth Longynough, daughter of David Longynough of Wylye, tiler,[1] born Thursday 30 March, baptised Monday 3 April.

1568 Ralph Henwood, firstborn son of Hugh Henwood of Wylye, blacksmith, and of Maud his wife, born Saturday 1 April, baptised Sunday 2 April.

1569 Alice Smyth, second daughter of Edward Smyth the younger of Wylye, labourer, and of Alice his wife, born Sunday 13 August, baptised Sunday 20 August.

1570 Joan Gullyford, first daughter of Maurice Gullyford of Deptford,

1   *tegularii*

labourer, and of Mary his wife, born Friday 6 October, baptised Sunday 8 October.

1571 Henry Hobbes, second son of Thomas Hobbes of Wylye, labourer, and of Alice his wife, born Thursday 2 November, baptised Sunday 5 November.

1572 Elizabeth Smyth, firstborn daughter of Thomas Smyth of Wylye, husbandman, and of Edith his wife, born Monday 5 February, baptised Friday 9 February.

1573 Jane and Millicent Locke, infant twins, the second and third daughters of Robert Locke of Wylye, labourer, and of Jane his wife, born and baptised Tuesday 6 February.

1574 Francis Coales, third son of William Coales *alias* Hart of Deptford, labourer, and of Agnes his wife, was born Sunday 25 February, baptised Monday 26 February.

1575 These nine baptisms were conducted in this year 1620
By John Lee Bachelor of Divinity, rector; Thomas Crockford Bachelor of Arts etc, assistant; Richard Eyles of Wylye, married, and John Locke of Wylye, unmarried, husbandmen, churchwardens.

1621/2

1576 Jane Locke, — daughter[1] of John Locke of Wylye, labourer, or husbandman, and of Joan his wife, born Sunday 6 May, baptised Tuesday 8 May.

1577 Julian and Jane Taylour, twin daughters of John Taylour of Wylye, husbandman etc, and of Joan his wife, born Tuesday 8 May, baptised Thursday 10 May.

1578 Frances Henwood, firstborn daughter of Hugh Henwood, now of Deptford, blacksmith, and of Maud his wife, born Monday 17, baptised Thursday 20 September.

1579 William Hill, fourth son of William Hill of Wylye, tailor etc, and of

1   a space follows *filia*

Grace his wife, born Tuesday 2 October, baptised Wednesday 3 October.

1580 Thomas Hillman, second son of John Hillman, of Wylye, tailor etc, and of Edith his wife, born Monday 3 December, and baptised[1] Sunday 9 December.

1581 Robert Eyles, second son of Richard Eyles *alias* Hicks of Deptford, husbandman, and of Maud his wife, born Wednesday 12 December, baptised Friday 14 December.

1582 John Patient, third son of Henry Patient, yeoman, now the farmer of the manor of Deptford, and of Joan his wife, born Tuesday 8 January, baptised Sunday 13 January.

1583 These eight baptisms were conducted in this year 1621
By John Lee, Bachelor of Divinity, rector; Thomas Crockford, Bachelor of Arts etc, assistant; John Lee the younger, Bachelor of Arts, curate; John Selwood of Deptford, married, and John Locke of Wylye again, unmarried, husbandmen, churchwardens.

1622/3

1584 Cecily Gamlin, — daughter[2] of Nicholas Gamlin of Wylye, labourer, and of Mary his wife, born Saturday 6 April, baptised Sunday 7 April.

1585 Anne Baker, second daughter of Robert Baker *alias* Chate of Wylye, woodworker, and of Mary his wife, born Tuesday 9 April, baptised Wednesday 10 April.

1586 Edward Wadland, firstborn son of Thomas Wadland, of Wylye, labourer, and of Edith his wife, born and baptised Monday 3 June.

1587 James Locke, firstborn son of Robert Locke, of Wylye, labourer or husbandman, and of Jane his wife, born Saturday 22 June, baptised Sunday 23 June.

---

1   *baptizat' fuit* has been inadvertently omitted
2   a space follows *filia*

1588 Arthur Brian, firstborn son of John Brian, of Deptford, brewer,[1] and of Joan his wife, born Monday 15 July, baptised Wednesday 17 July.

1589 Eleanor Barnes, firstborn daughter of John Barnes of Wylye, husbandman, and of Elizabeth his wife, born Friday 26 July, baptised Sunday 28 July.

1590 Frances Selwood, firstborn daughter of Thomas Selwood, of Deptford, labourer, and of Frances his wife, born Tuesday 17 September, baptised Sunday 22 September.

1591 Thomas Hughes, firstborn son of William Hughes, *alias* Clearke, of Wylye, tailor, and of Joan his wife, born Monday 23 September, baptised Tuesday 24 September.

1592 Margaret Coales, third daughter of William Coales, *alias* Hart, of Deptford, labourer, and of Agnes his wife, born Monday 28 October, baptised Friday 1 November.

1593 Edward Smyth, firstborn son of Edward Smyth the younger of Wylye, labourer, and of Alice his wife, born Sunday 10 November, baptised Wednesday 13 November.

1594 John Smyth, firstborn son of Christopher Smyth, of Deptford, butcher etc, from Eleanor his second wife, born Friday 6 December, baptised Sunday 8 December.

1595 Philip Bush, firstborn son of Philip Bush of Deptford, shepherd, and of Margery his wife, born Sunday 29 December, baptised the following Wednesday, 1 January.

1596 William Titford, firstborn son of William Titford, of Wylye, shepherd, and of Rachel his wife, born Sunday 9 February, baptised Wednesday 12 February.

1597 Joan Eyles, second daughter of John Eyles, *alias* Hicks, of Wylye, husbandman, and of Cecily his wife, the earlier, larger, and stronger of twins, born Friday 7 March, etc, baptised in the church at a public baptism on Saturday 8 March.

1   *cervisiarii*

1598 Cecily Eyles, third daughter of that same John and Cecily his wife, the later, smaller and weaker of those twins, born on that same Friday etc, and baptised privately at home the same night by the hands of the pastor of this congregation, Friday 7 March.

1599 Jane Spring, firstborn daughter of David Spring, *alias* Kent, of Wylye, labourer, and of Christian his wife, born Sunday 23 March, baptised Monday 24 March.

1600 These sixteen Baptisms were served in this year 1622
By John Lee the Elder, Bachelor of Divinity etc, rector; John Lee the younger, Bachelor of Arts, fully a Priest, curate; Thomas Kent of Deptford, yeoman; John Taylor of Wylye street, husbandman and brewer,[1] churchwardens.

1623/4

1601 Edward Kent, fourth son of Richard Kent of Wylye, husbandman, and of Susan his wife, born Thursday 27 March, baptised Saturday 29 March.

1602 Mary Locke, third daughter of John Locke of Wylye, labourer, etc, and of Joan his wife, born Monday 4 May, baptised the Sunday next following, 11 May.

1603 Richard Wayle, second son of Richard Wayle of Wylye, sieve-maker, and of Margaret his wife, born Friday 16 May, baptised Sunday 18 May.

1604 Joan Hobbes, fourth daughter of Thomas Hobbes of Wylye, labourer, and of Alice his wife, born Wednesday 4 June, baptised Sunday the feast of the Holy Trinity, 8 June.

1605 Joan Smyth, firstborn daughter of Thomas Smyth of Wylye, husbandman, and of Anne his wife, born Tuesday 10 June, baptised Sunday 15 June.

1606 Honor Potticarie, firstborn daughter of Thomas Potticarie, of

1   *cervisiario*

Wylye, husbandman, and of Catherine his wife, born Friday 27 June, baptised Sunday the feast of St Peter, 29 June.

1607 Elizabeth Hilman, firstborn daughter of John Hillman of Wylye, husbandman and tailor, and of Edith his wife, born Wednesday 29 October, baptised Sunday 2 November.

1608 Maud Henwood, second daughter of Hugh Henwood of Deptford, blacksmith, and of Maud his wife, born Wednesday 5 November, baptised Sunday 9 November.

1609 William Wadland, second son of Thomas Wadland of Wylye, labourer, and of Edith his wife, born Sunday 14 December, baptised Sunday 21 December.

1610 Mary Gullyfoord, second daughter of Maurice Gullyford of Deptford, labourer, and of Mary his wife, born Wednesday 4 February, baptised the Sunday before Lent,[1] 8 February.

1611 Jane Locke, fourth daughter of Robert Locke, of Wylye, now a husbandman, and of Jane his wife, born Thursday 12 February, baptised the first Sunday in Lent, 15 February.

1612 David Connerike, firstborn son of David Connerike, by nationality an Irishman, by condition a servant, etc, and of Joan Wadland his wife, born Wednesday, the feast of Matthew, 25 February, baptised the third Sunday in Lent, 29 February.

1613 These twelve baptisms were conducted in this year 1623
By John Lee the elder, Bachelor of Divinity, etc, rector; John Lee the younger, Bachelor of Arts, priest, curate; Joel Gyrdler of Wylye mill, clothier, and John Hillman of Wylye, husbandman and tailor, churchwardens.

1624/5

1614 John Barnes, firstborn son of John Barnes, of Wylye, husbandman, and one of the churchwardens for this year, etc, and of Elizabeth his wife, born Tuesday 8 June, baptised Sunday 13 June.

1   *in carnisprivio*

1615 Joan Patient, fourth daughter of Henry Patient of Deptford manor, yeoman, and of Joan his wife, born Tuesday[1] 22 June, baptised Sunday, etc, 27 June.

1616 Mary Hill, third daughter of William Hill of Wylye, now a husbandman, etc, and of Grace his wife, born Thursday 22 June, baptised Sunday, and also the feast of James, 25 July.

1617 John Potticarie, first-born son of Guy Potticarie of Wylye, yeoman, and of Margery his wife, born Wednesday 18 August, baptised Tuesday, the feast of Bartholomew, 24 August.

1618 John Gamlin, second son of Nicholas Gamlin of Wylye, labourer, and of Mary his wife, born Thursday 2 September and baptised Sunday, etc, 5 September.

1619 John Hughes, second son of William Hughes *alias* Clearke of Wylye, now a tailor, and of Joan his wife, born Saturday 20 November, baptised on Advent Sunday 28 November.

1620 Thomas Long, first-born son of Edward Long *alias* Longynough of Wylye, tiler, and of Christian his wife, born Sunday, etc, 26 December, baptised Saturday 1 January.

1621 Edith Hobbes, fifth daughter of Thomas Hobbes of Wylye, labourer, and of Alice his wife, born Monday, etc, 27 December, baptised the following day, Tuesday, etc, 28 December.

1622 Alice Baker, third daughter of Robert Baker, *alias* Chate, of Wylye, woodworker, and of Mary his wife, born Wednesday 29 December, baptised the Saturday aforesaid, 1 January.

1623 These nine baptisms were conducted in this year 1624
By John Lee the elder, Bachelor of Divinity, rector; John Lee the younger, Bachelor of Arts etc, curate; Edward Smyth of Wylye the elder, husbandman, and John Barnes of Wylye, husbandman, churchwardens.

---

1   *die die Martis*, the repetition is presumably a mistake

1625/6

1624 Joan Covey, fourth daughter of William Covey of Deptford, yeoman, and of Eleanor his wife, born Saturday 26 March, baptised Sunday 27 March.

1625 John Furnell, second son of Richard Furnell of Wylye, labourer, and of Jane his wife, born Tuesday 29 March, baptised Friday 1 April.

1626 Edith Hillman, second daughter of John Hillman of Wylye, tailor etc, and of Edith his wife, born Friday 13 May, baptised Sunday 15 May.

1627 Robert Sutton, first son of John Sutton of Wylye, ploughwright, and of Susan his wife, born and baptised Sunday 22 May.

1628 Grace Smyth, second daughter of Thomas Smyth of Wylye, husbandman, and of Anne his wife, born and baptised Sunday, the feast of the Holy Trinity, 12 June.

1629 Christopher Potticarie, firstborn son of Thomas Potticarie of Wylye, husbandman, and of Catherine his wife, born Saturday 13 August, baptised Sunday, the ninth after Trinity, 14 August.

1630 Hugh Coales, fourth son of William Coales, *alias* Hart, of Deptford, labourer, and of Agnes his wife, born Monday 22 August, baptised Wednesday, the Feast of St Bartholomew, 24 August.

1631 Elizabeth Smyth, the third daughter of Edward Smyth of Wylye, labourer, and of Alice his wife, born on Sunday the 28 August, baptised on Sunday 4 September.

1632 Christopher and Jane Davies, infant twins, the first son and first daughter of Robert Davies of Gillingham,[1] Dorset, yeoman and of Melior his wife, born Tuesday 6 September in the house of Guy Everley of Wylye, yeoman. The girl being extremely weak was baptised in a private baptism the same day, as speedily as could be, The boy being stronger was baptised in a public baptism the next day, to wit Wednesday 7 September.

1633 Richard Furnell, third son of William Furnell of Wylye, husbandman,

1   *Guillingham*

and of Lettice his wife, born Wednesday 5 October, baptised Sunday 9 October.

1634 Bridget[1] Conrike, first daughter of David Conrike, Irishman, now of Wylye, labourer, and of Joan his wife, born Thursday 6 October, baptised also on Sunday, 9 October.

1635 Christopher Henwood, second son of Hugh Henwood of Deptford, blacksmith,[2] and of Maud his wife, born at Deptford on Tuesday 13 December, baptised at Fisherton on Sunday 18 December, since the excessive swelling of the waters from melting snow threw down the bridges and breached the footpath to Wylye.[3]

1636 Robert Locke, second son of Robert Locke, of Wylye, husbandman, and of Jane his wife, born Tuesday 3 January, baptised Wednesday 4 January.

1637 Richard Titford, second son of William Titford of Wylye, shepherd, and of Rachel his wife, born the same Tuesday 3 January, baptised Sunday 8 January.

1638 Guy Potticarie, second son of Guy Potticarie of Wylye manor, yeoman, and of Catherine his wife, born Saturday 4 February, baptised Sunday 5 February.

1639 These sixteen baptisms were conducted in this year 1625
By John Lee Bachelor of Divinity, rector; Thomas Crockford Bachelor of Arts, assistant; John Lee Bachelor of Arts, priest and John White, priest, curates; William Locke and Thomas Potticarie of Wylye, husbandmen, churchwardens.

1626/7

1640 Margaret Patient, fifth daughter of Henry Patient of Deptford manor, yeoman, and of Joan his wife, born Friday 16 June, baptised Sunday 18 June.

1 *Brigeda*
2 *operarii* has been altered to *fabri-ferrii*
3 *quando quidem aquarum nimius ex nive liquefacta tumor pontes disiecerat iterq'*
    pedestre ad Wiliam abruperat

1641 William Bush, second son of Philip Bush of Deptford, shepherd, and of Margery his wife, born Friday 4 August, baptised Sunday 6 August.

1642 Sarah Harvey, fourth daughter of John Harvey of Wylye, husbandman, and of Mary his wife, born Thursday 10 August, baptised Sunday 13 August.

1643 Eleanor Kent, — daughter[1] of Richard Kent, of Wylye, husbandman, and of Susan his wife, born Friday 15 September, baptised Sunday 17 September.

1644 William Paradise, firstborn son of Humphrey Paradise of Wylye, but from Wilton, weaver, and of Mary his wife, born Tuesday 19 September, baptised Sunday 24 September.[2]

1645 Joan Spring, second daughter of David Spring, *alias* Kent, of Wylye, labourer, and of Christian his wife, born Friday 22 September, baptised the aforesaid Sunday 24 September.

1646 Joan Barnes, second daughter of John Barnes of Wylye, husbandman, and of Elizabeth his wife, born Monday 9 October, baptised Sunday 15 October.

1647 Henry Baker, illegitimate son of Susan Baker of Wylye a poor servant woman etc, born and baptised Sunday 22 October.

1648 Susan Potticary, illegitimate daughter of Amy Potticarie of Wylye, girl of a freeholding family, etc,[3] born Monday 23 October, baptised Friday 27 October.

1649 John Locke, third son of John Locke of Wylye, now a husbandman, and of Joan his wife, born Sunday 5 November, baptised the following Sunday, 12 November.

---

1   a space follows *filia*
2   Following this entry is a marginal sum which subtracts 1626 from 1697 and arrives at 71
3   *puellae ingenuae etc*

1650 Frances Furnell, third[1] daughter of William Furnell of Wylye, husbandman, and of Lettice his wife, born Sunday 3 December, baptised the following Sunday, 10 December.

1651 James Sutton, second son of John Sutton of Wylye, ploughwright, and of Susan his wife, born Saturday 24 February, baptised Sunday 25 February.

1652 These twelve baptisms were conducted in this year 1626
By John Lee Bachelor of Divinity, rector; John White priest, curate; Thomas Crockford Bachelor of Arts, assistant; James Rebecke of Wylye, but from Bapton, and William Hill of Wylye manor, husbandmen, churchwardens.

1627/8

1653 John Wadland, third son of Thomas Wadland of Wylye, labourer, and of Edith his wife, born Tuesday 10 April, baptised Wednesday 11 April.

1654 Elizabeth Conrike, second daughter of David Conrike of Wylye, labourer, and of Joan his wife, born Tuesday 12 June, baptised Wednesday 13 June.

1655 Jane Scammell, first daughter of Thomas Scammell of Deptford, labourer, and of Mary his wife, born Thursday 14 June, baptised Sunday 17 June.

1656 Joan Potticarie, second daughter of Thomas Potticarie of Wylye manor, husbandman, and of Catherine his wife, born Wednesday, the feast of St James the Apostle,[2] baptised Sunday 29 July.

1657 Martha Smyth, third daughter of Thomas Smyth of Wylye, husbandman, and of Agnes his wife, born Saturday 11 August, baptised Sunday 12 August.

1658 Richard Eyles, third son of Richard Eyles, *alias* Hickes, of Deptford, yeoman, and of Maud his wife, born Friday 31 August, baptised Sunday 2 September.

1   *tertia* altered from *secunda*
2   25 July

1659 William Potticarie, third son of Guy Potticarie of Wylye manor, yeoman, and of Margery his wife, born Friday 12 October, baptised Sunday 14 October.

1660 Another Robert Locke, third son of Robert Locke of Wylye manor, husbandman, but the first son of Robert and of Archillis or else (as she is commonly called) Artillis, his second wife, born[1] — , baptised Sunday 21 October.

1661 John Hillman, third son of John Hillman of Wylye, tailor etc, and of Edith, his wife, born Monday 22 October, baptised Sunday 28 October.

1662 William Covey, the second[2] son of William Covey of Deptford, yeoman, and of Eleanor his wife, born Thursday 25 October, baptised the same Sunday, 28 October.

1663 Henry Hobbes, third son of Thomas Hobbes of Wylye, labourer, and of Alice his wife, born Saturday 27 October, baptised the same Sunday, 28 October.

1664 Sarah Denmead, daughter unlawfully conceived of William Denmead *alias* Coldpie, formerly of Langford, now of Wylye, labourer, and of Elizabeth Longynough, who was his little prostitute,[3] now (as she becomes)[4] his wife, born Sunday 9 December, baptised Monday 10 December.

1665 John Smyth, second son of Edward Smyth of Wylye, husbandman, and of Alice his wife, born Friday the feast of St Thomas the Apostle,[5] baptised the following Sunday, 23 December.

1666 Hugh Gamlin, third son of Nicholas Gamlin of Wylye, labourer, and of Mary his Wife, born Friday 8 February, baptised Sunday 10 February.

1667 John Paradise, second son of Humphrey Paradise of Wylye, weaver,

1   a space is left and no date given
2   *tertius* has been crossed out
3   *meretricula*
4   *ut fit*
5   21 December

and of Mary his wife, born Friday 29 February, baptised Sunday 2 March.

1668 These fifteen baptisms were conducted in this year 1627
By John Lee Bachelor of Divinity, rector; John White, priest, curate; Thomas Crockford of Arts etc, priest, assistant; Anthony Ballard of Wylye, but from Bapton, and Henry Patient of Deptford manor, yeomen, churchwardens.

1628/9

1669 Agnes Coales, fourth daughter of William Coales, *alias* Hart, of Deptford, shepherd, and of Agnes his wife, born Saturday 5 April, baptised Palm Sunday 6 April.

1670 John Henwood, third son of Hugh Henwood of Deptford, blacksmith, and of Maud his wife, born Saturday 21 June, baptised Tuesday, the feast of Saint John the Baptist, 24 June.

1671 John Moonday, firstborn son of John Moonday of Wylye, fuller, and of Martha his wife, born Wednesday 13 August, baptised Sunday 17 August.

1672 Edith Titford, second daughter of William Titford of Wylye, shepherd, and of Rachel his wife, born Tuesday 4 November, baptised Sunday 9 November.

1673 Elizabeth Barnes, third daughter of John Barnes of Wylye, yeoman, one of the churchwardens for this year, and of Elizabeth his wife, born Wednesday 19 November,[1] baptised Sunday 23 November.[2]

1674 Jerome Potticarie, firstborn son of Nicholas Potticarie of Wylye, yeoman, etc, and of Bridget his wife, born and baptised Sunday 7 December.

1675 Elizabeth Scammell, second daughter of Thomas Scammell of Deptford, labourer, and of Mary his wife, born Ash Wednesday,[3] 18 February, baptised the first Sunday in Lent, 22 February.

1 corrected from 18 November
2 *secundo* has been over-written by *tertio*
3 *cinericeo*, corrected from *carnisprivio*

1676 Thomas Haytor, firstborn son of Richard Haytor of Wylye, tailor, and of Mary his wife, born Tuesday 10 March, baptised Saturday 14 March.

1677 Jane Potticarie, first daughter of Guy Potticarie of Wylye manor, yeoman, one of the churchwardens for this year, and of Margery his wife, born Tuesday 24 March, 1628, baptised Wednesday, the feast of the Incarnation, 1629.[1]

1678 These nine births occurred, but eight baptisms (see above) were conducted in this year 1628
By John Lee Bachelor of Divinity etc, rector; John White priest, curate; Thomas Crockford of Arts etc, priest, assistant; Guy Potticarie and John Barnes, yeomen, churchwardens.

1629/30

1679 Richard Tilley, firstborn son of Richard Tillie now of Deptford manor, but from Erlestoke,[2] tailor, and of Mary his wife, born at Deptford on Saturday 21 March 1628. He was baptised at Fisherton on account of flooding of the waters between Deptford and Wylye (more on this is to be seen in the Fisherton register)[3] on Thursday 26 March 1629.

1680 Anne Spring, second daughter of David Spring, *alias* Kent, of Wylye, labourer, and of Christian his wife, born Easter Sunday, 5 April, baptised the Monday in Easter week, 6 April.

1681 Eleanor Long, *alias* Longynough, first daughter of Edward Long, *alias* Longynough, of Wylye, tiler, and of Christian his wife, born Friday 17 April, baptised Sunday 19 April.

Subsequent baptism entries in this register, 1629-35, are written in English in a different hand, and in Latin, 1636-54, when the sequence ends.

---

1   25 March (1629)
2   *Stoake Com'*
3   *prout etiam videre est in registro Fishertonia*

Burials

conducted with due ceremony partly in the church and partly in the graveyard of Wylye in the county of Wiltshire, from the year of the Incarnation 1581, and thereafter.

1581/2

1682 Thomas Clearke, buried 3 April.

1683 John Selin, buried 28 February.

1684 John Selin, brother of the same, also buried 28 February.

1685 James Sanger, buried 3 March.

1582/3

1686 William Baker, son of Thomas Baker the younger, buried 11 June.

1583/4

1687 Maud Smyth, buried 17 June.

1688 Thomas Mascall, buried 20 July.

1689 Prudence Smyth, buried 17 October.

1690 Julian Locke, buried 28 September.

1584/5

1691 Edward Smyth the elder, buried 13 July.

1692 Alexander Smyth, buried 25 July.

1693 Mary Moonday, buried 23 October.

1694 Thomas Gullyford, buried 25 October.

1695 —, the wife[1] of Thomas Gullyford, buried 16 November.

1696 William Selin, buried 25 November.

1697 John Bar, buried 6 December.

1698 John Baker, buried 10 December.

1585/6

1699 Joan Freestone, buried 14 June.

1700 Elizabeth Oliver, buried 15 July.

1701 Giles Mathewe, buried 25 July.

1702 William Mascall, buried 25 November.

1703 John Moore, buried 7 January.

1704 Agnes Moore, buried 17 January.

1705 Christian Harries, buried 24 February.

1586/7

1706 Christian Wornell, buried 13 July.

1707 Philip Oliver, buried 10 June.

1708 Philip Spring, buried 14 August.

1587/8

1709 Philip Ayles, buried 20 June.

1710 Dorothy Taylour, buried 30 July.

1   A space is left for the forename

1711 Margery Ayles, buried —.[1]

1712 William White, buried 25 August.

1588/9

1713 Honor Potticarie, buried 23 May.

1714 Agnes Locke, daughter of Martin Lock, buried 24 May.

1589/90

1715 Philip Ayles, buried 7 August.

1716 Dorothy Baker, buried 6 March.

1590/1 [no entries]

1591/2

1717 Sibyl Baker, buried 8 June.

1718 Catherine Baker, buried 12 August.

1592/3

1719 Bathalin Smyth, buried 29 June.

1720 Guy Stiffe, buried 2 July.

1721 Maud Selin, buried 13 March.

1593/4

1722 Robert Bellie, buried 27 March.

1723 Catherine Hillman, buried 4 April.

1   no date is given

1724 Joan Stiffe, buried 19 April.

1594/5

1725 John Cullymore, buried 15 June.

1726 Joan Harries, buried 29 June.

1595/6

1727 George Harries, buried 8 May.

1728 Thomas Moonday, buried 10 May.

1729 Christian Locke, buried 22 August.

1730 Margaret Wayle, buried 20 September.

1731 Martin Locke, buried 9 October.

1732 Edith Holloway, buried 16 October.

1733 Richard Barnes, buried 17 October.

1734 Richard Taylour, buried 15 January.

1596/7

1735 Catherine Scarlet, buried 29 April.

1736 Alice Cox, buried 10 January.

1737 Roger Peareman, buried 16 January.

1738 Alice Peareman, buried 24 January.

1597/8

1739 Robert Idney, buried 24 April.

1740 Henry Clearke, buried 2 May.

1741 John Potticarie, buried 8 May.

1742 William Wandsborrough, buried 22 May.

1743 Jane Selin, buried 28 May.

1744 Richard Baker, buried 2 October.

1745 Susan Smyth, buried 4 October.

1746 Mary Baker, buried 14 October.

1747 Richard Cullymore, buried 20 November.

1748 Richard Mabill, buried 3 January.

1749 Susan Mabill, wife of the same Richard, buried 16 January.

1750 Elizabeth Hillman, buried 13 February.

1751 William Smyth, buried 1 March.

1598/9

1752 Melior Bowles, buried 25 March.

1753 Anne Baker, buried 3 April.

1754 Joan Skine, buried 6 April.

1755 William Bower, son of David, buried 25 June.

1756 John Smyth, buried 3 July.

1599/1600 [no entries]

1600/1

1757 Robert Lock, buried 24 April.

1601/2

1758 Richard Smyth, son of Christopher Smyth, buried 5 July.

1759 Alice Burt, widow, buried 6 July.

1602/3

1760 Richard Harries, buried 3 June.

1761 Margery Longynough wife of David Longeynough tiler,[1] buried 3 July.

1762 John Smyth, buried 2 January.

1603/4

1763 Richard Wandsborrough of — ,[2] buried 9 April.

1764 Joan Bakere, buried 19 April.

1765 John Oliver, buried 25 May.

1766 Brian Rawlins, buried 29 May.

1767 Joan Potticarie, wife of William Potticarie of Wylye, yeoman etc, buried 29 May.

1768 John Harries, buried 27 May.

1769 Elizabeth Bower etc, wife of Thomas Bower, rector of this church etc, buried 7 August.

1770 Thomas Chate, buried 18 August.

1   'tiler' is written in English
2   a space is left, and no place given

1771 Alexander Card, buried 20 August.

1772 Joan Mathewe, buried 28 August.

1773 John Mathew, buried 30 August.

1774 John Clearke, buried 1 September.

1775 William Card, buried 4 September.

1776 David Bower of Wylye, brewer etc, buried 8 September.

1777 Elizabeth —,[1] servant of the same David, buried 21 September.

1778 John Barnes of Deptford, buried 23 September.

1779 William Crutchel, buried 30 September.

1780 William Barnes of Wylye, buried 10 October.

1781 William Baker of — ,[2] buried 29 October.

1782 Edith Barnes, buried 4 November.

1783 John Baker, buried 12 December.

1784 Joan Potticarie of Wylye, widow, very elderly head of household, etc,[3] descended from the gentry family of the Topps of Stockton, died at the end of February, and buried in the choir of Stockton church aforesaid, near to her husband, 1 March.

1785 Alice Wadland, buried —.[4]

1786 Memorandum that a plague in the Autumn of 1603 is said to have carried off certain of these.

1 a space is left, but no surname given
2 a space is left, and no place given
3 *materfamilias perantiqua etc*
4 no date is given

1604–5 [no entries][1]

1606/7

1787 Christian Moonday, wife of Robert Moonday of — ,[2] buried 21 July.

1788 Michael Selwood, firstborn son of John Selwood, now of Deptford, tailor, and of Jane his wife, buried 28 June.[3]

1789 John Pierson, buried 29 July.

1607/8 [no entries]

1608/9

1790 Edith Steevens of — ,[4] widow, buried 1 April.

1791 Margaret Nightingale of — ,[5] buried 11 May.

1792 Thomas Spring, son of Henry Spring of Wylye the younger, buried 20 September.

1793 Margaret Potticarie, a very small infant daughter of John Potticarie of Wylye, clothier, and of Eleanor his wife, buried — March.[6]

1609/10

1794 Alice Oliver, buried 4 April.

1795 Alice Newman, buried 5 June.

1796 Edward Smyth, buried 6 July.

1   a later hand has written here in English 'Lord have mercy on us for Chst's sake'
2   a space is left, and no place given
3   this entry is out of sequence, unless July is intended
4   a space is left, and no place given
5   a space is left, and no place given
6   a space is left, but no date given

1797 Robert Moonday, buried 28 December.

1798 Edward Imber of Deptford, husbandman etc, buried 8 January.

1799 Agnes Steevens, buried 16 February.

1800 John Gullyford, buried 18 March.

1801 Guy Cullymore, buried 24 March.

1610/11

1802 Thomas Cleark, buried 27 March.

1803 Olive Locke, buried 22 July.

1804 Eleanor Everley, wife of John Everley, of Wylye, yeoman, buried 2 November.

1611/12

1805 John Selwood, a little boy, second son of John Selwood of Deptford, tailor and husbandman at the same time, and of Jane his wife, buried 25 August.

1806 Mary Pierson, daughter of John Pierson, *alias* Taylour, of Wylye, husbandman etc, buried 20 February.

1612/13

1807 John Baker, son of Thomas Baker of Wylye, buried 9 April.

1808 John Rocksborrough,[1] son of John Rocksborrough of Deptford, but from Stockton, shepherd etc, buried 6 May.

1809 Joan Rocksborrough, daughter of the same Rocksborrough etc, buried 8 May.

1 This surname is given as Rexby in the bishop's transcript relating to this and the following entry

1810 Margaret Idney, buried 10 March.

1811 Margaret Steevens, buried 24 March.

1613/14

1812 George Mabil of Wylye, a poor elderly man etc, buried 26 March.

1813 John Smyth, buried 23 June.

1814 John Eyles, *alias* Hicks, of Wylye street, husbandman etc, buried 20 August.

1815 Agnes Kent, wife of Thomas Kent of Deptford, yeoman, from the freeholding family of May of Langford etc, buried 11 September.

1816 Elizabeth Taylor, —[1]

1817 Bridget Lake, —[2]

1818 Christian Baker, buried 16 October.

1819 Alice Eyles, *alias* Hicks, widow, relict of the aforesaid John Hicks etc, buried 1 February.

1614/15

1820 Elizabeth Bower, a girl,[3] third daughter of Thomas Bower, rector of this church, and of Elizabeth his previous wife, deceased, buried 4 May.

1821 Mary Potticarie, firstborn daughter of John Potticarie of Wylye, clothier etc, and of Eleanor his wife, buried 30 June.

1822 Joan Starre, daughter of Thomas Starre, *alias* Warminster, of Wylye, tailor, and of his wife —,[4] buried 22 August.

1   no date given
2   no date given
3   *puella*
4   a space is left, but no name given

1823 Matthew Locke, — son[1] of Martin Locke, formerly of Wylye, deceased etc, and of Joan his wife, etc, buried 27 August.

1824 Eleanor Furnell, wife of William Furnell, of Wylye, husbandman, buried 26 November.

1825 John Dewe of Wylye, husbandman, head of a household, buried 2 January.

1826 Elizabeth Smyth, widow, relict of — Smyth,[2] buried 8 February.

1827 Eleanor Cuddimore, widow, relict of — Cuddimore,[3] buried 25 February.

1828 Christobel Cuddimor, buried 26 February.

1829 Judith Patient, — daughter[4] of Henry Patient, now of Wylye, husbandman, and of Joan his wife, buried 2 March.

1830 Anne Selwood, — daughter[5] of John Selwood, of Deptford, cobbler[6] and husbandman, and of Jane his wife, buried 7 March.

1615–16 [no entries]

1617/18[7]

1831 William Potticarie, of Wylye, yeoman, begetter by two wives of many children, peacefully fell asleep in Christ, and was buried in the choir of the church 27 February.

---

1   a space is left before *filius*
2   spaces are left for the husband's forename and place
3   spaces are left for the husband's forename and place
4   a space is left after *filia*
5   a space is left after *filia*
6   *sutor'* (not followed by *vestiarii*, which would signify a tailor)
7   a space is left before the entries for 1617, suggesting that the entries have been copied from another register, from which the page detailing 1615, 1616 and the first part of 1617 was missing

1832 Eleanor Potticarie, wife of John Potticarie of Wylye gentleman, troubled mother of many children, piously and peacefully died and was buried in the church 4 March.

1833 Before these two last burials there were given two holy addresses[1] by the Reverend Thomas Bower, rector of this church.

1618/19

1834 Edith Bellie, a little elderly woman of 80 years, etc, wife of Henry Belly of Wylye, husbandman, a truly old man, etc, died 14 June, buried 15 June.

1835 Catherine Baker, a poor little elderly woman, wife of Thomas Baker, *alias* Chate of Wylye, the younger, though in years the elder,[2] a poor little man, died 15 September, buried 16 September.

1836 Anne Bower, gentlewoman, born into the family of the Husseys, esquires of Edmondsham,[3] Dorset, was firstly wife of a certain Thomas Virgin, gentleman, of Dorset. Then with his decease after various troubles endured by her in Ireland, Wales, and finally in Ireland by both land and sea, she was secondly married as the second wife of the Reverend Thomas Bower, rector of this church. She was a lady of truly tender mercy for the poor and of most praiseworthy name, mother of four sons by Virgin and of one by Bower, all of whom she leaves surviving her. She died on Sunday 15 November, about 55 years old (as we may arrive at by reckoning), and was buried in the choir of the church on Wednesday 18 November.

1837 John Locke a little infant, — son[4] of John Locke of Wylye, labourer, and of Joan his wife, born 28 November, baptised 30 November, died and buried 13 January.

1838 Henry Spring, *alias* Kent, an elderly man 70 years old, of Wylye, formerly a husbandman, of very good standing among his neighbours, But before his death (for such is the fickleness of human affairs) he was

---

1   *conciones*
2   *vita tamen senior'*
3   *Edemundsham*
4   a space is left after *filius*

reduced by a changing fortune to lamentable poverty, He died 17 February, buried 18 February.

1839 Reverend Thomas Bower, rector of this church, of whose life these stages have been discovered. He was born in the town of Mere, offspring of a freeholding family there, educated in the liberal arts from boyhood by the outstanding innate care of his parents. He accomplished his studies, so that step by step he moved on towards distinguished places. While still a young man he entered service in the post of secretary[1] to the splendid prelate John Pierce, then bishop of Salisbury. At Christ Church,[2] Oxford, he achieved both degrees in Arts. Bidding farewell to the Academy, he returned to the aforesaid bishop and took the holy orders of a minister.

He obtained the rectory of the church of Pentridge in Dorset,[3] and through his lord the aforesaid bishop he held for some time a post as domestic chaplain[4] at the court of Queen Elizabeth of happy memory. Meanwhile, because he came into favour with the most noble Henry, earl of Pembroke, he was admitted to receive this rectory of Wylye, and so that he could lawfully retain both benefices, within the Pembroke circle,[5] he was now (as it fully appears)[6] enrolled as one of the chaplains of the Honourable Edward, earl of Hertford. Leaving behind the household of the court, he turned his attention to the countryside and his private affairs through his spirit and intelligence.[7]

He married two wives in succession, both very dignified ladies,[8] remembered above, by whom he gained five children, Samuel and James, sons, and Susan, Honor, and Elizabeth. He was a man of happy natural talents, with abundant learning, many-faceted knowledge, fluent eloquence, reverent dignity, wise through long experience of affairs,[9] full of careful advice from his continual experience of business, and (to express it in a word) equipped with almost all the endowments of nature and art. To him there seemed nothing lacking from the desired happiness of his

1   *loco amanuensis iuvenis adhuc inservit*
2   *Aede Christi*
3   *Pentrigianiae in agro Dorsettensi ecclesiae rectoriam*
4   *sacellani loco familiare*
5   *Pembrochiano numero*: the intended meaning is not entirely clear
6   *(ut videtu' pleno)*
7   *ruri se, et privatis institutis, pro genio suo et ingenio addixit*
8   *matronas gravissimas*
9   *longo reru' usu prudens*

worldly life apart from repose from his business. Of what remained he gave up his soul to God, his body to the earth, and his positions to his successors; and he peacefully fell asleep in Christ on Tuesday 23 February, about one o'clock in the afternoon. He was 65 years old, as he himself calculated not long before death.

And there is moreover one other matter which we feel it not unworthy to add by way of observation. Like a good shepherd, his care ended, the follower of his sheep brought together by his faith in Christ, finally this year he went to join the Lord's flocks in heaven.[1] He was buried in the choir of his church of Wylye at the hands of — Ingram,[2] curate of Pentridge church, after a holy funeral address[3] by his neighbour and devoted assistant Thomas Crockford, vicar of Fisherton.

1840 There were these six funerals in the year 1618, the last that of Thomas Bower, rector.
[Conducted] by Thomas Crockford, for almost the whole year assistant; Richard Kent of Wylye, husbandman, William Hoskins of Wylye, weaver, and Nicholas Potticary of Wylye, yeoman, churchwardens.

1619/20

1841 Richard Rives, a young unmarried labourer, etc, servant of Richard Eyles *alias* Hicks of Deptford, husbandman, died Sunday 31 October, buried Monday 1 November.

1842 Reginald Crosse, infant first son of Henry Crosse of Wylye, labourer and of Dorothy his wife, died and buried on Thursday 18 November.

1843 Henry Bellie of Wylye, an elderly husbandman and widower, retired, almost 90 years old (as may be reckoned), died Monday 26 December and buried Tuesday 27 December.

1844 Thomas Hillman, firstborn son of John Hillman of Wylye, tailor,[4] and of Edith his wife, an infant evidently new-born, died Thursday 20

1   *Sicut bonus pastor, cura defunctu, oves Christi fidei suae com'issas, secuuto', ultimo hoc anno, ad D'mini greges in caelum co'migravit.* The sentiment, if not the syntax, is evident.
2   a space is left for the forename
3   *contionem*
4   *vestiarii* (here not prefixed by the usual *sutorii*)

January, buried Friday 21 January.

1845 Thomas Starre *alias* Warminster of Wylye, tailor, head of a household, almost 53 years old, father of three sons by one wife who survives him, died Saturday 5 February, buried Sunday 6 February.

1846 There were these five burials in the year 1619, being the first year of the rectory of John Lee, Bachelor of Divinity, who was lawfully inducted on Monday 5 April at the hands of Thomas Crockford, vicar of Fisherton, assistant; George Ditten, Scholar of Oxford, curate; John Locke of Wylye, married, and William Cleark of Wylye, unmarried, husbandmen, churchwardens.

1620/1

1847 Alice Crutchill, a poor little old woman etc, wife or widow of a certain labourer, John Crutchill, late of Wylye but who absconded; she died and was buried on Monday 27 March.

1848 Ralph Henwood, a new-born infant, firstborn son of Hugh Henwood of Wylye, blacksmith, and of Maud, his wife, died and buried on Thursday 6 April.

1849 Emma Young (commonly called Emma Barter) of Wylye, a poor little old widow, more than 80 years old etc, died Sunday 14 May, buried Monday 15 May.

1850 Thomas Wayle of Wylye, an elderly weaver and poor widower more than 60 years old etc, died Wednesday 7 June, buried Thursday 8 June.

1851 Thomas Baker, *alias* Chate, of Wylye, a poor widower, by trade a blacksmith, by condition an almsman, the younger of two brothers of the same name, though he himself was elderly, almost 70 years old. He died Saturday 10 June, and was buried on Sunday, the feast of the Trinity, 11 June.

1852 Elizabeth Furnell, a feeble[1] little elderly woman, wife of Humphrey Furnell of Wylye, an elderly husbandman. She was descended from the

1   *decrepita*

Larkhams of Ufton in Berkshire, died on Sunday 16 July, buried Monday 17 July.

1853 An infant without forename, first daughter of John Dewe of Wylye, blacksmith, and of Honor his wife. Born on Wednesday 27 September, she was unexpectedly taken by death without the sacrament of the font, died and was buried Thursday 28 September.

1854 William Vallies, *alias* Wise, of Wylye, a poor unmarried almsman 70 years old more or less, died Sunday 24 December, buried Monday 25 December, the Nativity of the Lord Himself.

1855 Jane and Millicent Lock, infant twin daughters of Robert Locke of Wylye, labourer, and of Jane his wife, were born, baptised, died and were buried on Tuesday 6 February.

1856 Martha Lee, wife of John Lee, rector of this Church etc. She was raised, etc, in the city of Oxford, a woman almost 36 years old, mother of two sons and of one daughter, consort of one man. She fell into a wasting consumption[1] and, bearing witness to her Christian faith, piously and calmly she fell asleep in the Lord. She died at Wylye on Friday 9 February, and was buried in the cathedral church of Salisbury on Saturday 10 February.

1857 There were these eleven burials in the year of the Lord 1620
By John Lee, Bachelor of Divinity, etc, rector; Thomas Crockford, Bachelor of Arts etc, assistant; Richard Eyles, *alias* Hicks, of Deptford, married, and John Locke of Wylye, unmarried, husbandmen, churchwardens.

1621/2

1858 Jane Locke, — infant daughter[2] of John Locke of Wylye, labourer, and of Joan his wife, died and buried on Sunday 13 May.

1859 Elizabeth Smyth, infant daughter of Thomas Smyth of Wylye, husbandman, and of Edith his wife, died and buried on Tuesday 3 July.

1860 John Bysse, a newcomer and labourer, in the category of a stranger, but the brother of James Bysse of Wylye, labourer, died and buried

1   *in morbu' atrophiae*
2   a space is left after *filia*

Saturday 21 July.

1861 John Wayle, infant son of Richard Wayle of Wylye, sieve-maker, and of Margaret his wife, died Thursday 16 August and buried Friday 17 August.

1862 John Baker of Wylye, a poor labourer and almsman etc, the troubled father of many children, died and was buried on Thursday 30 August.

1863 Honor Dewe, wife of John Dewe of Wylye, blacksmith, descended from the freeholding Potticaries of this parish, almost 40 years old, died Wednesday 17 October, buried Thursday 18 October.

1864 Francis Coales, an infant, third son of William Coales, *alias* Hart, of Deptford, labourer, and of Agnes his wife, died Tuesday 23 October, buried Wednesday 24 October.

1865 Mary Bush, an infant, third daughter of Philip Bush of Deptford, shepherd, and of Margery his wife, died Thursday 8 November, buried Friday 9 November.

1866 John Baker, a small boy almost seven years old, the illegitimate son of a certain Christabel Baker, a poor woman (while she lived) late of Wylye, deceased; he died Sunday 9 December, buried Monday 10 December.

1867 Richard Wadland of Wylye, an elderly man, by trade a weaver, by condition a pauper, the troubled father of some children, etc, died and buried Saturday 15 December.

1868 There were these ten burials in the year 1621
By John Lee, Bachelor of Divinity, etc, rector; Thomas Crockford, Bachelor of Arts etc, assistant; John Lee the younger, Bachelor of Arts, curate; John Selwood of Deptford, married, and John Locke of Wylye, unmarried, husbandmen, churchwardens.

1622/3

1869 Richard Kent, second son of Richard Kent of Wylye, husbandman, and of Susan his wife, a small boy almost five years old, died and buried on Monday the twentieth of May.

1870 Edward Wadland, a small baby recently born and baptised, the firstborn son of Thomas Wadland of Wylye, labourer, and of Edith his wife, died and was buried Wednesday 5 June.

1871 John Prewett of Cannington, Somerset, a very elderly[1] freeholder and head of a household (as is stated), more than 90 years old. He had been summoned to London to give essential testimony, and on his return from there he was struck by a fatal sickness and died at the lodging house of William Lock in Wylye street on Friday 8 November. He was buried in the graveyard of our church on Saturday 9 November.

1872 John Potticarie of Wylye, but from Stockton, gentleman clothier, the widower of one wife, Eleanor, and her sole husband, the troubled father of ten children. Having suffered the varying fickleness[2] of the world, and the frightening blows of the Devil himself,[3] he piously and peacefully fell asleep in Christ on Sunday, the Feast of the Presentation of Christ,[4] and so was himself presented to Christ. He had his burial in his ancient place, which was not disproportionate,[5] on Thursday 6 February, after a holy address by John Lee, pastor[6] of this church. His body was given to the earth in the church, next to the body of his wife, under the three upper benches in the south row.[7] He was in the climacteric year of his age (as we understand it).[8]

1873 Joan Williams of Wylye, a poor woman, wife of a certain runaway scoundrel,[9] Richard Williams, but herself of a harmless life. She was related by marriage to the Hillmans of this neighbourhood, and almost 41

1　*antiquus*
2　*variam . . . inconstantia'*
3　*ipsiusq' Satanae terrificos conflictus*
4　2 February
5　*non inaequalem*: the implication of this curious remark is unclear
6　*propastorem*
7　*sub tribus superiorib' subselliis, in serie australi*
8　Climacterics were reckoned to occur at nine-yearly intervals through life. This is probably a reference to what was also known as the 'Grand Climacteric', or 9 x 7 years, the 63rd year of one's life, when a critical decline was supposed to begin.
9　*fugitivi nebulonis*

years old, the troubled mother of one daughter. She had a wretched[1] life and exchanged it for a better, died and buried Saturday 15 February.

1874 There were these five burials in the year 1622
By John Lee the elder, Bachelor of Divinity, etc, rector; John Lee the younger, Bachelor of Arts, etc, curate; Thomas Kent of Deptford yeoman, and John Taylor of Wylye street, husbandman and brewer, churchwardens.

1623/4

1875 Thomas Hillman, an infant not yet two years old, second son of John Hillman of Wylye, tailor, one of the churchwardens for this year, and of Edith his wife, died and was buried on Thursday 26 June.

1876 William Warren, a certain poor man from Sherborne,[2] etc, drawn to Deptford as an incomer for harvest work, became ill and died on Wednesday 13 August, buried in the graveyard of Wylye on Thursday 14 August.

1877 David Long, commonly known as Longynoughe, of Wylye, a poor tiler once widowed, the father of many children, about 70 years old (as may be reckoned), etc, died and was buried Wednesday 27 August.

1878 Joan Hobbes, an infant of almost seven months, fourth daughter of Thomas Hobbes of Wylye, labourer, and of Alice his wife, died and was buried on Saturday 24 January.

1879 Joan Locke of Wylye, widow, the relict of Martin Locke, weaver, etc. She was descended from the Belly family, husbandmen, and died Sunday 15 February, buried Monday 16 February.

1880 There were these five burials in the Year 1623
By John Lee the elder, Bachelor of Divinity, etc, rector; John Lee the younger, Bachelor of Arts, etc, curate; Joel Gyrdler, clothier, and John Hillman, tailor,[3] churchwardens.

---

1   *misella*
2   *Shirborniensis*
3   *sutor*, not followed by *vestiarii*, so 'cobbler' may be intended

1624/5

1881 Two premature baby girls, third and fourth children, but second and third daughters, of William Covey of Deptford, yeoman, and of Eleanor his wife, born Thursday 22 April. The first was born utterly lifeless (as it was reported), but the second was just[1] alive. Both were left unbaptized, and yet they had a religious burial in the graveyard, below the north side of the choir, near the body of their maternal grandmother —,[2] once the consort of Thomas Kent of Deptford, freeholder, on Friday 23 April.

1882 Christopher Smyth of Deptford, butcher, a poor man more or less 60 years old, twice married, the troubled father of several children, died Saturday 16 October, buried Sunday 17 October.

1883 John Fowler, a young unmarried labourer, servant of Richard Eyles, *alias* Hicks, of Deptford, yeoman, descended from a Warminster family of labourers, died Monday 8 November, buried Tuesday 9 November.

1884 There were these four burials in the Year 1624
By John Lee the elder, Bachelor of Divinity, etc, rector; John Lee the younger, Bachelor of Arts, etc, curate; Edward Smyth of Wylye the elder, and John Barnes of Wylye, husbandmen, churchwardens.

1625/6

1885 William Marshman of Deptford, a youth and a poor almsman,[3] son of William Marshman formerly of Deptford, labourer, etc, died and, buried Friday, the feast of the Incarnation of the Lord, 25 March.

1886 Elizabeth Baker, a poor widow, relict of John Baker, formerly of Wylye, labourer, deceased, from the family of the Furnells, husbandmen also of Wylye. She was a woman a little more or less than 50 years old, troubled mother of many children, etc, and she died and was buried on Saturday 28 May.

1887 Robert Sutton, an infant, first son of John Sutton of Wylye, ploughwright, and of Susan his wife, died Friday 3 June, buried Saturday

---

1   a word is illegible here, through damage or erasure
2   a space has been left for the name
3   *adolescentulus, paupercul', eleemosynarius*

4 June,[1] the eve of Pentecost.

1888 Thomas Kent, an unmarried husbandman, a little more or less than 38 years old, the eldest son by birth[2] of Thomas Kent of Deptford, yeoman, etc. He was wounded on Friday, the feast of St John the Baptist,[3] by an unlucky fall in the town of Wilton from a country vehicle headfirst on to stony ground which fractured his skull.[4] He died on Wednesday, the feast of St Peter,[5] and was buried in a religious manner in the graveyard of Wylye at the hands of the pastor John Lee, after a holy funeral address by Francis Edwards, the most excellent pastor of Woodhay[6] church, Hampshire, on Friday 1 July.[7]

1889 A certain citizen (as it is understood) of London, a maker of caps,[8] who was fleeing from a raging plague[9] in the city, unfortunately brought the sickness away with him. He grew fatally ill on the road, and breathed out his lamentable soul, after declaring his Christian faith with repeated wailing.[10] After his death he had his burial (as he had requested) with all manner of caution and haste, at the expense of this parish,[11] in the field near the king's highway where it leads westward out of the village, on Thursday 14 July.

1890 Jane Davies, an infant twin, first daughter of Robert Davies of Gillingham, Dorset, yeoman, and of Melior his wife, died and buried Thursday 8 September.

1891 Joan Patient, an infant, a little beyond the first year of her life, first daughter of Henry Patient of Deptford manor, yeoman, and of Joan his wife, died Sunday 25 September, buried Monday, 26 September.

1 the dates have been corrected from 2nd and 3rd
2 *filius natu maxim'*
3 24 June
4 *casu infaelici de vehiculo rusticano, in terram lapidosum, in oppido Wilton, precipitat' capitis fractura vulneratus*
5 29 June
6 presumably East Woodhay, since nearby West Woodhay lies in Berkshire. Francis Edwardes is recorded as curate at East Woodhay in 1633 (CCEd)
7 1 June has been lightly corrected to 1 July
8 *galerioru' opifex*
9 *pestem . . . saevientem*
10 *crebrii . . . ejulationibus*
11 *sumptibu' huius parochiae*

1892 An infant with no forename, son of William Gullyfoord of Deptford, labourer, and of Margaret his wife, was stillborn on Monday 7 November, and buried Tuesday, 8 November.

1893 Richard Furnell, a small baby slightly more than two months old, third son of William Furnell of Wylye, husbandman, and of Lettice his wife, died and was buried Sunday 8 December.

1894 Robert Lock, a very delicate[1] infant, second son of Robert Lock of Wylye manor, husbandman, and of Jane his wife, died and buried Tuesday 10 January.

1895 Jane Lock, the wife of Robert Lock just before written, and actually the daughter of John Brian of Langford, and the mother of the infant also just before written, and of three further children. She was a woman almost 30 years old, and died soon after the childbirth; buried Sunday 22 January.

1896 Tamsin Longynough, third daughter of David Longynough, formerly of Wylye. She was a poor servant woman nearly 30 years old, etc, died and buried Saturday 11 March.

1897 There were these twelve burials in the year 1625
By John Lee, Bachelor of Divinity, rector; Thomas Crockford, Bachelor of Arts, assistant; John Lee the younger, Bachelor of Arts, curate; John White, priest, curate; William Locke and Thomas Potticarie of Wylye, husbandmen, churchwardens.

1626/7

1898 Richard Taylour of Wylye, an elderly husbandman, almost 80 years old, the only husband of an only wife, and troubled father of several children of both sexes, etc. He was suddenly snatched by death, and he died unseen[2] in his bed at night in a storm, on Tuesday 28 March, and was buried Thursday 30 March.

1899 Susan Potticarie, the illegitimate daughter of Anne Potticarie of Wylye, etc, a little infant more than two months old, died and was buried

1   *tenerrimus*
2   *inobservatu'*

on Tuesday 2 January.

1900 Joan Vallies, a poor little elderly almswoman who was never married, almost 70 years old, etc, died and was buried on Saturday 27 January.

1901 There were these three burials in the year 1626
By John Lee Bachelor of Divinity, rector; John White, priest, etc, curate; Thomas Crockford, Bachelor of Arts, priest, etc, assistant; James Rebecke of Wylye, but from Bapton, and William Hill of Wylye, husbandmen, churchwardens.

1627/8

1902 Eleanor Barnes, firstborn daughter of John Barnes of Wylye, husbandman, and of Elizabeth his wife, a little girl almost five years old, died and was buried on Tuesday 29 May.

1903 Margaret Oakeford, a poor little elderly widow, relict of John Oakford, formerly of Wylye, husbandman deceased. She was descended from the family of the Bellies, husbandmen of Wylye, died Wednesday 2 January, buried Thursday 3 January.

1904 Henry Hobbes, a little baby little more or less than three months old, the third son of Thomas Hobbs of Wylye, labourer, and of Alice his wife, died and was buried on Thursday[1] 7 January.

1905 Mary Bower, of Wylye, an elderly widow, almost 80 years old. She was twice widowed, firstly by — Hill,[2] secondly by David Bower, of Wylye, brewer, deceased. She died on Wednesday 13 February, buried Thursday 14 February.

1906 An infant embryo without fore-name, the son of — Gullyford[3] of Deptford, labourer, and of Margaret his wife, stillborn, and buried without delay[4] on Sunday 17 February.

1907 Thomas Hillman of Wylye, once widowed, an elderly husbandman

---

1   *recte* Monday
2   a space has been left for the forename
3   a space has been left for the forename
4   *expedite*

almost 80 years old, ancient clerk of this parish church (chosen and approved by the rectors).[1] He was a most loving father of one son and one daughter, and a man especially pious and upright. He returned his Christian soul to God and died on Wednesday 20 February, buried Friday 22 February.

1908 A little infant without forename, first son of Robert Baker *alias* Chate of Wylye, woodworker, by Mary his second wife, was born, died, and buried on Monday 3 March.

1909 There were these seven burials in this year of 1627
By John Lee Bachelor of Divinity, etc, rector; John White, priest, curate; Thomas Crockford, of Arts etc, assistant; Anthony Ballard of Wylye, but from Bapton, and Henry Patient of Deptford manor, yeomen, churchwardens.

1628/9

1910 Christian Long, *alias* Longynough, a poor unmarried woman, almost 40 years old, etc, one of the daughters of David Long, *alias* Longynough, formerly of Wylye, tiler, etc, died and was buried[2] on Saturday 5 April.

1911 John Furnell, a little boy almost three years old, second son of Richard Furnell of Wylye, and of Jane his wife, died and was buried on Monday 12 May.

1912 Margaret Clearke of Wylye, a poor little elderly widow, almost 70 years old, descended from the family of the Smyths, husbandmen of Wylye, etc, died and was buried on Saturday 6 December.

1913 A little infant without forename, second son of Robert Baker *alias* Chate of Wylye, woodworker, by Mary his second wife, was stillborn and buried on Tuesday in the week before Lent,[3] 17 February.

1914 Mary Smyth of Wylye, a poor unmarried woman almost 40 years old, daughter[4] of a certain Edward Smyth, formerly of Wylye, tailor, and

1   *(eligentib' et approbationib' rectorib')*
2   *sepulta, die* has been repeated in error
3   *in carnisprivio*
4   *filii* presumably written in error

of Joan his wife, died and, buried Saturday 14 March.

1915 Humphrey Furnell, of Wylye, husbandman, an extremely elderly man, almost 90 years old, etc, was reported to have died suddenly at Heytesbury[1] on Wednesday 18 March, and to have been buried there on Thursday 19 March.

1916 There were these six burials in this year of 1628
By John Lee Bachelor of Divinity, etc, rector; John White, priest, curate; Thomas Crockford, of Arts etc, assistant; Guy Potticarie and John Barnes of Wylye, yeomen, churchwardens.

Subsequent burial entries in this register, 1629-35, are written in English in a different hand, and in Latin, 1636-44, when the sequence ends.

1   *Haytesburiae*

APPENDIX
THE WILL AND PROBATE INVENTORY OF THOMAS CROCKFORD, 1633-4

This is a transcript of the will of Thomas Crockford, with probate inventory, proved in Salisbury consistory court in 1634 (WSA P1/C/153).

In the name of God Amen. The eleaventh daye of September An'o D'ni 1633. I Thomas Crockford of Fisherton Dollimer in the Countie of Wiltis Clercke Viccar of Fisherton aforesaid beinge reasonable well of bodye & of indifferent good memorie doe make & ordayne this my last will & testament as hereafter followeth: First I bequeath my soule to almieghtie god my maker & redeemer and my bodye to bee buried in the parish Churche of Fisherton Dollimer aforesaid. As for my temporall goods & chattells. I doe dispose of them in this manner & forme followinge. Inprimis w'th the xxv^{li} that is due to mee from Mr John Topp of Stockton I doe give & bequeath to my 5 children nowe livinge the som'e of fourtie pounds of lawfull English money equally to bee devided among them. Their sev'all porc'ons w'thout any interrest to bee paid att such sev'all tymes as in order they shall severally one after the other accomplish the full age of one & twentie yeres. And yf any or either of them shall fortune to dye or decease before hee shee or they shall accomplish the age of xxi yeres aforesaid that then the porc'on or porc'ons belonginge to the deceased shall bee paid to the survivors of them. It'm I give & bequeathe to my kinswoman Frances Sheerelock one ewe worth 5^s or 5^s in money after one moneth next ensuinge my decease. It'm I give to my servant Symon Woolfe my ould breeches & doublett to bee d'd to hym after one moneth next ensuinge my decease. It'm I give towards the benefitt of the Churche of Fisherton Dollimer aforesaid one shillinge. It'm I give to Thomas the son of Joell Doutey my godson one shillinge, It'm all the rest of my goods & chattells moveable & unmoveable of what kinde soev' they bee I give & bequeath to my nowe wife Joane Crockford whome I doe appointe & ordayne to bee whole & sole executrix of this my last will & testam't. It'm my will is that yf either of my said 5 children shall fortune to bee married before hee or shee shall accomplish the full age of one & twentie yeares w'thout the consent & good likinge of my said wife their mother that then the porc'on of either of them soe beinge married shall remaine to the use & disposinge of my said wife Joane Crockford. It'm I doe ordayne and appointe Jerom Goffe of Stockton & Robert Ailes of Fisherton Dollimer aforesaid to bee the overseers of this my last will & testament. In witness whereof I have hereunto sett my hand & seale the daye & yere first above written.

Signed D'cti Thomae Crockford
Witnesses hereunto Tho. Merest Cl'icus
Jerom Goffe
Robert Ailes

1634
A true Inventorie of all the goods and Chattells of Thomas Crockford Clerck, of Fisherton Dallimer late Viccar deceased, taken & prised by Jerom Goffe, Robert Eyles al's Hix, James Rebeck and John Ingrom sen. Prisers the eighthe daye of Aprill An'o D'ni 1634.

His wearinge Apparrell.
Inp'mis one Cloake one Cassock Coate one gowne w'th all the rest of his appar'll woollen lynnen hatts, capps, shooes bootes & spurrs – x^{li}

In the little chamber being the middle chamber where hee died.
It'm one tester bedsteed matted & corded w'th one feather bedd, two feather boulsters, 2 downe pillowes one paire of sheetes 1 pair of blanketts one cov'led one greene rugge – viij^{li}
It'm one square table board, 4 ioyned stooles of tymber w'th one little box – x^s
It'm one chest 2 coffers one little cupbord w'th locks & keyes to them all belonginge – xvj^s
Item one warminge panne one paire of tongues w'th one fire panne & one paire of iron doggs – vij^s

In the inner chamber over the hall.
It'm one tester bedesteed w'th one flock bed & all thappurtenances thereunto belonginge – iiij^{li}
It'm one greate cheste one greate cupbord 2 coffers - ij^{li}

In the chamber over the kitchinge.
It'm 2 ould bedsteeds w'thout matts or cords one standinge bedsteed w'thout a tester w'th one flock bed & its appurtenanc's one truggle

bedsteed w'th one flock bed & its appurtenanc's – v^{li}

In the hall

It'm one table board w'th one carpett & 2 cussions, 2 formes & 6 ioyned stooles – ij^{li}

It'm one square table board, 2 ioyned tymber chaires – x^s

It'm 2 liverie side cupboards – xiij^s 4^d

It'm 2 andirons in the chimney – iiij^s

In the kitchinge.

Of timber houshold stuffe:

It'm one table boarde 2 formes 2 chaires one little chaire for a childe 2 little stooles one Amerie – x^s

It'm one yottinge vate one meshinge vate – x^s

It'm 3 cowles 6 trendalls 1 silte 2 powdring tubbs 2 ould tubbs, 3 pailes & one churne – xxx^s

Item 3 dozen of trenchers 1 dozen of woodden dishes w'th one paire of billowes – ij^s

It'm one yest hurdell - vj^d

summe is 36^{li} 12^s 10^d

In the kitchinge

Of Brasse and Iron

Inp'mis one fornace p'sed att – xxvj^s viij^d

It'm 4 kettles – xxvj^s viij^d

It'm 3 brasse crocks – xxx^s

It'm 2 skilletts one bastinge ladle one skimmer one brasse chaffing dishe & 2 brasse candlesticks – x^s

It'm one pestle w'th its morter of brasse – iiij^s

It'm 3 spitts, one drippinge panne one minsinge knife one cleever one beife-pricker 2 paire of pothookes – x^s

It'm one paire of andirons 2 paire of hangings in the chimney & a crooke – vj^s viij^d

It'm one pile one iron colerake, one paringe iron – iij^s iiij^d

It'm one hooke 2 hatchetts 3 wadges of iron & steele – v^s

It'm one shovle & one spade – j^s

It'm 2 brondirons & one fryinge pan – vj^s

Of pewter

It'm one flagon one boale one bason – x^s

It'm 4 deepe platters 3 broade platters – xviij^{s}
It'm 5 pottingers 4 servinge dishes – xij^{s}
It'm 3 pewter dishes 2 saltes 6 saucers & one dozen of spoones – vij^{s}
It'm 2 pewter candlesticks 2 pewter chamber potts – v^{s}

In the butterie.
It'm 9 barrells & 3 horses to beare up the barrells – xxx^{s}
It'm one leatherne bottle – ij^{s}

In the barne.
It'm the wheate therein p'sed att – v^{li}
It'm the bareley therein – 13^{li}
It'm 10 bushells of malte – ij^{li}
It'm one wymmowinge sheete 2 sacks 2 baggs 2 seives 1 halfe bushell &
one pecke – x^{s}
It'm one forke w'th 3 iron prongs one ould halfe bushell & 1 threshould
– xij^{d}
It'm all the haye prized att – vi^{li}
It'm 2 corne pikes one dunge pike – xviij^{d}

In & about the barten.
It'm 2 loade of wood – x^{s}
It'm one planck boarde one ladder – iij^{s}
It'm 2 woodden piggs troughes – xij^{d}

In the feild.
It'm the wheate nowe growinge thereon – xij^{li}
It'm 3 halfes of oates growinge – xxx^{s}
It'm one dozen & halfe of hurdells – iij^{s}

Of beasts livinge.
It'm 3 kine – vij^{li}
It'm 46 sheepe & 4 lambs – x^{li}
It'm 4 piggs – ij^{li}

summe is 65^{li} 17^{s} 10^{d}

Of flesh.
Inp'mis 6 flitches of bacon & 1 flitche of beeife – iiij^{li}

Of naperie & lynnen.

It'm 4 paire of sheetes, 2 of lockheram and 2 of canvas – ij^{li} 13^s 4^d

It'm one holland bedsheete – xvj^s

It'm 3 paire of pillowbees – x^s

It'm 6 table cloathes, 3 of lockerham 3 of canvas – x^s

It'm 1 dozen of diaper napkins – xij^s

It'm 1 dozen of other napkins – vj^s

It'm one holland towell 1 diaper towell 1 lockerham towell 1 canvas towell – v^s

Of div's other things in div's places.

Inp'mis 338 bookes – xxx^{li}

It'm one howse att Warminster beinge leasehould p'sed att – xl^{li}

It'm in the kitchinge 6 shelfes & 1 bacon rack w'th its 4 crookes or hookes – vj^s

It'm one bridell & saddle – 5^s

It'm one muskett gunne w'th its rest one headpeice one sword bandeleers bullett bagge & mould – xxx^s

It'm some smale trifles in & about the howse – xij^d

summe is 81^{li} 14^s 4^d

The whole summe & valewe of the goods & chattells doth amounte to clxxxiiij^{li} & v^s

.

INDEX OF NAMES

Unless prefixed by 'p.' (for a page number) references are to entry numbers in the text or roman page numbers in the introduction. A few long biographical entries are printed in bold. No attempt has been made to distinguish between individuals having the same name, and two or more may occur in the same text entry. Variant spellings of surnames have been combined under that most frequently found, with other forms noted in brackets, and cross-referenced if not adjacent to the form used. Common forenames have been abbreviated, as follows:

Alex	Alexander		Margt	Margaret
Chris	Christopher		Nic	Nicholas
Edm	Edmund		Phil	Philip
Edw	Edward		Ric	Richard
Eliz	Elizabeth		Rob	Robert
Geo	George		Rog	Roger
Hen	Henry		Thos	Thomas
Jas	James		Wm	William
Jn	John			

— Agnes, 583
  Eliz, 1303, 1414, 1418, 1777
  Thos, 1415
Abbat
  Eliz, 403
  Wm, 125
Abell, Edith, 1327
Acrigge (Acrig. Acrigg)
  Joan, 1184
  Mary, 1007
  Nathaniel, 1038
  Rebecca, 1017, 1229
  Ric, 1017, 1213
  Susan, 1007, 1017, 1038, 1213, 1229
  Wm, 837, 842n, 1007, 1017, 1038, 1072,
    1079, 1184, 1213, 1229
Adams, Ric, 637
Aford
  Edw, 292
  Mary, 292, 476
  Rob, 476
  Rog, 292

Agre
  Amy, 946
  Ric, 946
Ailes see Eyles
Albright, —, 827
Aldridge, Ambrose, 1292
Alford (Alfoord)
  Frances, 814
  Grace, xiii, 801
  Joan, xiii, xxxii, 811
  Thos, xiii, 801, 811, 814
  family, 1208
Amor
  Eliz, 1268
  Matthew, 1303
Andrewes (Andrews)
  Agnes, 626
  Eleanor, 11, 205, 481, 734
  German, 547
  Isabel, 497
  Joan, 53, 431, 628, 1088
  Jn, 43, 53, 66, 74, 100, 197, 205, 255,

GENERAL INDEX

This is an index of places, occupations, and selected subjects. Places are Wiltshire parishes unless otherwise stated. Bapton, Deptford, Fisherton Delamere, Stockton and Wylye, which occur on almost every page, have not been indexed. Occupations are followed by the consistent or most frequent Latin word or words translated; husbandman (*agricola*), labourer (*operarius*) and yeoman occur very frequently and are omitted. Unless prefixed by 'p.' (for a page number) references are to entry numbers in the text or roman page numbers in the introduction.

WILTSHIRE RECORD SOCIETY
(AS AT MARCH 2020)

President: DR NEGLEY HARTE
Honorary Treasurer: IVOR M. SLOCOMBE
Honorary Secretary: MISS HELEN TAYLOR
General Editor: MS CLAIRE SKINNER

Committee:
DR V. BAINBRIDGE
DR D.A. CROWLEY
DR J. HARE
S.D. HOBBS
DR T. PLANT
MRS S. THOMSON
K.H. ROGERS

Honorary Independent Examiner: C.C. DALE

PRIVATE MEMBERS
Note that because of recent legislation the Society no longer publishes members'
addresses in its volumes, as it had done since 1953.

Honorary Members
OGBURN, SENR JUDGE R W
SHARMAN-CRAWFORD, MR T

ADAMS, MS S
ANDERSON, MR D M
BADENI, COUNTESS JUNE
BAINBRIDGE, DR V
BARNETT, MR B A
BATHE, MR G,
BAYLIFFE, MR B G
BENNETT, DR N
BERRETT, MR A M
BERRY, MR C
BLAKE, MR P A
BOX, MR S D
BRAND, DR P A
BROCK, MRS C
BROWN, MR D A
BROWN, MR G R
BROWNING, MR E
BRYSON, DR A
CARTER, MR D
CAWTHORNE, MRS N

CHALMERS, MR D
CHANDLER, DR J H
CLARK, MR G A
CLARK, MRS V
COLCOMB, MR D M
COLLINS, MR A T
COOPER, MR S
CRAVEN, DR A
CROOK, MR P H
CROUCH, MR J W
CROWLEY, DR D A
CUNNINGTON, MS J
DAKERS, PROF C
D'ARCY, MR J N
DODD, MR D
DYSON, MRS L
EDE, DR M E
ENGLISH, MS K
GAISFORD, MR J
GALE, MRS J
GHEY, MR J G
GINGER, MR A
GODDARD, MR R G H
GOUGH, MISS P M

GRIFFIN, DR C
GRIST, MR M
HARE, DR J N
HARTE, DR N
HAWKINS, MR D
HEATON, MR R J
HELMHOLZ, PROF R W
HENLY, MR C
HERRON, MRS Pamela M
HICKMAN, MR M R
HICKS, MR I
HICKS, PROF M A
HILLMAN, MR R B
HOBBS, MR S
HOWELLS, DR Jane
INGRAM, DR M J
JOHNSTON, MRS J M
JONES, MS J
KEEN, MR A.G
KENT, MR T A
KITE, MR P J
KNEEBONE, MR W J R
KNOWLES, MRS V A
LANSDOWNE, MARQUIS OF

LAWES, MRS G
MARSH, REV R
MARSHMAN, MR M J
MARTIN, MS J
MATHEWS, MR R
MCCREE, DR P
MOLES, MRS M I
MONTAGUE, MR M D
MORLAND, MRS N
NAPPER, MR L R
NEWBURY, MR C COLES
NEWMAN, MRS R
NICOLSON, MR A
NOKES, MR P M A
NOYCE, MISS S
OGBOURNE, MR J M V
OGBURN, MR D A
PARKER, DR P F,

PATIENCE, MR D C
PERRY, MR W A
PLANT, DR T
POWELL, MRS N
PRICE, MR A J R
RAILTON, MS A
RAYBOULD, MISS F
RAYMOND, MR S
ROBERTS, MS M
ROGERS, MR K H
ROLFE, MR R C
ROSE, MR A
SAUNT, MRS B A
SHELDRAKE, MR B
SHEWRING, MR P
SKINNER, MS C
SLOCOMBE, MR I

SMITH, MR P J
SPAETH, DR D A
STONE, MR M J
SUTER, MRS C
SUTTON, MR A E
TATTON-BROWN, MR T
TAYLOR, MISS H
THOMSON, MRS S M
VINE, MR R E
WADSWORTH, MRS S
WILLIAMSON, MR B
WILTSHIRE, MR J
WILTSHIRE, MRS P E
WOODFORD, MR A
WOODWARD, MR A S,
WRIGHT, MR D P
YOUNGER, MR C

UNITED KINGDOM INSTITUTIONS

Aberystwyth
    National Library of
    Wales
    University College of
    Wales
Birmingham. University
    Library
Bristol
    University of Bristol
    Library
Cambridge. University
    Library
Cheltenham. Bristol
    and Gloucestershire
    Archaeological
    Society
Chippenham
    Museum & Heritage
    Centre
    Wiltshire and Swindon
    History Centre
Coventry. University of
    Warwick Library
Devizes
    Wiltshire Archaeological
    & Natural History
    Society
    Wiltshire Family History
    Society
Durham. University
    Library

Edinburgh
    University Library
Exeter. University Library
Glasgow. University
    Library

Liverpool. University
    Library
London
    British Library
    College of Arms
    Guildhall Library
    Inner Temple Library
    Institute of Historical
    Research
    London Library
    The National Archives
    Royal Historical Society
    Society of Antiquaries
    Society of Genealogists
Manchester. John Rylands
    Library
Marlborough
    Memorial Library,
    Marlborough College
    Merchant's House Trust
    Savernake Estate Office
Norwich. University of
    East Anglia Library
Nottingham. University
    Library

Oxford
    Bodleian Library
    Exeter College Library
Reading. University
    Library
St Andrews. University
    Library
Salisbury
    Bourne Valley Historical
    Society
    Cathedral Library
    Salisbury and South
    Wilts Museum
Southampton. University
    Library
Swansea. University
    College Library
Swindon
    Historic England
    Swindon Borough
    Council
Taunton. Somerset
    Archaeological and
    Natural History
    Society
Wetherby. British Library
    Document Supply
    Centre
York. University Library

INSTITUTIONS OVERSEAS

AUSTRALIA

Adelaide. University Library

Crawley. Reid Library, University of Western Australia

CANADA

Halifax. Killam Library, Dalhousie University

Toronto, Ont
Pontifical Inst of Medieval Studies
University of Toronto Library

Victoria, B.C. McPherson Library, University of Victoria

NEW ZEALAND

Wellington. National Library of New Zealand

UNITED STATES OF AMERICA

Ann Arbor, Mich. Hatcher Library, University of Michigan

Athens, Ga. University of Georgia Libraries

Atlanta, Ga. The Robert W Woodruff Library, Emory University

Bloomington, Ind. Indiana University Library

Boston, Mass. New England Historic and Genealogical Society

Boulder, Colo. University of Colorado Library

Cambridge, Mass.
Harvard College Library
Harvard Law School Library

Charlottesville, Va. Alderman Library, University of Virginia

Chicago
Newberry Library
University of Chicago Library

Dallas, Texas. Public Library

Davis, Calif. University Library

East Lansing, Mich. Michigan State University Library

Evanston, Ill. United Libraries, Garrett/Evangelical, Seabury

Fort Wayne, Ind. Allen County Public Library

Houston, Texas. M.D. Anderson Library, University of Houston

Iowa City, Iowa. University of Iowa Libraries

Ithaca, NY. Cornell University Library

Los Angeles
Public Library
Young Research Library, University of California

Minneapolis, Minn. Wilson Library, University of Minnesota

New York
Columbia University of the City of New York

Salt Lake City, Utah. Family History Library

San Marino, Calif. Henry E. Huntington Library

South Hadley, Mass. Williston Memorial Library, Mount Holyoke College

Urbana, Ill. University of Illinois Library

Washington. The Folger Shakespeare Library

Winston-Salem, N.C. Z.Smith Reynolds Library, Wake Forest University

LIST OF PUBLICATIONS

The Wiltshire Record Society was founded in 1937, as the Records Branch of the Wiltshire Archaeological and Natural History Society, to promote the publication of the documentary sources for the history of Wiltshire. The annual subscription is £15 for private and institutional members. In return, a member receives a volume each year. Prospective members should apply to the Hon. Secretary, c/o Wiltshire and Swindon History Centre, Cocklebury Road, Chippenham SN15 3QN. Many more members are needed.

The following volumes have been published. Price to members £15, and to non-members £20, postage extra. Most volumes up to 51 are still available from the Wiltshire and Swindon History Centre, Cocklebury Road, Chippenham SN15 3QN. Volumes 52-71 are available from Hobnob Press, c/o 8 Lock Warehouse, Severn Road, Gloucester GL1 2GA. Volumes 1-55 are available online, at www.wiltshirerecordsociety.org.uk.

30. *Abstracts of Wiltshire tithe apportionments*, ed. R.E. Sandell, 1975
31. *Poverty in early-Stuart Salisbury*, ed. Paul Slack, 1975
32. *The subscription book of Bishops Tounson and Davenant, 1620–40*, ed. B. Williams, 1977
33. *Wiltshire gaol delivery and trailbaston trials, 1275–1306*, ed. R.B. Pugh, 1978
34. *Lacock abbey charters*, ed. K.H. Rogers, 1979
35. *The cartulary of Bradenstoke priory*, ed. Vera C.M. London, 1979
36. *Wiltshire coroners' bills, 1752–1796*, ed. R.F. Hunnisett, 1981
37. *The justicing notebook of William Hunt, 1744–1749*, ed. Elizabeth Crittall, 1982
38. *Two Elizabethan women: correspondence of Joan and Maria Thynne, 1575–1611*, ed. Alison D. Wall, 1983
39. *The register of John Chandler, dean of Salisbury, 1404–17*, ed. T.C.B. Timmins, 1984
40. *Wiltshire dissenters' meeting house certificates and registrations, 1689–1852*, ed. J.H. Chandler, 1985
41. *Abstracts of feet of fines relating to Wiltshire, 1377–1509*, ed. J.L. Kirby, 1986
42. *The Edington cartulary*, ed. Janet H. Stevenson, 1987
43. *The commonplace book of Sir Edward Bayntun of Bromham*, ed. Jane Freeman, 1988
44. *The diaries of Jeffery Whitaker, schoolmaster of Bratton, 1739–1741*, ed. Marjorie Reeves and Jean Morrison, 1989
45. *The Wiltshire tax list of 1332*, ed. D.A. Crowley, 1989
46. *Calendar of Bradford-on-Avon settlement examinations and removal orders, 1725–98*, ed. Phyllis Hembry, 1990
47. *Early trade directories of Wiltshire*, ed. K.H. Rogers and indexed by J.H. Chandler, 1992
48. *Star chamber suits of John and Thomas Warneford*, ed. F.E. Warneford, 1993
49. *The Hungerford Cartulary: a calendar of the earl of Radnor's cartulary of the Hungerford family*, ed. J.L. Kirby, 1994
50. *The Letters of John Peniston, Salisbury architect, Catholic, and Yeomanry Officer, 1823–1830*, ed. M. Cowan, 1996
51. *The Apprentice Registers of the Wiltshire Society, 1817– 1922*, ed. H. R. Henly, 1997
52. *Printed Maps of Wiltshire 1787–1844: a selection of topographical, road and canal maps in facsimile*, ed. John Chandler, 1998
53. *Monumental Inscriptions of Wiltshire: an edition, in facsimile, of Monumental Inscriptions in the County of Wilton, by Sir Thomas Phillipps*, ed. Peter Sherlock, 2000
54. *The First General Entry Book of the City of Salisbury, 1387–1452*, ed. David R. Carr, 2001
55. *Devizes Division income tax assessments, 1842–1860*, ed. Robert Colley, 2002
56. *Wiltshire Glebe Terriers, 1588–1827*, ed. Steven Hobbs, 2003
57. *Wiltshire Farming in the Seventeenth Century*, ed. Joseph Bettey, 2005
58. *Early Motor Vehicle Registration in Wiltshire, 1903–1914*, ed. Ian Hicks, 2006
59. *Marlborough Probate Inventories, 1591–1775*, ed. Lorelei Williams and Sally Thomson, 2007
60. *The Hungerford Cartulary, part 2: a calendar of the Hobhouse cartulary of the Hungerford family*, ed. J.L. Kirby, 2007
61. *The Court Records of Brinkworth and Charlton*, ed. Douglas Crowley, 2009
62. *The Diary of William Henry Tucker, 1825–1850*, ed. Helen Rogers, 2009
63. *Gleanings from Wiltshire Parish Registers*, ed. Steven Hobbs, 2010
64. *William Small's Cherished Memories and Associations*, ed. Jane Howells and Ruth Newman, 2011
65. *Crown Pleas of the Wiltshire Eyre, 1268*, ed. Brenda Farr and Christopher Elrington, rev. Henry Summerson, 2012
66. *The Minute Books of Froxfield Almshouse, 1714–1866*, ed. Douglas Crowley, 2013

67. *Wiltshire Quarter Sessions Order Book, 1642–1654,* ed. Ivor Slocombe, 2014

68. *The Register of John Blyth, Bishop of Salisbury, 1493–1499,* ed. David Wright, 2015

69 *The Churchwardens' Accounts of St Mary's, Devizes, 1633–1689,* ed. Alex Craven, 2016

70 *The Account Books and Papers of Everard and Ann Arundell of Ashcombe and Salisbury, 1745–1798,* ed. Barry Williamson, 2017

71 *Letters of Henry Hoare of Stourhead, 1760–81,* ed. Dudley Dodd, 2018

72 *Braydon Forest and the Forest Law,* ed. Douglas Crowley, 2019

Further details about the Society, its activities and publications, will be found on its website, www.wiltshirerecordsociety.org.uk.